worship:

wonderful
and
sacred
mystery

worship:

wonderful
and
sacred
mystery

Kenneth W. stevenson

The Pastoral Press
Washington, DC

Acknowledgments

Acknowledgment is gratefully made to the respective publishers for permission to reprint, sometimes in edited form, the following: "'Ye Shall Pray for . . .': The Intercession," *Liturgy Reshaped*, Kenneth Stevenson, ed., (London: SPCK, 1982) 32-47; "Eucharistic Offering: Does Research into Origins Make Any Difference?", *Studia Liturgica* 15 (1982/1983) 87-103; "Eucharistic Sacrifice - An Insoluble Problem?", *Scottish Journal of Theology* 42 (1989) 469-492; "A Theological Reflection on the Experience of Inclusion/Exclusion at the Eucharist," *Anglican Theological Review* 68 (1986) 212-211; "The Origins of the Nuptial Blessing," *Heythrop Journal* 21 (1980) 412-416; "'Benedictio Nuptialis': Reflections on the Blessing of Bride and Groom in Some Western Mediaeval Rites," *Ephemerides Liturgicae* 93 (1979) 457-478; "Van Gennep and Marriage - Strange Bedfellows: A Fresh Look at the Rites of Marriage," *Ephemerides Liturgicae* 100 (1986) 138-151; "Marriage Liturgy: Lessons from History," *Anglican Theological Review* 68 (1986) 225-240; "The Ceremonies of Light: Their Shape and Function in the Paschal Vigil Liturgy," *Ephemerides Liturgicae* 99 (1985) 170-185; "Prayer over Light: A Comparison between the Easter Vigil and Candlemas," *Worship* 64 (1990) 2-9; Chapter 9, "Origins and Development of Ash Wednesday," is a paper delivered in the Liturgy Master-Theme at the Eleventh International Conference on Patristic Studies, Oxford, 19-24 August, 1991.

ISBN: 0-912405-90-2

The Pastoral Press
225 Sheridan Street, N.W.
Washington, D.C. 20011
(202) 723-1254

The Pastoral Press is the publications division of the National Association of Pastoral Musicians, a membership organization of musicians and clergy dedicated to fostering the art of musical liturgy.

Printed in the United States of America

Contents

Introduction

THIS BOOK IS THE RESULT OF THE KIND INVITATION FROM LARRY Johnson of The Pastoral Press to assemble together a collection of material on various aspects of liturgical history that have aroused my attention. The book comes in three sections, grouping together eleven articles that I have written over the past decade or so. Nearly all have in one way or another an oral origin, and nearly all are haunted by one or another of my books.

The first section consists of a few explorations of the eucharist. Chapter 1 was published in the *Festschrift* of my mentor, Geoffrey Cuming. It arose from a sermon on intercession I preached in Boston Parish Church, England, while serving there as Lecturer (Second Presbyter) in the late 1970s. It also linked in with a growing fascination with eucharistic sacrifice. Chapter 2 was delivered as a Communication at the meeting of the *Societas Liturgica* in Vienna, 1983, and was intended to serve as a preliminary report on certain researches that eventually bore fruit in the form of my *Eucharist and Offering* (New York: Pueblo, 1986). Chapter 3, by contrast, emerged as an extended comment on that book, in an attempt to look more closely at the contemporary debate on eucharistic sacrifice. I was glad to see it published in my homeland, Scotland. Both these chapters express my conviction that all Christian traditions need to look at their roots—and to each other—to see a much wider and deeper picture of the eucharist. Chapter 4—

some reminiscences of a personal kind—was prized from me by David Holeton as a preparatory paper for the International Anglican Liturgical Consultation held in Boston, Massachusetts in 1985.

The second section is devoted to the study of the marriage liturgy. Chapters 5 and 6 were preliminaries to my first book on that subject, *Nuptial Blessing: A Study of Christian Marriage Rites* (London: SPCK, 1982; New York: Oxford University Press, 1983). A special concern was to elucidate the way in which marriage prayers were written; hence, first, the period of origins and, second, the multifarious texts of the Western Middle Ages. Chapter 5 was read as a Communication at the Oxford Patristic Conference, 1979; and part of Chapter 6 was read at the Fourth Nordic Colloquium for the study of Latin Liturgy, Oslo, 1978. The year 1983 saw our family spend the spring at the University of Notre Dame, when I was Visiting Professor for the spring semester. A patient class of graduates put up with what I had to offer, and chapters 7 and 8 eventually resulted. Aidan Kavanagh's invitation to write on the marriage liturgy for the Pueblo series on the reformed rites of the Roman Catholic Church required a changed perspective. Chapter 7 expressed this shift, and was read as a Communication at the *Societas Liturgica* in Boston in 1985. Chapter 8, on the other hand, began as a direct response to some of the discussions that went on in the Notre Dame classes.

The third section concerns the liturgical year. When I was asked to contribute to the Talley *Festschrift*, I had intended to write on Ash Wednesday, but pressures from the move to a new job meant that I had to offer instead an article already being published in *Ephemerides Liturgicae* on Candlemas. For this duplication I apologize without reservation. Chapter 9 was read in the Liturgy Master-Theme at the Oxford Patristic Conference, 1991, and it is meant, somewhat late in the day, "for Tom." Chapters 10 and 11 have a slightly different origin. Chapter 10 complements material on Holy Week piety and the Easter Vigil as written up in my little book, *Jerusalem Revisited: The Liturgical Meaning of Holy Week* (Washington, D.C.: The Pastoral Press, 1988). It was read as a paper at the meeting of the British Society for Liturgical Study, 1984. Finally, comparisons are not always unpleasant; in liturgy they are the spice of life, especially when about ceremonies of light. The last chapter was read as a Communication at the meeting of *Societas Liturgica* in York in 1989.

The pages that follow are "oral" in origin in another sense. They are frequently the result of personal or distanced contact with other scholars, snatched conversations at conferences, a request to talk or even preach on a subject that is so dear to me that it is part of my life. Some of the conclusions often resulted from a lone early morning walk with the Guildford rectory dog, Alcuin, a border-terrier of some note. He has shared many a fateful moment with me at that time of day.

Apart from my time at Notre Dame, the whole of my ministry has been spent in the Anglican pastorate, though I have been able to combine parish work with teaching from time to time, e.g., as Chaplain and Lecturer at Manchester University. I am a historian, trained in that nebulous Anglican discipline, historical theology. I am therefore all too conscious that much of the material that has been worked over through the years and which is expressed in lightly revised form in the pages that follow would yield different treatments, other conclusions, were the author a systematic theologian or someone trained in the human sciences. However hard we try to look at the data from new perspectives, our vista is still a limited one. I am conscious, too, that because of their mainly oral origins, these chapters will contain what an American once described as "Britishisms." I hope that not too many translations-in-the-mind are necessary to grasp what the author is trying to articulate. The intention behind my meaning is usually to examine afresh, whatever the service, whatever the era in question, that subtle, fascinating genius of liturgy—the marriage of text and context. *What* we say or sing, and *how* and *when* we say or sing it contributes in large measure to *why* that is our speech or song before the Lord.

I come from a long line of clergy, and it is therefore appropriate for me to dedicate this miscellany to my various forebears, in particular to the two archetypes: on my father's side, to Isak Sidenius, the son of a Lapp fur-trapper in Norway, who became a dean in the Danish Church in the mid-eighteenth century; and, on my mother's side, to Christian Jessen, who was "hofpraest" (court chaplain) at Augustenborg, in south Jutland, around the same time. I know that they both loved books—and so did their seed.

Kenneth Stevenson

First Sunday in Advent, 1991
Guildford, England

EUCHARIST

1

"Ye Shall Pray For . . ."
The Intercession

IF YOU COMPARE THE EUCHARISTIC INTERCESSION IN THE 1662 PRAYER Book with the corresponding provisions in the Church of England Alternative Service (1980), you will find it hard to see any similarities, other than the topics for prayer which they have in common. But even this is not entirely true, because the conventional sequence of praying for the church, the world, the suffering, and (if you are daring) the departed is no longer mandatory in the new orders.

If you look further afield, the new American Episcopal Prayer Book is rich in different forms of intercession, with several patterns and ingredients; and the Roman Missal of Paul VI gives even less direction than either of these modern Anglican compilations. Clearly, to compare the new intercessions with the old is—without exaggeration—like comparing chalk with cheese.

In the face of what amounts to a liturgical revolution, there can be little doubt that much confusion surrounds Christian congregations on prayer in general, and intercession in particular; and it is my purpose to clarify the aims—theological, liturgical, and pastoral—which might help redirect contemporary intercession, and, in the process, to discuss some of the problems thrown up by new language in prayer. If liturgy is the Cinderella of theological studies, then the intercession is certainly the Cinderella of liturgical studies. It is an item of regular worship which is too important to ignore because it occupies a central position in the eucharist—indeed, one might almost say that it is the *pivot* on which the liturgy of the word moves forward to the liturgy of the sacrament: and the current renewal of non-eucharistic worship means that the intercession is no longer, if it ever was, specifically the "prayer of the *faithful*."

Furthermore, because of its central position, the intercession has become increasingly isolated. In the old days, it seemed as if the entire liturgy was made up of different prayers, which were jumbled together without much coherence, unless you had a good knowledge of liturgy. Now it stands in stark loneliness, and we often appear not to know what we do with it, largely because we have not thought it out.

The result is that the intercession may seem like A.A. Milne's "Expotition to the North Pole," in which the church bumbles along, not quite sure of where it is going, and not even unanimous about what it is doing . . . Put in liturgical terms, this "Expotition" is a sort of *à la carte* diet of fancy, liturgical experimentation; some enjoy the indulgence, like Pooh-Bear, but others, like Eeyore, clearly do not.

WHAT IS INTERCESSION?

If much of liturgical renewal is, at its best, a *retour aux sources*, then any theological renewal which accompanies it, however nervously, should constitute a return to *fundamentals*. In public worship we are dealing with theology, and Regin Prenter was right to affirm once that "the liturgy of the church is theological. It speaks to God and Man about God and Man." Reinterpreting the *lex orandi lex credendi* motto attributed to Prosper of Aquitaine, Prenter offers us a stern warning against a liturgy which does not heed theology, and against holding to a theology which is divorced from the praying life of the church. Nowhere is this tension more acute than at the point in public worship when the Christian assembly offers to God its own needs and the needs of the whole world. *How* a person intercedes is a reflection of what that person really believes, whether such prayers are uttered in public on Sunday morning after much preparation, or are the silent, spontaneous thoughts and yearnings of the individual which one's circumstances provide.

Long ago Augustine wrote that "God does not ask us to tell him about our needs in order to learn about them, but in order that we may be made capable of receiving his gifts."[1] It is a sound principle that good theology emerges from Christian life as it is experienced, and Augustine wrote those words to clear one befuddled mind (a woman called Proba) concerning the need for intercessory prayer, which during his time was still an integral part of the eucharistic liturgy.

Intercession is the way the Christian builds up a relationship with God so that the person may discern God's will, and try to carry it out. This is the exact opposite of the theology of prayer which arises from so many extempore (and prepared) utterances, a feature of church life which we may with some justification caricature as the "let us pray—here is the news" syndrome. By all means, "pray for all people according to their needs," but the danger is that God is presented to the assembly as some power whose mind has already been made up, and it is the purpose of repetitious, intense, fulsome, and even sentimental prayers to *alter* it. But intercession is a means of identification with the world, not an escape, and so there are three dimension to it which are all vital.

Our Relationship with God

The first is the obvious one—our relationship with God. The Christian spiritual tradition, manifested in the Bible and reinforced in the lives of the saints, is one which affirms that God is our friend and companion. It therefore follows that, just as you don't go straight up to a stranger and ask for five pounds, you will not begin your relationship with God by demanding what you want at the time. This is why the classic liturgies of the past do not usually begin with intercession, and, if they do, (as in the old processional litany at Rome), the petitions are general and do not mention specific ends. Herein lies an important psychological and theological truth—that we understand God better in our worship if we come to intercession after adoration, and in penitence.

As usual, the best liturgies are those which have a structure, an internal logic, which is not there just for tradition's sake. Furthermore, our intercessions commit us again to pray, so that if, for example, we are praying about someone dying of cancer, we are ready to receive God's gifts and rejoice in a recovery, however temporary, or adjust painfully to the end of a human life. Most intercessory prayers are about very ordinary things, but when we stop to look at them in relation to the real heights and depths of human experience, we begin to see how *ambivalent* intercessory prayer is. We are two-faced because we are frightened, and regular prayer serves as a constant soothing of that fear into a relationship of love with perfect love. Anthony Bloom puts it this way: "we believe and we do not believe at the same time, and faith shows its measure by overcoming its own doubts."[2]

Those with Whom We Pray

The second level is the relationship with those *with* whom we pray. It is a fine thing that the Anglican tradition insists on a Book of *Common* Prayer, which contains the belief and the prayer of one branch of Christianity. Similarly, the new daily office of the Roman Church is called "The Prayer of the Church." Again and again, we find the need to reassert the obvious, that prayer is a corporate activity, not just with angels and archangels, but with other Christians now. Human nature has a genius for making prayer individualistic; too many people in the past have spoken of liturgical prayer in the eucharist as "Me and My Lord," and clergy still describe saying the offices as "saying *my* office." One of the lessons which religious communities have much to teach the rest of the present-day church is the discipline of being physically near other Christians during daily prayer and worship. Even if monks do not like each other, the necessity of being next to each other several times a day can help them to accept their dislike and to heal it.

Those for Whom We Pray

The third level is the relationship with those *for* whom we pray. And it is those *people*, not those *situations*. A peculiar habit of contemporary society is to dehumanize people, until they become situations, whether on-going, crisis-ridden, or processed. When I listen to special intercessions in public worship which reflect these secular tendencies, I often think of the bold phrases of some of the classical formulas, which are by contrast so personal and at the same time so theological. This example is the ninth of the Roman Catholic Good Friday biddings, which is personal in style, yet universal in scope:

> Let us pray
> for those who serve in public office,
> that God may guide their minds and hearts,
> so that all may live in true peace and freedom.

Effective intercession, therefore, needs to be real to the people who are praying, and also apposite. As Geoffrey Wainwright has succinctly written: "the test of sincere intercession is the commitment to corresponding action."[3] You cannot pray for anyone without involving yourself.

But this involvement varies. There are some items of prayer which can imply activity, for instance, visiting the sick. There are other subjects of prayer which can involve no activity other than being better informed and contributing financial help, for instance, to the homeless of the Third World. The *effect* of the prayer, however, is to make us more Christ-like in being open to the needs of others, and this is why those liturgies are most helpful which somehow build into their structures a form of prayer which includes certain widely spread themes in a regular pattern.

PRAYER AND LANGUAGE

At this stage in the discussion, it is worth taking the opportunity to explore the critical question of the language of prayer, since it sometimes comes home with a vengeance in the intercession, because of the freedom that is now generally allowed.

Some years ago Michael Ramsey made three criticisms of the Anglican Prayer Book tradition. He suggested that it suffered from being too verbose, too preachy, and too cerebral.[4] His observations in fact point up three symptoms of the contemporary west which stand in contrast to previous ages, in particular sixteenth-century England. We will consider them one by one.

Dislike for Length of Speech

It is clear that we do not like length of speech, because many are naturally suspicious of verbosity, whether from politicians, the pulpit, or from the media in general. You have to earn the right to be listened to at length; you cannot assume it.

This means that modern prayers measure their effectiveness as means of communication by their epigrammatic structure and content, which probably explains why patristic rather than medieval or reformed patterns have served as the models for so many new compositions; and if you don't like the anaphora of Hippolytus, there is still the early version of Basil of Caesarea.[5] But while one struggles to work out a new style of liturgical language which is both incarnate in this world as it is now, and redemptive in lifting us from the quagmire of present human existence to beyond, what one loses in a somewhat arid style is gained in structure. You don't have to be a liturgist to listen to a variety of anaphoras, ordination prayers, or nuptial blessings and hear certain common themes, which are expressed in different ways. Variety is the spice of life, particularly when that life is lived in chunks of common experience rather than superlatives of high-flown excellence that don't speak to us any longer.

Preachiness

Preachiness is the second criticism referred to by Ramsey, and it is probably the most obvious today in all modern services when they are presented and performed badly. What Anglicanism evolved in the sixteenth century appears to us today as preachy, although it did not appear so then. But preachiness we are certainly all indulging in to excess. When a service, still worse a whole liturgical tradition, becomes intent at getting at congregations, and telling them what they should believe, or more commonly what they should be doing, worship ceases to uplift, but simply pours out, and that with much emptiness. Many celebrations suffer from piling high more and more "things" on the congregation's mind, whether in unnecessary "introductions," superfluous "welcomes," aggressively activist "notices," or just ill-prepared sermons and intercessions. As Ulrich Simon wrote somewhat rhapsodically and caustically several years ago, "God still remains to be found."[6] Worship must recover some sense of *adoration* if it is to be alive and healthy, and the adoration must start from the heart, and not just consist of words. Part of our problem is that we expect the meaning of things to leap to our eyes and ears, and we no longer like to grow in understanding—everything must be immediate. Furthermore, the anxiety to make a "totality" out of the liturgy naturally means that many wish to relate the intercessions to the theme of the readings and sermon. There is little evidence of this in antiquity—quite the reverse, in fact—and Paul De Clerck's magisterial study of the intercession in the west singles out this modern trend as being a quite new feature of the liturgy.[7] Many are the occasions when it is both appropriate and praiseworthy, but there is a danger of making the intercession into a repeat performance of the sermon, with the result that the liturgy loses some much needed subtlety, the *universal* dimension of prayer is lost, and it ceases to be prayerful. Worship needs more care, more preparation; not least in the intercession. To borrow Bernard of Clairvaux's well-known image, it needs to become more like a bowl, and less like a funnel.

The Cerebral Aspect of Worship

This naturally leads us to Ramsey's third criticism, the cerebral aspect of worship. Once again, it is a mistake which can be as easily identified today as in sixteenth-century England. Are modern liturgies, or more accurately, are the ways modern liturgies are *presented*, too cerebral, too much addressed to the *mind* of the people, and insufficiently addressed to the *heart*? There is a danger of liturgical language becoming too literalistic in its style, and failing to give birth to new images. The Prayer Book Eucharist and the Tridentine Mass in time developed extraneous compensations, but these proved inadequate (as in the case of sentimental Anglican hymnody), or else downright distorting (as in the case of individual Roman devotions). This state of things becomes intolerable because of its theological inconsistency.

Christian worship at its best leans on the wholesome psychology of Judaism: "Thou shalt love the Lord thy God with all thy *heart*, and with all thy *soul*, and with all thy *mind*, and with all thy *strength*." The sophisticated westerner can find this hard to take, but William Temple was right in pointing out that, when religion neglects one part of the human personality, that aspect is bound to return in a disfigured, even a warped form.[8] This means that liturgical language, as well as the style of the liturgical celebration, should evoke a response from the imagination and the affections, as well as the will and the intellect. As long as they fail to do this, our rites and our services will continue to be noted for dull competence rather than sparkling brilliance. The acid test is really that language in worship should identify with the worshipers but also "stretch" them; it should speak to the people but also uplift them.

What are the implications of this for liturgical intercession? Simply this: intercessions are frequently the most verbose, the most preachy, and the most cerebral ingredients in the eucharistic celebration, and this holds good also of non-eucharistic worship. This is because they are long-winded, in that they hammer home ideas instead of suggesting them; because they are written (or uttered) in order to needle people, instead of trying to help them to pray; and because they are boldly intellectual, in that they hand out information and nothing more. Of course there are occasions when one or other of these aspects is needed, particularly if local circumstances make it appropriate, for example, willingness to spend money on an extra organ-stop after a sparse Christian Aid Week. But these heavy possibilities of intercession should not become the norm. Benedict was right in recommending that prayers are better when they are short. Dean William Perry was justified in criticizing the old Absolution in Morning and Evening Prayer for containing "hardly anything except information." And the Psalmist cried in despair not for a new mind but for a new heart . . .[9]

The liturgy, however, has to carry a great deal. While theologians may challenge any number of traditional dogmas or details of biblical exegesis, *and* get away with it, the moment a change is made in public worship, questions are asked. A theologian's blunder has far fewer repercussions than a liturgist's; and, what is more, liturgy is where most people receive and digest their theology, for good or ill. The handshake or bear-hug (enjoyed or disliked) at the Peace expresses forgiveness and reconciliation as a prelude to the eucharist; and a sweet hymn to the cross encapsulates personal feeling about the atonement more effectively than a series of challenging sermons. Prayer from the heart is the mirror of what we really believe; as De Boer has bluntly put it, "the most adequate prayer will be the silent prayer, for when we are silent we are one, and when we speak we are two."[10]

This line of thinking has its advantages, but it also has its drawbacks. It is possible—and probably frequent—that people use the language of the church to hide behind, and in the old days, the hieratic language of Tudor England or medieval Rome served as a kind of cushion from the self-exploration (even the self-examination) which the plainness of new language inevitably provokes. For example, Anglicans could have difficulties over passages from the Nicene Creed (which, after all, was written in the fourth century, and takes no account of theological development in the many centuries since), but these were concealed, deliberately or not, beneath the subtle combination of Cranmerian prose and Merbecke's chant.[11] The so-called new translation when it is *said* has a different feel altogether, and makes the most somnolescent believer wake up!

But the tension may go deeper still, and consist of a dichotomy between faith as it has been handed down, and belief as it is actually experienced. Anglicans have long been used to this schizophrenia,[12] which often appears in church members as well as theologians and clergy, whose personal *belief* is radical and questioning, but whose *spirituality* is formal and conservative. It may well be only in the public intercession of the church that these two contrary aspects can resolve themselves. The great high-flown periods of the anaphora can pass over their heads and hearts, but new-style intercessions, which often insist on particularity, cannot escape their critical eye. Intercession is for them, for everyone, near the bone—and rightly so.

Another way in which people can hide from their doubts through using old language is coming to light in the protest against what many call the "absence of mystery" in new services. It is difficult to define what is meant by this phrase. It may be lack of dignity, even lack of the security which time-honored forms possess. The Canon was muttered after the ringing of the *Sanctus* bell at a far altar; or the Prayer for the Church Militant was enunciated by an urbane and cultured gentleman who happened to be ordained. Yes—we have lost something; but I suspect that much of this "mystery" (so called) is really about atmosphere in worship—where people sit, how the church is lit, the pace at which prayers are read or sung, as well as the tone of voice used by those conducting the service. All this, and much more, has changed in so many churches alongside the change in liturgical language. Many people do yearn for the old days, and they probably would have done the same in 1549, when the first Book of Common Prayer was introduced, had they been alive then. They certainly have their predecessors.

But the pilgrim church has to go forward on its way, and pitch its tent in new and often quite unfamiliar territory. The circumstances which we mention in our intercessions are different from the past. We are experiencing the hand of God in our worship in consequently different ways from, say, fourth-century Syria, eighth-century France, sixteenth-century Germany, just to take three formative eras in the history of the church. We may have lost out on beauty of language, but this is a subjective matter in many ways, and in any case, beauty is a deceptive companion in the quest for truth, and many criticisms of new services could be met by preparing and presenting them with greater care.

LITURGICAL STYLES AND TENDENCIES

Paul De Clerck's study of the development of the intercession in the west has thrown a great deal of light on the forces which help to shape this too long neglected ingredient in the eucharist. It is, perhaps, a pity that the energies of liturgists should have been so much focused in recent years on the eucharistic prayer, for although the fruits of their labors speak for themselves in the consensus which is now so apparent between the churches on what should make up an anaphora, more study of intercession in the past before the recent divisions might have helped to clarify and scrutinize texts.

Nonetheless, many of the intercessions in the new books have drawn on ancient models, Latin as well as Byzantine (as witness the new American Prayer Book), but never to the point of anachronism.[13] You can pray an antiquarian anaphora more easily than an intercession, especially if the former employs a rich biblical catalogue of creation and redemption motifs, and the latter prays for non-existent catechumens and the Holy Roman Emperor.

Four tendencies can be discerned in modern intercessions. They overlap, but they are still distinct.

The Tendency to Particularize

The first is the tendency to *particularize*, to which we have already alluded. A glance at contemporary texts proves this immediately, as witness the occurrence of the word "particular." We are more likely to pray for the sore toe of the person who delivers the mail than for the ailments of Her Majesty's public servants. Like the diptychs of old, particular intercessions have a specific reference, but the danger is that they fossilize, they lose their particularity, because they are unthinkingly repeated.

Particular intercessions of this kind come in two quite different forms, and should not be confused. Pray for Zimbabwe by praying to God, or by asking the congregation; in other words, it is a case of using either the petition ("we pray for . . .") or the bidding ("Let us pray for . . ."). The biddings/collect sequence from the Roman Good Friday services makes this plain and clear.

The Tendency to Generalize

Another tendency is to *generalize*. Although not so fashionable, it is still a framework behind prayers of intercession which allow for both "free" and "set" portions, and this is the method that was espoused in some recent Church of England rites for the eucharist. Whether or not these options are always used, they serve to universalize the scope of the intercessions, and may also prevent the community from becoming too bound up in its own pet concerns. Generalizing intercessions are in the same genre as the ancient collect.

It is a pity, however, if the free compositions of modern intercessions are invariably particular, never general. The new

Roman Divine Office contains many fine litanies at morning and evening prayer which are frequently general in style, meditating on the theological mystery of the day or occasion, a most successful feature, which often combines succinctness with force. At Christmas and Easter there are opportunities in the eucharist to bring theology into intercessions, for example, in commemorating the dead on Easter Day.

Combining Word and Prayer

A third feature is to *combine word and prayer*. Not so common as the others, this method requires skill and flair, qualities not in abundance. If the occasion demands, the leader of the intercession may wish to direct attention to a specific theme by a short "sentence" (whether taken from Scripture or a Christian writer, or composed for the occasion); and it is followed by a silence and a short collect-type prayer. (The procedure can be repeated, over a number of topics, or different aspects of the same theme.) Such a scheme has much in common with the old Embertide biddings between the readings, or the Hispanic "Paschal Prayers." The similarity is that readings provoke prayer; the difference is that these readings should be short and to the point.

Involvement

The fourth tendency is by far the most distinctive in recent centuries, *involvement*; it is indeed a mark of the revolution which has happened so quickly. The intercession is split up among different participants, who exercise a diaconal function, and the prayers are summed up in a series of prayers or a final collect by the president. Taking this a stage further, the intercession may contain a number of responses said or sung by the congregation, like the *Kyrie eleison* of old; or the responses may be different each time, and easily followed because printing service-sheets is much easier than it was.

History has its own lessons to teach about this. The responses should be real responses to prayer, and not become an excuse to sing elaborate chants, unless the talent is obvious and appropriate. Different voices should blend together, so that the congregation does not get so distracted that the intercession is no prayer, but like a bad chorus from a Greek tragedy. The principle of involvement is a fine one, and needs to be worked at.

Of these four types, the first is probably going to be the commonest for the foreseeable future, together with the fourth, precisely because of the scope that they give. But they need to be kept in balance, so that general universalizes particular, and monologue tempers involvement. It is interesting to note that Geoffrey Willis, in his study of the Good Friday prayers, has demonstrated that the biddings are older than the collects, and probably date back as far as the third century.[14] Here is a remarkable testimony to the reluctance of intercession to adapt to new ways on special occasions. But where the litany adapted on ordinary occasions, the local rites of Western Europe were very much in the hands of local liturgists, and De Clerck's work on the Franco-Gallican *dicamus omnes* shows how risky is the business of linking set intercessions closely to a particular age, especially if subsequent ages are less interested in development and change, and slavishly use forms which no longer have meaning for them.

Yet another area of development today is clearly a minority interest, but sound and pastoral, and this is to *introduce intercessions into the anaphora*. Daring are the churches which do this, particularly if they allow liberty as well. The new Roman anaphoras contain intercessions, but in relatively set forms, whereas the "Common Eucharistic Prayer" (Prayer D in the American Prayer Book) is the most significant contemporary example, in which there is a structure with (mandatory) general themes, to which may be added special subjects *ad libitum*. Engberding made the study of eastern anaphoras his life's work, and he has shown that it is precisely in the intercessions that the various local versions of the prayer of St. Basil (on which Prayer D is based) exhibit the most variety, because a number of local styles and interests were in operation in this part of the anaphora as it was reaching a developed form, whether in Syria, Byzantium, Alexandria, or Armenia.[15] This should encourage rather than inhibit us, whether in the direction of appropriate freedom, or in order to recover the practice of anaphoral intercession, which is so logical after the communion epiclesis, when the church prays for the blessing of the Spirit on its life of faith.

Whatever form is used for intercession (litany, biddings and/or collects, free prayer), history demonstrates the advantages of having a big pastoral heart, in praying for real needs (e.g., the Stowe Missal, which is the first extant litany composed in Latin), and combining this with a good selection of topics (e.g., the *Deprecatio Gelasii*, one of the finest forms of intercession in antiquity). Another lesson is that—as with so many parts of the liturgy—good forms of intercession spread from one place to another on their own inherent quality, and (given imaginative handling) adapt to local circumstances. The history of Christian worship is a nervous compendium of progress and regression, and even if the intercession has to embody on its way theologies which become outdated (e.g., praying selfishly for good weather, knowing that scientifically this makes things difficult for other inhabitants of the earth), the fact remains that at its best it continues to set before God's people their work and God's work, in ways that are sound and clear.

SOME PASTORAL ISSUES

Apart from problems arising from liturgical technique, there are some basic personal conditions which the public prayer of the church has to carry, and these become more acute with the introduction of freer forms of intercession.

Unanswered Prayer

One is the old question of *unanswered prayer*. Intercessions which repeatedly mention people by name, and their physical, mental, or spiritual condition, run the risk of demanding what God may not give. For instance, if we pray for a regular communicant of the church who is seriously ill, the feelings aroused in the eucharistic gathering may be high, even emotional, and everyone naturally wants that person to recover. A diagnosis of "terminal illness" may lead to the ministry of the laying-on of hands and anointing (if these have not happened before). It could be that the person recovers to live a long time, or has a temporary reprieve, or dies.

In this context it is just as well that we have set forms of prayer to fall back on, because over the weeks or years specific requests will change, as the praying community adjusts to what is happening. Generalized prayer for the suffering (fine examples of which are to be found in the Alternative Service Book and the American Prayer Book) help to gather up the more specific petitions, which are not "answered," if the person for whom the prayer is made is going to die soon. The interplay of the official (general) text and the local (specific) insertion marks an important pastoral transition which the liturgy should express.

The Absence of God

Another problem is the spiritual condition which has recently been described as the *absence of God*.[16] Many people feel this absence at different points in their lives, even in different parts of the same year, and the human sciences of psychology, psychoanalysis, and psychiatry have done much to clarify what brings on these bouts or conditions, whether they be caused by external or biochemical stress. The church cannot turn its back on these natural phenomena among her own members, nor should they be marked off as sinful, in the way that the ancients described *accidie,* which, in our opinion, overlaps with the mental and physiological conditions which feel spiritual emptiness, and, in the case of the believing Christian, can often lead to unnecessary feelings of guilt. Some people are more prone to this than others.

Apart from an obvious concern to accompany the healing ministries of the secular world, the Christian community has a duty to proclaim the cry of dejection from the cross as an authentic part of Christian experience, and one which can (and should) find appropriate expression in public prayer. Assuming that this should not become a masochistic indulgence through undue frequency or intensity, the vital question is, how should it be expressed?

There are occasions when not just individuals but entire congregations sense the absence of God, though this will not happen frequently. When it does, the atmosphere of the celebration will probably be heavy, because of spiritual deadness, when nothing means anything, preaching seems empty, the sacraments feel lifeless. The liturgical year embodies a natural rhythm of waiting and barrenness (Advent and Lent), jubilation and splendor (Christmas and Easter), reflection and plain sailing (the "green" Sundays). But at the heart of the personal deadness lies the intercession, which should offer up the emptiness of the community, or the individuals, as a deepening of relationship with God—for God's absence implies that the relationship is there, even if it is not felt. Prayers for church, world, suffering, and departed take on a new dimension, which hymn- writers in the past have often been the only artists within the liturgy with the courage to explore, such as the Dane, Bernhard Severin Ingemann, whose manic "Igennem nat og traengsel" is well-known in English as "Through the night of doubt and sorrow" or his compatriot, Nikolai Grundtvig's "er du modfalden, kaere ven?" ("are you downcast, dear friend?").

Prayer and the Departed

For many, an added difficulty arises at that stage which every Christian has to face sooner or later—*prayer and the departed*. Whether one be Catholic, Protestant, or somewhere between, bereavement will certainly make any Christian more aware of the need to express in prayer some relationship with the person who has died. As usual, the two traditional extremes offer their wares, with one side insisting on prayer *for* the departed and prayer *by* the saints, and the other side adhering to the Reformed principle of thanksgiving *only* for those who have gone before in faith.

Some find these explanations inadequate, and they are more than likely to be found so at the point of bereavement, even if the Catholic gets a thoroughly-paschal funeral, or the Protestant gets a joyful send-off. On the one hand, although the notion of "the remedial fire" is still alive, purgatory itself seems unreal, and actually underplayed in modern Catholicism. On the other hand, only to give thanks for some locks up grief, which is so necessary; and to consign others to the fires of hell is a Protestant legacy which effectively puts the church in the place of God. Donald Allchin has written with great perception on this question. He maintains that there is an instinct which perceives not only the world beyond at the moment of death, but a fellowship and communion of saints embracing

those left behind and those who have gone before.[17] The Alexandrian Anaphora of Basil contains so much of beauty and antiquity, among which numbers a finely-phrased intercession of
the departed, couched in strongly eschatological ideas, which
are at once biblical, catholic, and tender:

> Since, Master, it is a command of your only-begotten Son that
> we should share in the commemoration of your saints, vouch-
> safe to remember, Lord, also those of our fathers who have
> been well-pleasing to you from eternity . . . [Then follows a list
> of faithful ones, and the reading of the diptychs] . . . Give them
> rest in your presence; preserve us who live here in your faith,
> guide us to your kingdom, and grant us your peace at all times;
> through Jesus Christ and the Holy Spirit.[18]

* * * * * *

Liturgical renewal certainly affects the style, the language,
and even the attitudes to intercessory prayer. But it has gone
much further than that. Comparatively little help has been giv-
en to this crucial part of Christian worship,[19] and, in consequence, we are witnessing what amounts to a creation *ex nihilo*. Through being deprived of the old and familiar, we have
had to start again, and so there is set before us the opportunity
to rediscover what intercession really is. Even if we have little
to say, the starting point is that intercession, isolated though it
may be from other parts of the liturgy, is one of the supreme
and costly privileges of the Christian.

So the tensions and the upsets and the time taken to prepare
intercession—all these are hiccups that are worth while. Why?
Because the real purpose of intercession is to express the essential dimensions of the Christian faith . . . that we are friends
of God, because we are his adopted sons and daughters . . .
that we are committed to each other, in a sacramental and living communion . . . and that we are resolved to serve them in
the world, and to participate in its joy and pain. The offering
of intercession, therefore, should feel for these three vital sensitivities, in which language and symbol become lost in wonder, love, and praise, and the liturgy becomes a mere vehicle
of God's redeeming power.

Notes

1. Augustine, Second Letter to Proba, VIII, 17, quoted by P. Baelz, *Prayer and Providence* (London: SCM, 1968) 112, n. 22, where Baelz gives a paraphase of the original; see PL 33:501.

2. A. Bloom, *Living Prayer* (London: Libra Books, 1966) 71.

3. G. Wainwright, *Doxology* (London: Epworth, 1980) 355.

4. Quoted from M. Duggan, *Through the Year with Michael Ramsey* (London: Hodder and Stoughton, 1975) 162.

5. M. Hatchett, *Commentary on the American Prayer Book* (New York: Seabury, 1980) 374-375, 377-378.

6. U. Simon, "Unliturgical Remarks on Eucharistic Liturgy," *Theology* 74, no. 611 (May 1971) 207.

7. P. De Clerk, *La "Prière universelle" dans les litugies latines anciennes*, Liturgiewissenschaftliche Quellen und Forschungen, vol. 62 (Münster: Aschendorff, 1977) 311ff.

8. F.A. Iremonger, *William Temple* (Oxford: Oxford University Press, 1948) 327; Temple is quoted in some observations on the characteristics of the Lancashire folk, but they can be applied less restrictedly.

9. Rule of St. Benedict, ch. 20 ("Reverence in Prayer"); W. Perry, *The Scottish Prayer-Book—Its Value and History* (Cambridge: Cambridge University Press, 1929) 54; Psalm 51:10.

10. P.A.H. De Boer, *Fatherhood and Motherhood in Israelite and Judaean Piety* (Leiden: Brill, 1974) 53.

11. Kenneth Stevenson, ed., *Authority and Freedom in the Liturgy*, Grove Liturgical Study, vol. 17 (Bramcote: Grove, 1979) 30f.

12. Michael Ramsey, *Jesus and the Living Past* (Oxford: Oxford University Press, 1980) 56, where Ramsey describes the more extreme variety of this tension as a "spiritual *tour de force.*"

13. *The Book of Common Prayer* (New York: Seabury, 1979) 383-395.

14. G. Willis, *Essays in Early Roman Liturgy*, Alcuin Club Collections, vol. 46 (London: SPCK, 1964) 45-47.

15. H. Engberding, in various articles entitled "Das anaphorische Fürbittgebet," *Oriens Christianus*, e.g., on Armenian Basil, 51 (1967) 29-50; others include 45 (1961) 20-29; 46 (1962) 33-60; 47 (1963) 16-52; 49 (1965) 18-37; and 50 (1966) 13-18.

16. Wainwright, *Doxology* 42f.; see F. Paget, *The Spirit of Discipline* (London: Longmans, 1933) for the famous essay on *accidie*. See also the excellent exploratory book by Gordon Mursell, *Out of the Deep: Prayer as Protest* (London: Darton, Longman and Todd, 1989).

17. A.M. Allchin, *The World Is a Wedding* (London: Darton, Longmann and Todd, 1978) 68ff.

18. R.C.D. Jasper, G.J. Cuming, eds., *The Prayers of the Eucharist* (London: Collins, 1980) 36f; see J. Doresse, E. Lanne, eds., *Un Témoin archaïque de la liturgie copte de S. Basile*, Bibliothèque du Muséon, vol. 47 (Louvain, Presses Universitaires, 1960) 24ff.

19. The excellent little book, Michael Vasey, *Intercessions in Worship*, Grove Worship, vol. 77 (Bramcote: Grove, 1981) is a notable exception. A more general work is Lukas Vischer, *Intercession* (Geneva: World Council of Churches, 1980), combining profundity with constructive and eirenic comment.

2

Eucharistic Offering:
Does Research into Origins
Make Any Difference?

AT THE RISK OF RUSHING IN WHERE ANGELS FEAR TO TREAD, I WILL try to make some suggestions and guidelines for a specifically liturgical study of eucharistic offering, on the basis of the many anaphoras of the Eastern Churches. By way of introduction, perhaps I should give some explanation for my motivations in this regard.

I was nurtured in the Scottish Episcopal Church, and grew up with its eucharistic liturgy. At one stage of my education in that church, a priest showed me a copy of the Scottish Liturgy of 1764, which in the eighteenth and nineteenth centuries was usually celebrated after a synaxis taken from the (English) 1662 liturgy. The priest carefully explained some of the features of difference between the Scottish and the English eucharists, beginning, naturally, with the epiclesis, in its traditional West Syrian position. But he also pointed out that in the anamnesis, the words "which we now offer unto thee" appeared immediately after reference to the holy gifts, and, moreover, that this clause was printed in large capital letters.[1]

I was not yet aware of the full implications of this insertion. But it is significant that the words *were* inserted, thereby implying that England was inadequate in its more Protestant stance, and although the Scottish Episcopal tradition had been increasingly infected by the eighteenth-century Non-Jurors with their "higher" sacramental theology, this influence was only building upon a "Laudian" High-Churchmanship which can be seen in the liturgy of the Scottish Prayer Book of 1637.[2] Nonetheless, these words were *inserted* in order to express a particular theological emphasis within the total eucharistic action.

As a student at Edinburgh University during the late 1960s, I was involved in the issue as to whether the student Chaplaincy should adhere to using the (slightly modernized) Scottish Episcopal liturgy at the eucharist, or should open its arms to the majority of the English students, who were becoming familiar with the liturgy contained in the so-called "Series 2" eucharistic order. Now, that order had been proposed in a form which included the words, "we offer this bread and this cup," but Evangelical pressure in the Church of England had removed those words, and substituted for them, "we make the memorial . . .", thus deleting the poisonous verb "to offer."[3]

As a seminarian, I made a doctoral study of the eucharistic liturgy of the Catholic Apostolic Church, which is a nineteenth-century sect that has now disappeared with which my family was associated, and which had interesting and unique ecumenical, liturgical, and charismatic pretensions, about which I have written elsewhere.[4]

When I defended the dissertation, the first point made by the external examiner was that I had omitted one source, and this source was the verb in the anamnesis of that rite. In English, it was, "we present," a less loaded word than "we offer," a fact I had noted in my commentary. But, suggested the examiner, was this verb surely not taken from the anamnesis in Greek Mark, *"proethêkamen,"* "we presented"?[5]

All three of these experiences, the Scottish Liturgy of 1764, the English controversy over "Series 2," and the composition of the Catholic Apostolic Liturgy, in time convinced me of the following principles lying behind eucharistic offering as expressed in the liturgy: (1) antiquity knows of no uniform treatment of the theme within the eucharistic prayer; (2) we are on surer ground when we talk *imprecisely* about eucharistic offering, *if* we are to use ancient anaphoral themes and structures as our models; (3) the ancient anaphoras developed *organically*, whereas those areas of Western Protestantism which have sought to inculcate more overt sacrificial ideas into their liturgies have done so *self-consciously*.

The way offering and sacrifice are handled in the main anaphoras of the Eastern Churches, as these are to be found in the pages of *Prex Eucharistica*,[6] reveals a number of significant points of variety:

1. A West-Syrian/Byzantine focus on anamnesis-epiclesis: offering the gifts for consecration and communion. Such an essential movement is discernible in the archetype, the *Apostolic Tradition* of Hippolytus.

2. An East Syrian concept of offering which was "unitive," as witness the (supposedly early) formula in the Addai and Mari dialogue prior to the anaphora.[7]

3. An Armenian reticence on offering in the anamnesis, though still stressing the "sacrifice of praise" at other points in the anaphoral traditions.

4. A tantalizing Egyptian focus on past-tense verbs in the anamnesis, which could be interpreted to point back to the placing of the gifts on the altar, or the offering before the intercessions in the preface.

5. In all of them, sacrificial language appears in regard to the anaphora as a sacrifice of praise and thanksgiving, but also as making

6. a close connection between those who have offered the gifts and the anaphora itself, as witness the frequent mention of the "offerers" in the intercessions. (Such an insight, by the way, has a great deal to teach us today about the sacrificial character of intercession.[8])

The last two of those conclusions are important, not only for present ecumenical convergence, but also in demonstrating the internal unity of the eucharistic prayer in the various traditions of antiquity. Taking the first four each in turn, some clarification is in order.

THE WEST SYRIAN/BYZANTINE ANAPHORA

The "archetype" for this anaphora is that of Hippolytus,[9] despite the problems which surround that text. The movement of ideas within the prayer regarding offering seems to be:

1. Telling the story;
2. Offering the gifts in remembrance;
3. Praying for the work of the Spirit in the eucharistic celebration.

Ligier may well be right in suggesting that the narrative of the institution and the anamnesis were a recent addition to the prayer;[10] nonetheless, as the reconstructed text stands, the gifts are presented to God for God's blessing, but the words "oblation of the church" could be taken to mean not the eucharistic gifts so much as the whole eucharistic celebration. In other words, an imprecise formula, reminiscent of the use of the word "sacrifice" of the eucharist in *Didache* 9 and 14, where the context implies the *whole* celebration.[11]

The Basil anaphoral tradition expands on this sequence of ideas considerably. The early Alexandrian text, edited by Doresse and Lanne,[12] contains a number of interesting features. (Although it only starts just before the institution narrative, we can surmise from the later Coptic Alexandrian recension that there was no offering in the preface, unlike the [even later] Byzantine version.) The first is that at the epiclesis, prayer is made for the Spirit to make "these gifts that are set before you . . . holy of holies"; an imprecise and allusive treatment of eucharistic consecration. The second is that at the commemoration of the departed, there is no conscious division into two groups, the saints and the remainder. Now, the eastern tradition does not make such a distinction explicitly; this anaphora, in language reminiscent of the Jewish Passover embolism, asks God "to remember" the faithful saints and fathers of the church.

Faced with these two theological "primitivisms" (which are also of ecumenical significance), the Doresse-Lanne Greek retroversion's use of an aorist verb at the anamnesis ("we presented") is tantalizing. Raes criticized this as an Egyptian symptom, since the anaphora of Mark uses this verb in the anamnesis, the offering in Mark being located early on in the preface. But it is not just the *tense* of the verb which has altered, it is the verb itself—"present" instead of "offer." Both words have sacrificial *nuances*, but the second has them more easily, as the English translation shows. Granted that the Coptic text dates from the seventh century, we could allow for ample time for the anaphora to have been Egyptianized. But Gregory Dix was criticized for having taken liberties with the text of the *Apostolic Tradition*. My own conclusion is that "we presented" is authentic, and is an "early" symptom of the tradition represented by Basil. The movement of offering within this prayer, therefore, is essentially one of "gift." The "story" is recounted in the preface and post-*Sanctus*. The gifts "were presented" before the anaphora began (no offertory-theology here, merely reference to a functional act), so that when the anamnesis comes, the dominant theme is that of remembrance, especially when the descriptive expressions are taken into account, "your own from your own gifts," and "that are set before you" in the epiclesis. Moreover, the prayer for "those who offer these gifts to you, and those for whom they are presented" in the ensuing intercessions strengthens this theme.

The later Alexandrian version of Basil adds little to this interesting original. The verb in the anamnesis is "we offer," in line with Hippolytus, and also Chrysostom, James, and *Apostolic Constitutions* VIII.[13] A few small words are added at the epiclesis and the prayer for the offerers, but the scheme remains theologically the same. However, when we come to the Byzantine version,[14] the additions are greater, as one would expect, because the entire anaphora has undergone considerable expansion. Near the beginning of the preface, thanks are given to God for Christians being able "to offer to you with a contrite heart and a humble spirit this our reasonable service," and toward the end of the preface, God is praised for "enabling the whole reasonable and intelligent creation" to "do you service and render you unending praise."

For the first expansion, the parallel is with Greek Mark, where the offering of "reasonable *and unbloody* service" occurs in the preface, though if Geoffrey Cuming and others are right, the tradition represented by the Strasbourg papyrus may be no "mere" fragment but a complete anaphora.[15] Is Basil influenced by Mark? It would seem that he (whoever was the author of this Byzantine version) certainly was. For the second expression, the word "render" is another verb with sacrificial overtones, and it is used in the *Trisagion* prayer of the Byzantine liturgy.[16] But the parallel is less direct for position in the anaphora; in Chrysostom praise is not "rendered," but God is asked to "receive" this "ministry," an oblique expression which was probably originally intended to refer to the whole priestly Body of Christ.[17]

Another addition comes just before the institution narrative: "And he left us memorials of his saving passion, these things which we have set forth." Allowing for the expansion of an anaphora, it is probably necessary to repeat certain themes in order to hold it together: thus, at the end of such a full account of the life of Christ, it is needful to refer to the gifts just before the narrative of the Last Supper. What is interesting is that the verb is not only past, but *perfect*-tense (whereas in the early Alexandrian version, and in Greek Mark, the verb in the anamnesis is *aorist*). Could the author have been familiar with the early Alexandrian version? This is certainly a remote possibility.

After the institution narrative, there is a similar desire to hold together the anaphora in its expanded format, with the repetition of "Therefore, Master, we also . . ." at the start of the anamnesis and epiclesis. At the end of the anamnesis, the *Grottaferrata G b VII* text reads "and offering you from your own, in all and through all." Later versions revert (?) to the indicative ("we offer"). It is conceivable that by using the participle form, the purpose is to emphasize thanksgiving and memorial, instead of offering.[18]

Another repetition of a theme comes in the epiclesis, "approach your holy altar," and with "having set forth the likeness of the holy body and blood of your Christ." And the prayer for the offerers is similarly expanded.

As far as the eucharistic offering is concerned, however, the Byzantine version does not alter much from the Alexandrian version used by the Coptic Church. The dominant theme is that of "gift," but it is set in the context of "story" and "response," as the full catalogue of salvation history before the narrative and the full intercessions after the epiclesis demonstrate. The internal logic of this tradition is that sacrifice of praise is offered to God in the first part of the anaphora, and the gifts are offered in the anamnesis for consecration and communion, which involves sacrificial intercession, as the church responds to the social context of the eucharist.

THE EAST SYRIAN ANAPHORA

In the present texts of the East Syrian anaphoras, the *cusha-pas* (prayers of inclination) form an important part of what might be called the more developed spirituality of the eucharistic liturgy. These have been usefully studied by Bryan Spinks,[19] who has also gone on to study the whole concept of offering in the anaphoras of Theodore and Nestorius, where he works out an ingenious and persuasive sequence of ideas. It is worth comparing their complexity with Addai and Mari, where the notion of sacrifice involves no sequence whatever, but appears to be "unitive."[20] Moreover, the juxtaposition of thanksgiving and offering is abundantly plain from the start, in the formulas used in the dialogue. In the third *Gehanta*, the eucharist is described as "the commemoration of the body and blood of your Christ which we offer to you upon the pure and holy altar as you have taught us"; and the ensuing epiclesis in that prayer recalls Hippolytus, "and rest upon this oblation of your servants," which we would interpret imprecisely, along the lines of the *Didache* rather than later western medieval theology. Addai and Mari may yet be more primitive than Hippolytus, or (for that matter) early Alexandrian Basil. Taking us right back to the Semitic roots of Christian euchology, it speaks of the eucharist in dynamic terms, and with no internal sequence of ideas. Simplicity, indeed, requires such a theological starkness.

THE ARMENIAN ANAPHORA

The Armenian anaphora of James[21] provides us with a good example of adaptation, and it may, indeed, be paralleled in the way in which Twelve Apostles was "Syriacized," if the original of Twelve Apostles came from Greek West Syria.[22] At the anamnesis of Armenian James, which is shorter than both the Syriac and Greek versions, we "remember" the saving acts of Christ, and then "shout and say: spare us, Lord . . .," thus leading into supplication in the epiclesis, where the bread is "set before." After the petition for consecration, the priest prays that God "receive from our hands the gifts of your body and blood of Christ," which is the nearest the east ever gets to offering the body and blood of Christ, but is a less strong expression, and simply means "accept" in the sense of ratify consecration.

The anaphora of Athanasius is a complex prayer.[23] During the post-*Sanctus*, "we offer thanks to you . . . you gave us your only-begotten Son . . . victim and anointed, lamb and heavenly bread, archpriest and sacrifice . . ."; this is deliberately paradoxical language, in order to heighten the reality of Christ in the account of the "story." At the anamnesis we encounter the Basil formula, "we offer you your own from your own, in all and for all," but this comes after the eucharistic action has been described as "offering before you this mystery of the saving body and blood of Christ" (compare, once again, with Addai and Mari, "the commemoration . . . which we offer to you . . ."). The epiclesis prays for the Spirit "on these gifts set before," and the intercessions refer repeatedly to "by this sacrifice." All in all, Athanasius amounts to an interesting and original composition, bringing together both Greek and Syriac features.

The anaphora of Gregory Nazianzen, which Gabrielle Winkler has suggested was written by Gregory himself, is perhaps the most striking of all the Armenian prayers.[24] In the post-*Sanctus* the priest prays, "let us offer this sacrifice as an odor of your sweetness" (Phil 4:18, an expression found elsewhere including many Syriac anaphoras). The anamnesis begins with "we offer you, Lord, these oblations given to us by you on this altar": this parallels Addai and Mari, as well as Basil. It goes on to record the saving acts, and includes a remembrance of the three persons of the Trinity, in which "we offer blessing and glory to the Holy Trinity," and "with everlasting glorification we offer this sacrifice and confess this to be the deified body and blood." The epiclesis is brief, twice referring to the "memorial," and the intercessions plead "through these gifts" and "through these things" on four occasions. Gregory Nazianzen thus contains significant Syriac features (eastern and western), which include the expanded anamnesis, the stress on sacrifice of praise, and the sacrificial references in the intercessions. The juxtaposition of "sacrifice" and "memorial" is perhaps a symptom of the continuing need to define the eucharist in ways which were contemporary to the compiler of the prayer.

THE JACOBITE AND MARONITE ANAPHORAS

At this stage I want to look briefly at some features of the many Syriac anaphoras of the Jacobite and Maronite collections. Eight characteristics can be discerned from them.

1. The offering-verb is frequently absent from the anamnesis (as Twelve Apostles), except when the anaphora stresses the sacrifice of Christ as its particular emphasis (e.g., Timothy, Severus, and others).[25]

2. The "offering" of praise is a *nuance* which comes over more easily in Syriac than in Greek; compare the use of "render" in the Byzantine Basil anaphora at the end of the preface. This shows how local language inevitably colors the way in which prayer (not just anaphoral prayer) is composed and understood.[26]

3. "Gifts" are repeatedly referred to as "oblations" in the epiclesis, but the offering is usually at the start of the intercessions, "we offer for . . .," thus sharpening the sacrificial character of intercession.

4. Sometimes there is prayer at the end of the epiclesis for the *acceptance* of the offering, as *sharar*, and Greek Mark, but not Basil, James, or Chrysostom (except in the latter immediately prior to the *Sanctus*).[27]

5. The anamnesis is flexible: sometimes the life of Christ is extended back to his *birth*, usually it is extended forward to the *second coming*, thus mingling the historical and the eschatological.[28]

6. A few anaphoras seem to want to redefine the concept of anamnesis in psychological terms (e.g., James of Edessa).[29]

7. Intercessions invariably include prayer for the offerers.

8. Theological emphases vary, as they should within a rich anaphoral tradition. Sometimes the focus is on "story," sometimes on "gift," sometimes on "response," but all three mingle happily together. What is beyond dispute is that the anamnesis sequence of "remembering . . . we offer" is *not* part of this tradition at all, but is a Greek West Syrian feature. The current preoccupation with Greek West Syrian models of anaphoral prayer needs to be offset by a proper balance when looking at antiquity. Already in the Syriac *Testamentum Domini* the notion of thanksgiving is strengthened in the anamnesis, an idea which provides an earnest of future Syriac developments.

THE EGYPTIAN ANAPHORAS

In Egyptian prayers the science of liturgical research advances more tangibly. There seems to be a growing opinion to support the notion that in the Strasbourg papyrus (fourth-fifth century) we have no "mere" fragment, but a complete anaphora. Like all good hypotheses, it should explain rather more than it assumes, and I am convinced that Geoffrey Cuming's study[30] will stand as a landmark in the history of the study of Egyptian liturgy. If it is complete, then the full liturgical formula is one of offering the whole eucharist early in the anaphora, as a sacrifice of praise and thanksgiving, with the old and oft-quoted passage from Malachi 1:11 following it, serving as explanation, comment, and "rounding off" the introductions; the anaphora then moves into intercession, which opens by referring to the eucharist as an "offering." The *Deir-Balyzeh* papyrus and the Louvain fragments (both sixth century) lead the way in adding the remainder of the anaphora, which eventually includes two epicleses, sandwiched by institution narrative and anamnesis, this latter with a past-tense verb.[31]

The past-tense verb, then, is the result of a subsequent "addendum" to the anaphora, if Strasbourg is complete. In Strasbourg, the offering of the sacrifice of praise comes immediately after the mention of the eucharistic action "through Jesus Christ . . . with the Holy Spirit," which itself comes soon after the start of the anaphora, which in turn follows the placing of the gifts on the altar.[32] Still assuming Strasbourg is complete, therefore, we can discern the logic (however allusive) of the God-ward and the human-ward in the eucharist; the gifts, the sacrifice of praise and thanksgiving, and the sacrifice of intercession. In this latter connection it is interesting to note that incense is directly connected with the intercession in Renaudot's text of Coptic Mark, perhaps inspired by Malachi 1:11, and here Gregory Dix might conceivably be right in one of his inspired guesses that Malachi 1:11 became a biblical source for the theological (as opposed to the fumigatory) use of incense in the liturgy. (The *sharar* also has incense at its intercessions.)[33]

In the development of Mark, various linguistic "retouches" can be seen in the process, but the movement of offering still remains, under the later clothing. Serapion's structure partially reflects it, with the repeated insistence of the past-tense verb.[34] If, however, Strasbourg is incomplete, the offering-logic remains much the same, except that it has evolved organically rather than piecemeal.

I have dwelt on these eastern prayers at some length because they contain so much richness and diversity that without them our story is a bare one. Suffice it to say that the *Didache*[35] provides us with the first eucharistic formula—*thusia*, which later recurs in *Apostolic Constitutions VIII*, Greek Mark, and other prayers. However, this word is from *Didache* 14, and therefore probably the later addition, which was made in order to give precision to the moral qualities of the Christian eucharistic life; but the language used, together with the use of Malachi 1:11, points to a unity between the eucharistic action and the living sacrifice of the Christian community, in faith and good works. Problems over the *Didache* still abound, but it still need not be seen as the archetype for the whole story, particularly when one considers what Aidan Kavanagh has written about the various ways in which baptism was perceived and ritually expressed in East Syria, West Syria, and Rome.[36] Nonetheless, that concluding part to the eucharist in the *Didache* was written neither by Thomas Cranmer in 1549, nor by Gregory the Great in the sixth century. Again and again we liturgists have to guard against trying to read back into the past texts what later formulations and theological infighting have obscured.

Different kinds of literary and theological variety, too, are discernible in the *super oblata* prayers of the various Latin sacramentaries, as well as among the offertory prayers of the later medieval west. The *postpridies* of the Mozarabic tradition also reveal a rich combination of eastern and western ideas, from "epiclesis" to "acceptance," and we even find the expression "holocaust" as a liturgical shorthand for the eucharist.[37] However, it is in the so-called *super oblata* prayers that the transition towards Carolingian notions of priesthood and eucharist can be seen, for in these prayers are to be found the key to what prayer writers expected the eucharist to do, which is an essential aspect of any discussion of eucharistic offering.

* * * * * * *

It will have become apparent by now that an important method in our quest is *historical and literary*: how and when what formulas were developed and why. In conclusion, let me make some further observations, as criteria to what I hope will be a truly ecumenical quest. For even allowing for the fact that the eastern prayers which we have looked at were not written in an atmosphere of theological controversy, they still have some important lessons to teach us.

1. It is important to try to "get behind" the words, in order to find out how they were understood. For an Anglican, this is an appropriate area of concern because of the manifestly wide gap between the intentions of Thomas Cranmer in his eucharistic theology and the intentions of subsequent Anglicans. For example, if Cranmer was Zwinglian in his theology (an epithet which I do not necessarily regard as a criticism, although Gregory Dix who popularized the notion obviously did), his notions of eucharistic presence and offering are far from that which is depicted, for example, on the frontispiece of Charles Wheatly's *Rational Illustration of the Book of Common Prayer*,[38] where, in a classical-designed church, a priest stands in surplice and academic hood, at the north end of a commodious altar, with a mass of elegantly clad communicants devoutly kneeling, and the Lamb of God is atop, in the clouds, eternally offering himself at the north end of the heavenly altar. How a prayer is actually "heard" may indeed vary from the original intentions of the writers of the prayer. On the Roman Catholic scene, if David Holeton's researches are to be heeded, a shift in understanding may well explain why *munus* and *oblata* in Leo the Great refer to the whole eucharist, and not to the gifts, and that the title *super oblata* (which dates only from the seventh century) is anachronistic, at least in reference to the earliest of those prayers, even though that title sums up well the intentions of the later writers.[39]

2. Eucharistic liturgy also knows the process of inserting entirely new prayers (or other material), as the expression of a subsequent age, or even as a gloss upon what is happening. Extra prayers, usually of a devotional kind for the priest, can be divided approximately into three groups: those which duplicate material from the anaphora itself; those which interpret an action in the liturgy (e.g., at the offertory); and those which

express the penitence and unworthiness of the priest.[40] Comparable to this development is the role played, particularly among Protestant Churches, of hymnody. In Lutheranism hymnody was there from the start, and most Lutherans in this day look on their hymnody as a source of their eucharistic spirituality. The same is true of Methodists, who in the Wesleys have a rich quarry from which to construct a theology of eucharistic offering which heeds the protests of many of the Reformers that Calvary must not be undermined, but also reflects what might be described as that instinct for continuity and tradition which has reared its head consistently among Churches of the Reformation since the sixteenth century.[41] Franck's tender hymn, "Schmücke dich, O liebe Seele," Charles Wesley's "Hosanna in the highest," and William Bright's "And now, O Father, mindful of the love"[42]—these examples (and others) all point to the way in which new material builds up a theology and a piety.

3. But we are still dealing with theology, however nebulously, and another essential criterion is concerned with the development and the conceptual framework of theological ideas. Commenting on the Church of England controversy, Leslie Houlden wrote that the problem with "most of the commonest formulations involving sacrificial language is that they start too far up the conceptual ladder; that is, they presuppose more fundamental theological concepts which seem not to be fully clear, like a mountain whose summit is exposed while the lower levels are shrouded in mist."[43] And it is this kind of radical criticism of the debate which throws into question a lot of the kind of writing which recent decades have witnessed, notably Francis Clark's study, which pays scant attention to the development of doctrine and its place in the liturgy, and has a preconceived idea of what "the Catholic theology" of eucharistic sacrifice is, into which everyone else must be fitted or not.[44]

Historical theology, in its search for origins, cannot overlook systematic theological questions. For example, in order to understand Cyprian's view of eucharistic sacrifice,[45] you have to be able to enter into a Neo-Platonic world of prototypes and antitypes. Inevitably, liturgy has to lag behind theological developments, and work out theological shorthand for that kind of formulation of ideas concerning the work of Christ and the worship of Christians in any given age. However, theology is not dominated by Neo-Platonism; it is so pluriform today, not just from an ecumenical point of view, but also within churches, that the challenge facing the liturgist who works with the methods of historical theology is to avoid relativizing everything into context, and instead to offer an overview which shifts perspectives, and enables us to understand how we have got to where we are today.

Finally, let me say that I am convinced that research into origins makes a considerable difference, for a greater understanding of origins will not make us "un-live" our past so much as illuminate a story which is ours, and which is deep in the memory of Christians with whom we share a communion, back through many generations. For without looking to the east in a romantic way, I think that the euchological riches of the anaphoral tradition of Basil of Caesarea have the potential to heal western division, for here is a spirituality and a theology of eucharistic offering which is bred from ancient imprecision, in which the "living sacrifice" of the people and the "sacramental action" of the church walk side by side. The "living sacrifice," so prominent in many patristic homilies, somehow left the western euchological scene, to return with a vengeance in the sixteenth century, but only after a long period in which the doctrine of atonement developed apart from eucharistic theology, in which latter eucharistic presence loomed so large that sacrifice was virtually excluded from the picture. What we badly need is something more wholesome, for at the end of the day, the eucharist is sacrificial in the sense that it is both the action of Christ in us now as well as being our response to his saving work.[46] It is important to realize that sacrifice—*thusia*—was a common-coin expression in early Christianity (cf. 1 Pt 2:5 where "spiritual sacrifices" refer to *all* worship), and that sacrifice was applied even to preaching by no less a person than John Chrysostom (*Hom.* 29.1 in *Rom.*).

In the west, we have been so preoccupied with "magic moments"[47] that we have failed to understand the internal unity of the eucharistic prayer, and thereby have failed to apprehend the inner dynamic of the eucharistic celebration itself. From this summary of a wider study of eastern anaphoras (and the whole notion of eucharistic offering in the liturgy down the ages), it is plain that three criteria of "story," "gift," and "response" are alive and vibrant in the many traditions represented in the east. "Story" is sacrificial, because we are recounting the mighty acts of God as events which are past but also present, in that they have a bearing on *us now*, so that to recount the Christian story in the eucharist is to proclaim realities which involve commitment by us, as God is committed to us in the first place.

"Gift" is also part of the eucharist, because we are feeding in the presence of God; the bread and wine assume a new context by the very fact of being set amid the actions and words of Christ, present in the power of the Holy Spirit. Some ancient anaphoras express this by offering the gifts at the anamnesis immediately prior to the epiclesis. Other ancient anaphoras do not find this necessary, but rather "present the memorial," to quote from the ecumenical *Lima* liturgy.

"Response" is not our Pelagian search for relevance. It is, rather, the work of Christ within us, as we seek to articulate the catholic concerns of the church, hence the supreme appropriateness of anaphoral intercession. Charles Gore had this to say on the whole subject in his masterly study of the doctrine of the holy eucharist published as long ago as 1901: "And in the self-oblation is the culmination of the sacrifice."[48] Intercession and self-oblation are so much part of the eucharistic action of Christ in us that they belong together, right in the heart of the celebration of the redeemed humanity, where we feast joyously on the gifts of God, and celebrate the story of that redemption in bread and wine.

Notes

1. W.J. Grisbrooke, *Anglican Liturgies of the Seventeenth and Eighteenth Centuries*, Alcuin Club Collections, vol. 40 (London: SPCK, 1958) passim.

2. Richard F. Buxton, *Eucharist and Institution Narrative*, Alcuin Club Collections, vol. 58 (Great Wakering: Mayhew-McCrimmon, 1976) 209ff.

3. Colin O. Buchanan, "Series 3 in the Setting of the Anglican Communion," in R.C.D. Jasper, ed., *The Eucharist Today* (London: SPCK, 1975) 16. There was no problem over this issue in the U.S.A.,

which had followed the Scottish lead and had developed this considerably; see T.J. Talley, "The Eucharistic Prayer: Tradition and Development," in Kenneth Stevenson, ed., *Liturgy Reshaped* (London: SPCK, 1982) 59ff.

4. Kenneth Stevenson, "The Catholic Apostolic Church: Its History and its Eucharist," *Studia Liturgica* 13 (1979) 21-45, and "The Liturgical Year in the Catholic Apostolic Church," *Studia Liturgica* 14 (1982) 128-134. See also Chapter 4 of this volume.

5. F.E. Brightman, *Liturgies Eastern and Western* (Oxford: University Press, 1896) 133.31.

6. A. Hänggi and I. Pahl, eds., *Prex Eucharisticum*, Spicilegium Friburgense, vol. 12 (Fribourg: Presses Universitaires, 1968) (hereafter *Prex*); and Kenneth Stevenson, "Anaphoral Offering: Some Observations on Eastern Eucharistic Prayers," *Ephemerides Liturgicae* 94 (1980) 209-228; this article has been summarized by B. Neunheuser in *Archiv für Liturgiewissenschaft* 24 (1982) 384. See also the key chapters, subsequently written in Kenneth Stevenson, *Eucharist and Offering* (New York: Pueblo Publishing Co., 1986) 10-73.

7. Bernard Botte, "L'Anaphore chaldéenne des apôtres," *Orientalia Periodica* 15 (1949) 269.

8. See Kenneth Stevenson, "Ye Shall Pray for: The Intercession," in *Liturgy Reshaped* 32-47. Reprinted as Chapter 1 of this volume.

9. *Prex* 80-81. The thanksgiving theme is amplified in the (expanded) version of the *Testamentum Domini* (*Prex* 221): "we offer you this thanksgiving."

10. Louis Ligier, "The Origins of the Eucharistic Prayer: From the Last Supper to the Eucharist," *Studia Liturgica* 9 (1973) 179ff. For a recent discussion of this notion of anaphoral evolution in terms of "slotting in" new material, see Bryan D. Spinks, *The Sanctus in the Eucharistic Prayer* (Cambridge: University Press, 1991) 104ff.

11. *Prex* 60-68.

12. J. Doresse and E. Lanne, eds., *Un Témoin archaïque de la liturgie copte de S. Basile*, Bibliothèque du Muséon, vol. 47 (Louvain: Presses Universitaires, 1960) 20-21; but see A. Raes, "Un nouveau document de la liturgie de S. Basile," *Orientalia Christiana Periodica* 26 (1960) 403-404; compare, in general, with Leonel L. Mitchell, "The Alexandrian Anaphora of St. Basil of Caesarea: Ancient Source of 'A Common Eucharistic Prayer'," *Anglican Theological Review* 58 (1976) 194-206. The text of this ecumenical eucharistic prayer is to be found in the American Episcopal *Book of Common Prayer* (New York: Seabury, 1979) 372-376, the (American) United Methodist *At the Lord's Table*, Supplement Worship Resources, vol. 9 (Nashville: Abingdon, 1981) 22-23, and the Canadian Anglican *Book of Alternative Services* (Toronto: Anglican

Book Centre, 1985) 207-210. This prayer deserves more attention from liturgists than it has so far earned.

13. See *Prex* 226-227 (Chrysostom), 248-252 (James), 92-93 (*Apostolic Constitutions* VIII).

14. Ibid. 236-237.

15. See below, p. 95ff; see also Kenneth Stevenson, "'The Unbloody Sacrifice': The Origins and Development of a Description of the Eucharist," in G. Austin, ed., *Fountain of Life* (Washington, D.C.: The Pastoral Press, 1991) 103-130.

16. Brightman, *Liturgies* 314.13 (see 370.11); see the same verb in Justin, *Apologia I* 65:3 (text in *Prex* 68-69).

17. *Prex* 224-225.

18. J.-P. Montminy, "L'Offrande sacrificielle dans l'anamnèse des liturgies anciennes," *Revue des sciences philosophiques et théologiques* 50 (1966) 395. I am indebted to Père P.-M. Gy, O.P. for drawing my attention to this important little study. It is interesting that the present participle should also appear in the American ecumenical prayer.

19. Bryan Spinks, "Priesthood and Offering in the *kussape* of the East Syrian Anaphoras," *Studia Liturgica* 15 (1982/1983) 104-118.

20. Bryan Spinks, "Eucharistic Offering in the East Syrian Anaphoras," *Orientalia Christiana Periodica* 50 (1984) 347-371. Spinks suggests that the intercessions in Nestorius and Theodore amount to a "pleading" of the sacrifice of Christ, which is celebrated in the institution narrative. I would prefer to see less subtlety in these two anaphoras than he suggests; but I welcome his corrective to the ideas put forward in my preliminary study, "Anaphoral Offering," see above, note 6. For the texts of Addai and Mari and *sharar*, see Bryan Spinks, *Addai and Mari—The Anaphora of the Apostles: A Text for Students*, Grove Liturgical Study, vol. 24 (Bramcote: Grove Books, 1980).

21. A. Baumstark, "Die armenische Rezension der Jacobusliturgie," *Oriens Christianus* 7/8 (1918) 14-25, esp. 17ff.

22. *Prex* 267; see below on Syriac anaphoras.

23. Ibid. 320-326.

24. Ibid. 327-331. The other Armenian anaphoras are equally interesting. Winkler's studies have recently culminated in a magisterial treatment of Armenian initiation rites: *Das armenische Initiationsrituale, Entwicklungsgeschichte und liturgievergleichende Untersuchung der Quellen des 3 bis 10 Jahrhunderts*, Orientalia Christiana Analecta, vol. 215 (Rome: Pontificium Institutum Studiorum Orientalium, 1982).

25. *Prex* 279 (Timothy), and 283 (Severus).

26. Spinks has shown this in his study of Nestorius where the Syriac *masqin* translates the Byzantine Basil *anapempei* ("renders"): see note 20 above.

27. See Spinks, *Addai and Mari* 19 ("and may this oblation be acceptable before you"), and *Prex* 108-109 ("receive, O God, the thank-offerings of those who offer the sacrifices . . ."); but this latter quotation comes during the anaphoral intercessions in Greek Mark.

28. This is discernible in Twelve Apostles, *Prex* 267; and also Maritas of Tagrit and Philoxenus, E. Renaudot, *Liturgiarum Orientalium Collectio*, vol. 2 (Frankfurt: Baer, 1847) 263, 302ff., and 312ff.

29. See Renaudot, *Liturgiarum* 372f. ("we inscribe your supernatural dispensation on the tablets of our hearts"). The institution narrative and anamnesis "unit" in many of the Syriac anaphoras is a restless entity: see, for example, the compression of the former in the anaphora of Thomas of Heraclea, A Raes, *Anaphorae Syriacae*, vol. 2.3 (Rome Pontificium Institutum Studiorum Orientalium, 1973) 341.5 (see Raes' description of this feature as an "anomaly," 333).

30. G.J. Cuming, "The Anaphora of Mark: A Study in Development," *Le Muséon* 95.1-2, 115-129; see H.A.J. Wegman, "Une anaphore incomplète?", in Van Den Broek and M.J. Vermaseren, eds., *Studies in Gnosticism and Hellenistic Religion* (Leiden: Brill, 1981) 432-449. The full study has been published, G.J. Cuming, *The Liturgy of Mark*, Orientalia Christiana Analecta, vol. 234 (Rome: Pontificium Institutum Studiorum Orientalium, 1990).

31. *Prex* 116ff. and (full text) 102ff.

32. Stevenson, "Anaphoral Offering" 223ff.

33. See E. Renaudot, *Liturgiarum*, vol. 1, 40; Gregory Dix, *The Shape of the Liturgy* (London: Dacre, 1945) 427f.; the *sharar's* incense prayer is in *Prex* 411. The sacrifice-incense-intercession movement is, I think, an important development not taken seriously enough by historians of ceremonial or theologians.

34. Stevenson, "Anaphoral Offering" 225f. and nn.

35. See chart in John McKenna, *Eucharist and Holy Spirit*, Alcuin Club Collections, vol. 57 (Great Wakering: Mayhew-McCrimmon, 1975) 46f.

36. Aidan Kavanagh, *The Shape of Baptism: The Rite of Christian Initiation* (New York: Pueblo Publishing Co., 1978) 51.

37. M. Férotin, *Le Liber Mozarabicus Sacramentorum et les manuscrits mozarabes* (Paris: Didot, 1912), e.g., nos. 125, 188, 206, 270, 279, 284, 306, 369.

38. Charles Wheatly, *Rational Illustration on the Book of Common Prayer* (London: Bettesworth, Innes and Rivington, 1720); see Buxton's important discussion of the shift in Wheatly's eucharistic theology discernible between the 1710 and 1720 editions, *Eucharist and Institution Narrative* 163.

39. David R. Holeton, "The Sacramental Language of St. Leo the

Great: A Study of the Words "Munus" and "Oblata," *Ephemerides Liturgicae* 92 (1978) 115-165.

40. For example, Brightman, *Liturgies* 309f., 319f. (Basil; and John Chrysostom), and 45ff. (James) for the Byzantine anaphoras. On duplication of material in the western offertory rites, and with particular reference to the new Roman Missal, see Niels Krogh Rasmussen, "Les rites de présentation du pain et du vin," *La Maison-Dieu* 100 (1969) 44-58.

41. J.E. Rattenbury, *The Eucharistic Hymns of John and Charles Wesley* (London: Epworth, 1948) 81-147.

42. Hymn 397 in *Hymns Ancient and Modern*, written by W. Bright, a Tractarian scholar; see M. Frost, ed., *Historical Companion to Hymns Ancient and Modern* (London: Clowes, 1962) 349f.

43. J.L. Houlden, "Sacrifice and the Eucharist," in *Explorations in Theology* (London: SCM, 1978) 80.

44. F. Clark, *Eucharistic Sacrifice and the Reformation* (Oxford: Blackwell, 1960); see review by E. Mascall, *Theology* 64 (1961) 310-316.

45. Cyprian, *Letters*, 63, 14.4, discussed by R.P.C. Hanson, *Eucharistic Offering in the Early Church*, Grove Liturgical Study, vol. 19 (Bramcote: Grove, 1979) 19; but John Laurance's work on Cyprian (Ph.D. Dissertation, University of Notre Dame, 1983) suggests alterations to the traditional view on "offering Christ" in Cyprian.

46. See Rowan Williams, *Eucharistic Sacrifice: The Roots of a Metaphor*, Grove Liturgical Study, vol. 31 (Bramcote: Grove, 1982) passim.

47. Compare our discussion of marriage rites and the role of the priest at the end of the Middle Ages in the west: Kenneth Stevenson, *Nuptial Blessing: A Study of Christian Marriage Rites*, Alcuin Club Collections, vol. 64 (London: SPCK, 1982; New York: Oxford University Press, 1983) 71 and 83, and passim on the historical background.

48. Charles Gore, *The Body of Christ* (London: Murray, 1901) 213; see also Kenneth Stevenson, *Eucharist and Offering* (New York: Pueblo Publishing Co., 1986).

3

Eucharistic Sacrifice:
An Insoluble Liturgical
Problem?

IT IS A WELL-KNOWN FACT THAT MANY A MODERN EUCHARISTIC
prayer shows signs of handling the relationship between the
Supper and Calvary with due care, even with some creative
ambiguity. For some, indeed, the very concept of offering is
fraught with problems which can only be faced in liturgical
formulas by having recourse to paradox. The bread and wine
are on the table, but they are neither "offered" sacrificially, nor
are they "held back" from the good purposes of God.[1] The act
of memorial is neither a re-enactment of Calvary nor is it an in-
significant feature of the church's life, as if all the eucharistic
community did was to bask in the sunshine of Christ's single
offering, and that is that. Yet many modern prayers are the direct result of creative movements such as liturgical research,
patristic theology, and the rapprochement between the churches that has been so much part of twentieth-century history.

The liturgical chickens usually come home to roost at one
or other of two places in the eucharist. The first is at the
point when the bread and wine are placed on the table (or
else, in some traditions, uncovered). What is said by way of
interpretation can speak volumes. The president may say
nothing at all; may quote 1 Chronicles 29—"of your own do

we give you"; or may yet say words that formally present the gifts to God, in sometimes quite elaborate language; another option is to point to Christ as the only offering, other than that of ourselves (Rom 12:1).

The second (but historically earlier) is in the eucharistic prayer. Whether or not the institution narrative is read beforehand as a "warrant," there is normally some prayer of remembrance (called *anamnesis*) which in effect says why the eucharist is being celebrated, what it intends to be and do. This prayer usually leads into the invocation of the Spirit (*epiclesis*) over the bread and wine and the communicants. (Sometimes, as in the new Roman rite, the epiclesis is "split," invoking the Spirit on the gifts earlier, before the narrative, and on the communicants, after the *anamnesis*.) The permutations of offering formulas as they are to be found in (or are absent from) the anamnesis are fascinating. Antiquity gives us few norms, as recent research demonstrates. But it is important to realize that the Reformation has induced considerable self-consciousness in the way this aspect of eucharistic discourse is handled in the new prayers of our time.

TRADITIONS

The Churches of the Reformation were clearly reticent about sacrifice in their liturgies.

In the Lutheran tradition, perhaps one of the most conservative is the Danish, in which the eucharistic rite consists of (a) preparation of the bread and wine (functional only), (b) bidding for thanksgiving, followed by the *Sanctus*, (c) *Agnus Dei* (usually in hymn form), (d) prayer for the presence of Christ, (e) Lord's Prayer, and (f) institution narrative. (There are slight variations, but this, in essence, reproduces Luther's *Deutsche Messe*.) What is noticeable, however, is the way in which hymnody plays a dominant role in the service. There are even traces, in some of the nineteenth-century hymn-writer Grundtvig's work, of some allusions to the eucharist as a spiritual sacrifice.[2] But it is one thing for the congregation to sing about it, another thing altogether for the priest to pray about it.

In the Calvinist tradition, one of the classic rites is that of the Scottish *Book of Common Order* (1564).[3] Here Knox simplifies and adapts Calvin's rite. The wordiness persists in the lengthy prayers of thanksgiving and supplication. Indubitably Christo-centric, these prayers enable the individual Christian to hover before Christ as the recipient of his eternal gifts, acceptable only in him. And yet, perhaps more faithful to Calvin's theolo-gy of the eternal sacrifice of Christ, the 1940 *Book of Common Order* makes so bold as to describe the eucharist as "pleading His eternal sacrifice, we Thy servants set forth this memorial."[4] As with Grundtvig in Denmark, so with Milligan in Scotland, the sacrificial metaphor adheres to the church, but when it ap-pears, it comes as a neat adaptation of tradition.

The Anglican rite is a varied one. It is well-known that Cranmer's 1552 rite needed some editorial touches in 1661 be-fore it could find acceptance at the Restoration. But these changes did not affect the substance of the rite, and it was left to the Scottish Episcopalians in the following century to give fullest expression to what could be called a Reformed Patristic view which might be characterized as follows:

(a) solemn placing of the bread and wine on the altar
(b) a full eucharistic prayer in which:
  —Christ's single offering is proclaimed
  —a full anamnesis of the work of Christ includes the
    offering of the gifts in memorial and . . .
  —in petition for the Spirit's descent to fulfill the
    intentions of the eucharist
  —self-oblation of the worshipers.[5]

Such a scheme has much to commend it. It safeguards Reforma-tion sensitivities about the unique character of Christ's work, and yet it gives the eucharist a powerful, ecclesial character which leans on the less self-conscious *nuances* of the West Syri-an anaphoras, on which the Scots and the English Non-Jurors relied so much in their research and liturgical reconstruction. Self-oblation, that deeply biblical (Rom 12:1) motif, which is one of Cranmer's finest expressions, is also brought into the or-bit of the eucharistic prayer (Cranmer had placed it in 1552 af-ter Communion). All the goods are in the shop-window.

For Methodists, such alterations to Anglican heritage are not so much to be found in any changes to the eucharist made in the 1784 *Sunday Service* (those do not affect sacrifice as it appears in the 1662 Prayer Book) but rather in the eucharistic hymns of the Wesleys. Liturgists are apt to underestimate the power and force of these fresh compositions, and perhaps even neglect the reason for their appearance at all. Methodism is reputed to have been "born in song." The theology of these hymns so contrasts with Cranmer's rite that it is tempting to suggest that they were composed as a mild corrective, to make up for what was taken to be absent. In the eucharistic hymns of the Wesleys are some very rich formulations, of which one example will suffice:

> Father, the grand oblation see,
> The death as present now with Thee
> As when He gasp'd on earth — *Forgive*:
> Answer, and show the curse removed,
> Accept us in the Well-beloved,
> And bid Thy world of rebels live.[6]

There is no fear of using bloodthirsty language, because at each stage, the central character of Calvary dominates, as well as the benefits accruing to the believer, the faithful participant. The Wesley door to eucharistic sacrifice is more pronounced than the Danish Lutheran, simply because there are so many hymns of this type. The potential effect of such hymnody on popular piety should not be overlooked.

The Missal of the Council of Trent (*Missale Romanum* 1570), however, shows a different liturgical progression altogether. The offertory prayers contained in that document are a conservative selection from the very full repertoire of such prayers as are contained in the local medieval missals.[7] These prayers all speak of sacrifice and offering, in preparatory terms, and while they avoid the more elaborate texts in use in some localities, they still use language unacceptable to the Reformers. Doubtless conservatism and anti-Protestant polemic make the removal of the key-formulation *Orate, fratres* unthinkable, because it speaks about the priest offering a sacrifice, with the people. The Canon remained, as far as sacrifice is concerned, unchanged. Thus with the Roman Catholic Church, we can detect no major changes, other than the intended systematization of missals by the very fact of issuing a missal that could be regarded as, in some sense, "conciliar," authoritative, a sign of loyalty to the Holy See. In the epoch of rubricism which followed, there was no scope for any moves to alter or soften any of the central parts of the 1570 Missal that could correspond to the cautious reappraisal of eucharistic sacrifice in the Lutheran, Calvinist, Anglican, and Methodist traditions cited earlier.

CONTEMPORARY SERVICE BOOKS

That same reappraisal is apparent in the contemporary successors to these traditions.

The 1978 (American) *Lutheran Book of Worship*,[8] though by no means typical of worldwide Lutheranism, adopts what could still be called a Lutheran line. Thus, at the preparation of the bread and wine, both creation as gift of God and justification by faith are held in balance:

> O Lord our God, maker of all things,
> through your goodness you have blessed us with these gifts.
> With them we offer ourselves to your service and dedicate our
> lives to the care and redemption of all that you have made, for
> the sake of him who gave himself for us, Jesus Christ our Lord.
> Amen.

This prayer seems to be handling the notion of "offertory" with carefully balanced tongs. In one of the eucharistic prayers (still an alternative to the more conservative pattern of thanksgiving and narrative), we encounter similar care:

> Therefore, gracious Father, with this bread and cup we remember the life our Lord offered for us.

But it is also clear from what follows that the eucharistic memorial is no mental activity, but a dynamic that involves consecration, sharing in the heavenly banquet, and joining with the prayers of the saints in heaven.

When we come to the 1979 *Book of Common Order*[9] of the Presbyterian Church of Scotland, the same emphases noted in the 1940 book are apparent:

> Therefore, having in remembrance his work and passion, we
> now plead his eternal sacrifice and set forth this memorial
> which he has commanded us to make.

Moreover, both the 1979 and the 1940 rites are able to offer the bread and cup before the thanksgiving, in language reminiscent of the corresponding prayer in the Catholic Apostolic Liturgy.[10] Paradox enters the scene, however, as no sooner are the gifts offered than there is a quotation from 1 Chronicles 29—all that is ours is already God's.

Anglicans show variety—yet again. Whereas the American *Book of Common Prayer* (1979) reproduces the Reformed patristic tradition developed earlier, the *Alternative Service Book* (1980) muddles through in somewhat pragmatic fashion. American Episcopalians place the bread and wine on the altar in silence (at least they are supposed to) and proceed to use a selection of eucharistic prayers which either offer a spiritual sacrifice of thanksgiving or offer the gifts in remembrance of Christ, or both.

> We celebrate the memorial of our redemption, O Father, in this sacrifice of praise and thanksgiving. Recalling his death, resurrection, and ascension, we offer you these gifts.[11]

As is well-known, this book, like others, contains the famous "Common" eucharistic prayer, based on the Alexandrian anaphora of Basil of Caesarea.[12] Anglicans in England, however, are more restricted in their anaphoral language. Less varied in style anyway, they preach the single and unique nature of Calvary, which is particularly obvious in the First Eucharistic Prayer:

> Therefore, heavenly Father,
> we remember his offering of himself
> made once for all upon the cross,
> and proclaim his mighty resurrection and glorious ascension.
> As we look for his coming in glory,
> we celebrate with this bread and this cup
> his one perfect sacrifice.[13]

The tension is particularly stark when setting the 1979 American and 1980 English books side by side. But comparable differences, though possibly less considerable in degree, can be discerned in worldwide Lutheran and Methodist rites. They show many things, most important of all that the reappraisal of sacrifice noted earlier takes on different speeds in different ecclesial traditions, and meets resistance that also differs in force. The 1980 book permits a diversity of practice at the preparation of the gifts, where there is even scope for using the Roman Catholic offertory prayers ("Blessed are you . . . through your goodness we have this bread/wine to offer . . ."). The "offertory-substitute" is a characteristic of High Church Anglicanism,[14] but all that it achieves when used in connection with an anaphora that is reticent about sacrifice is to give the preparation of the gifts an accentuation that is not harmonious at all.

American United Methodists have wrestled with the issue in a different way. The 1981 president's book, *At the Lord's Table*,[15] allows the bread and wine to be brought to the table or else uncovered. (That alternative can speak volumes about the Godward/Human-ward character of the eucharist, and it should be noted.) In the eucharistic prayers, however, the standard anamnesis which recurs in the various texts uses an ingenious periphrasis that is redolent of the Wesleyan hymnody. Rich in Hebrews Christology, it runs:

> Therefore,
> in remembrance of all your mighty acts
> in Jesus Christ,
> We ask you to accept this our sacrifice
> of praise and thanksgiving,
> which we offer
> in union with Christ's sacrifice for us,
> as a living and holy
> surrender of ourselves.

This is perhaps the most nuanced formulation we have seen so far. The eucharist is a memorial-sacrifice, but it is at one and the same time the action of Christ himself, through his heavenly intercession. Through it, the church offers itself in obedience (Rom 12:1, again!). Moreover, the expression "in union with" prevents any notion of immobilizing Christ, which is the fundamental pitfall of the English Anglican treatment of this theme. However, perhaps meeting some need for reticence, the 1986 *Book of Services* adopts a more cautious line:

> And so, in remembrance of your mighty acts in Jesus Christ,
> we offer ourselves in praise and thanksgiving
> as a holy and living sacrifice
> in union with Christ's offering for us
> as we proclaim the mystery of faith.

Lame by comparison, it still keeps the essential features of the earlier formulation, although the power of the phraseology seems to have been reduced somewhat. Here, nonetheless, is Wesleyan spirituality incarnated into liturgical ministerial text, and that is an achievement in itself.

The Roman Missal of 1970, when compared with its predecessor, steps out into pastures new. Signalled by the Second Vatican Council, and the 1965 *missa normativa*, there is immediately an atmosphere of simplicity. The offertory prayers have been reduced, though the *Orate, fratres* (which was gone in the 1965 draft) persists, even though the language is less loaded. The preceding prayers, however, are a happier replacement for the medieval-style orations. But by far the most significant is the principle adopted in having alternative eucharistic prayers, deliberately borrowed from the Eastern Churches, and thus pioneered in the west, holding out a fruitful example to Western Protestantism as it underwent liturgical revisions in its own way.

Much has been written about the Roman prayers,[16] which perhaps exemplifies the kinds of pressures exerted on the revisers to be cautious in this new path. Some are disappointed that EP II is not more faithful to the famous anaphora contained in Hippolytus' *Apostolic Tradition*. (The International Commission on English in the Liturgy has produced its own English text, perhaps as a result.)[17] Some may well be disappointed that EP III does not employ more rhetorical models from the Gallican/Visigothic tradition. (Perhaps that may provide a new and living way for native Hispanic liturgies.) Many are certainly disappointed in EP IV, which seems to correct the Alexandrian Basil original. (The International Commission on English in the Liturgy has also produced its own text of Basil, complete with the original shape and congregational acclamations.) At root, EP II adopts the Hippolytan pattern, similar to the type of formulation we have seen in the American Episcopalian book—offer the gifts in remembrance of Christ. EP III is more subtle, setting the eucharistic action early on in the context of Malachi 1:11, that time-honored patristic quotation,[18] and then, after the narrative, offering the whole eucharist as "this holy and living sacrifice," perhaps deliberately avoiding other more fulsome formulations. But EP IV goes over the top with the famous offending words, "we offer you his body and blood." (Aidan Kavanagh's waspish critique comes as a heart-felt plea from someone who is both ecumenically committed and a Byzantine rite Catholic, who therefore knows the Basil tradition first hand.)[19]

We may thus summarize these modern rites as follows.

The American Lutheran rite employs the offertory in a cir-cumspect manner in order to give right teaching about crea-tion (all is God's) and justification (Jesus gave himself for us) and that leads into the inevitable feature of self-oblation. In the anaphora we celebrate in memory of the one offering for us. Lutheran sensitivities are safeguarded.

The Scottish Presbyterian book tries to express Calvin's teaching on the eternal sacrifice. What the church does is to *plead* that sacrifice, and it is therefore natural that anamnesis leads on to epiclesis, since the pleading of the eternal event should have consequences for the present. When faced with such a forceful formulation, presenting the bread and cup be-fore the anaphoral prayer merely serves as a preparatory act.

The two Anglican books point up the differences of a rite (English 1980) that tries to accommodate Low Evangelicalism (preaching the single sacrifice in the anamnesis) with High Church ritual (allowing offertory prayers and ceremonies). Hardly satisfactory, it must take a firm second place to the American Episcopal rite, which keeps the offertory secondary, and only in the anaphora offers the gifts in memory of Christ's saving work. Coupled to that is the fact that the anamnesis leads into a single epiclesis (the English prayers have the "split" epiclesis, with all its attendant problems), so that the movement of remembering, offering, and praying for the con-secration-sanctification has a logical and inevitable flow.

The American United Methodist rite gives a nod in the di-rection of the offertory, though this is clearly optional. More interesting from a theological point of view is the sensitive handling of the anamnesis, where the intercession of Christ is the starting-point for the eucharistic memorial, a theme famil-iar to Reformation theology, and, indeed, to many Syriac anaphoras.

The Roman Catholic prayers show a deliberate down-grading of the offertory (the typography shows this too, though that does not necessarily reach popular piety immediately to change it), and three new attempts are made to look at eucharistic sacrifice, in the new prayers of the anaphora. Each has its own character, but the traditional Roman emphasis on offering persists in III, and particularly in IV: II remains relatively unscathed. But here, in a sense, is the same process we have noted in the other traditions. You cannot turn back the eucharistic clock. To reappraise the tradition means not looking to other fields where the grass might be greener, but rather looking to see how one's own pastures might grow and develop from where they are.

But there is one, unique theology and liturgy of the eucharist that has not been so far mentioned—the *Lima* Statement and its accompanying unofficial rite. The approach takes on a much wider approach to sacrifice than was possible in the sixteenth century:

> The eucharist is the great sacrifice of praise by which the Church speaks on behalf of the whole creation . . .
> The eucharist is the memorial of the crucified and risen Christ . . .
> The biblical idea of memorial as applied to the eucharist refers to this present efficacy of God's work when it is celebrated by God's people in a liturgy . . .
> The *anamnesis* in which Christ acts through the joyful celebration of his Church is thus both representation and anticipation. It is not only a calling to mind of what is past and of its significance. It is the Church's effective proclamation of God's mighty acts and promises . . .
> The eucharist is the sacrament of the unique sacrifice of Christ, who ever lives to make intercession for us . . .
> In Christ we offer ourselves as a living and holy sacrifice in our daily lives (Rom. 12.1, I Pt. 2.5); this spiritual worship, acceptable to God, is nourished in the eucharist.[20]

Adopting the kind of tactic espoused by many modern ecumenical documents, this statement moves all the time from the general to the particular, and thus manages to ensure that nothing is lost; to take one example, that the particularity of the eucharist does not compromise the general character of ordinary witness to Christ in daily living. On the other hand, it sets the church's thank-offering within the orbit of the work of

Christ in heaven, thus relying on that biblical image as a means of affirming that the work of Christ is eternal, not bound by the limits of history. Similarly, it takes care to imply that the very word *anamnesis* is analogical, that is to say that the concept of memorial does not make the eucharist a category of something else (that we do not fully understand), but rather is in a category entirely of its own. Unsatisfactory as this sort of theology may be for critical minds (it certainly has its limitations), the *Lima* language attempts, for the very first time in history, to straddle effectively the deep divides of the sixteenth century, and since.

Its liturgy[21] seeks further to resolve some of these tensions. One senses that behind some of the texts lies a determination to keep the sixteenth-century emphasis on the cross (shared by both Reformation and Catholic piety, in different ways) with the twentieth-century's emphasis on the *whole* of the life of Christ as a ministry of humble obedience, and therefore also one of sacrifice. Thus, before the *Sanctus*:

> At the last supper, Christ bequeathed to us the eucharist, that we should celebrate the memorial of the cross and resurrection, and receive his presence as food.

And in the anamnesis:

> Wherefore, Lord,
> we celebrate today the memorial of our redemption:
> we recall the birth and life of your Son among us,
> his baptism by John,
> his last meal with the apostles,
> his death and descent to the abode of the dead;
> we proclaim Christ's resurrection and ascension in glory,
> where as our Great High Priest
> he ever intercedes for all people;
> and we look for his coming at the last.
> United in Christ's priesthood, we present to you this memorial:
> Remember the sacrifice of your Son and grant to people everywhere the benefits of Christ's saving work.

When liturgical language waxes prolix, the limits appear boundless. Yet here we find a *total* anamnesis of Christ, which holds together two distinct paradoxes. On the one hand, there is the dialectic between the ministry of Christ and Calvary itself. On the other hand, there stands the unique offering of Christ, once and for all, over against the fact of the Christian eucharist, taking place in human history, in all its particularity. Paradox seems to underline this prayer. It certainly underlines the way offertory is treated in this rite, adapting as it does some of the material from the Roman Missal of 1970. What is interesting is the critique offered by the German Lutheran Frieder Schulz,[22] who identifies features in this liturgy, the anamnesis in particular, which will commend themselves more readily to the "Catholic" parts of the church, rather than the "Protestant" sections.

THREE THEOLOGIANS

At this stage it is appropriate to look at the work of a few writers who have either already made, or deserve to make, some impact on this discussion.

The first is Max Thurian, brother of Taizé, who was a member of the Faith and Order Commission of the World Council of Churches, and who took a part in drafting both the official *Lima* statement and the accompanying (but unofficial) liturgy. In 1959 he published his important study, *L'Eucharistie: mémorial du Seigneur, sacrifice d'action de grâce et d'intercession.*[23] The subtitles, in a sense, say it all. The eucharist is both a memorial of Christ and a sacrifice of thanksgiving and intercession. In other words, it does not just look back, it does something in the here and now. (Perhaps behind this truth lies a feeling after connecting anamnesis with epiclesis—memorial and invocation belong together.) Thurian's influence can be detected in the Taizé liturgies, with intercessions after the creed which "offer for" in the traditional eastern manner, and an anamnesis which states boldly:

Everything comes from you
and our only offering
is to remember your marvels and gifts.[24]

The secret of the Thurian approach is to spread sacrificial language right through the liturgy of the eucharist, not unlike the eastern rites or, for that matter, the Catholic Apostolic liturgy.[25] For him, the metaphor of sacrifice is vibrant and necessary, not an optional side-dish that goes down well with some religious traditions. For him, the very nature of worship is to offer ourselves, in the service of the Lord. Once again, the heavenly intercession of Christ forms the indispensable link between church on earth and church in heaven.

The second contributor to this debate is David Power, whose *The Sacrifice We Offer*[26] sets out to unravel the background and produce a contemporary evaluation of the Tridentine doctrine of the eucharistic sacrifice. Anything that adds to the picture here is bound to illuminate why certain people said certain things over four hundred years ago. Power distinguishes between *suffrage* and *propitiation*[27] and shows how, against considerable pressure to do otherwise, the Fathers of Trent deliberately refrained from defining *how* the eucharist is a sacrifice of propitiation. Appositely, he shows how the image of propitiation of the work of Christ (as opposed to the eucharist) is found for the first time expressed liturgically in the fourth-century anaphora of *Apostolic Constitutions VIII*.[28] Although Power has to admit that it *was* held to be a sacrifice of propitiation at Trent, one is left with the impression that Power would rather it had not; and also, from the point of view of Christology, that the theme of "propitiation" of the Father by Christ is not meant to be taken literally. It is a metaphor of passion, feeling, power, rather than one intended to convey the idea that Christ actually makes the Father forget his anger at us. (Propitiation-language has always been notoriously difficult to reconcile with the image of the loving God.)

Second, Power shows that the real problem for the Reformers with Trent ought to be with its view of the priesthood,[29] its function and rights. He even implies, in an illuminating concluding chapter, that perhaps the emotive atmosphere of the time inhibited a more radical reappraisal of the tradition. Certainly, the late medieval imperative formula at priestly ordinations that tells the new priest to offer Mass for the living and the dead does not reach back to the earliest liturgies. It has been readjusted drastically in the reformed Roman Catholic ordination liturgy. Here, one senses, is the obverse of the Lutheran-Methodist reappraisal: the people of God can sing about spiritual sacrifice, but the president of the assembly must watch what she/he says, in case it implies a function in some sense separate from that of the assembly. There is a great deal of psychological taboo behind those two attitudes, both Catholic and Protestant.

The third writer is Bryan Spinks, who has written on the eucharist in the Independent tradition (including Congregational and United Reformed) in England as well as the East Syrian anaphoras. In the former,[30] he shows how the influence of High Calvinism dominates the scene and influences some liturgies. He even goes so far as to suggest that Calvin was not, at the end of the day, a particularly good prayer-writer, he was really better at systematic theology. For Roman Catholics and Anglicans, his two books on the Independent tradition in England are a sobering reminder that it is possible (and was frequently the case) that Reformed Christians could use a simple liturgy but have a higher view of the sacrament than many within the Anglican Church. He also notes how the new eucharistic prayers of the English United Reformed Church are theologically richer and more varied than the texts contained in the 1980 Church of England *Alternative Service Book*. That much needed saying.

Spinks' other contribution shows how the East Syrian anaphoras[31] held together the paradox of Calvary and eucharist differently from the classical West Syrian prayers. Here, the action of eucharist and the intercession of Christ are brought together, and this may explain why intercession and invocation soon became standard features of anaphoral prayer. Fundamental to this approach, however, is the church's offering of praise in union with the saints and angels in heaven, and that hinges on Spinks' major preoccupation, the *Sanctus*.

From a systematic point of view,[32] Spinks sees in both the Independent and East Syrian texts signs of a more sensitive handling of the Christology of sacrifice. The church cannot offer Christ, because the Head and Body, though one, are united only by the action of the Head. We therefore cannot identify the self-offering and the eucharistic memorial with the sacrifice of the cross. The two must be separate; otherwise, to alter the image somewhat crudely, the church becomes the tail which wags the heavenly dog! For that reason, over-confident sacrificial language which avoids paradox is suspect.

SACRIFICE AND OFFERING

A fourth contributor to this series of eucharistic debaters is the writer of this chapter. In a monograph entitled *Eucharist and Offering*,[33] an attempt was made to look at the theme of sacrifice and offering in the major liturgies of east and west. Works of synthesis are necessarily limited in scope, and eucharistic sacrifice has a reputation for being a bit of a quagmire. To dare to tread in the mud seemed a rash venture, like rushing in where even the heavenly beings may get their wings soiled with the divisions of the church.

Nonetheless, someone had to try to do the job, infinitely more tricky than the (comparatively straightforward) themes of eucharistic presence and eschatology. Two main motivations lay behind the study, apart from the fact that a start was required, even by someone as inexperienced as this author.

First, there is a considerable *variety* over the way in which sacrifice is handled in these rites, particularly in the east, where (so far as we know) there has been no major schism on eucharistic sacrifice grounds. That is to say, anaphoras within the same tradition can vary from one another, to the extent that they can adopt quite different approaches, but there is never a sense that one is right and another is wrong. Applying such a rule of thumb to the west since the sixteenth century should embolden separated Christians to be less afraid of using prayer traditions that are different from their own, without the feeling that if one uses a prayer that does not place all the "correct" theologies within a bulging anaphora, somehow that eucharist is second class. Conversely, another type of Christian might be made to think that an anaphora that said too much about sacrifice and not enough about something else was, in some sense, wrong. We need to be more eucharistically relaxed about these matters.

The second motivation was that the churches today seemed to need a much wider view of sacrifice, *if they were to have one at all.* In one way, the critique of traditional sacramental models ought to make us question difficult theological truths, so that they are subjected to scrutiny. To be too precise about how the eucharist is a sacrifice is to court the same kind of theological and ecumenical disasters as the corresponding approach to eucharistic presence. Above all, the liturgy is not the place for doctrinal precision.

The wiser view offered in that study suggested an approach that latched on to three criteria, which recur throughout the various liturgies. One is the offering of "story." We recount the story of salvation in reading the word and preaching it. We also recount it in a different and more formal manner during the eucharistic prayer, or whatever corresponds to it; at that point, praise is offered to God for God's mighty acts. The story is our sacrifice of praise, because it is the story of God's engagement with us, God's commitment to us, as we try—yet again—to align ourselves with God's perfect and eternal will. This makes the tale of salvation history no mere "prelude" (to use the commonly mistaken view of what the *praefatio* means) but the way in which we set what we are doing with bread and wine within an eternal and yet historical context.

The second criterion is that of "response." We listen to the story, but we also act upon it, hearing and receiving the word, and praying for the needs of the world. We involve ourselves in the mighty acts of God by placing the eucharist in the context of that history of salvation that will go on. The church is not just the passive recipient—it is also the servant of Christ, who therefore dares to act boldly in imitation of him. To dare to "do" the eucharist is part of that response. It is, at root, the "Godward" aspect, the "deep structure" which evokes a response from men and women simply by coming together around that table.

The third criterion is that of "gift." Here we come to the most sensitive part of all, not just because of the controversies of the past, but because of the paradox that in bread and wine God speaks to us, in ordinary food that is itself the result of dying and rising, wheat crushed and baked, grapes crushed and fermented. In acted parable, as of old, Jesus plays it slant. The bread and wine are neither formally "offered" nor ritually "held back." They are just there, on the table, eloquent testimony of the parable to end all parables, that it is in dying that we live to him.

FOUR ROUTES THROUGH THE ANAMNESIS

What difference does this theological discussion make to the perennial liturgical question? It can illuminate the importance of the variety with which we are faced and it can also enable us to evaluate what is before us, so that we can see the advantages as well as the disadvantages. Roughly speaking, there are four separate routes through the anamnesis.

The first is the traditional West Syrian and Latin one, "Remembering . . . we offer." Such a style is to be found all over the east (except in the East Syrian tradition). It is also to be found in the Roman tradition, both before and after 1970. It is yet again to be found in the Scottish-American strand of Anglicanism since the Reformation. But each of these three branches of the family treats the matter differently. The eastern view (which is followed partly by the Anglican group mentioned just now) places a great deal of emphasis on the "story," so what we remember is full, historical, eternal. Moreover, what we *offer* is closely linked both with what is remembered and the invocation (epiclesis) which follows. All that the Anglican rites of this group tend to do to the scheme is to add the important Reformation glosses that Christ's sacrifice is unique, unrepeatable, once and for all. The Roman texts, however, suffer the disadvantage of carrying a great deal of sacrificial weight for the simple reason that for much of its history, the Roman Church used an anaphora (the Canon—now EP I) that was almost entirely dominated by the theme of offering. The "split epiclesis" does not help matters, as it can imply, for those who think the *verba Christi* consecrate, that the oblation of the gifts in the anamnesis is, in some sense, an offering of Christ's body and blood, which is what EP IV actually says. The advantage, therefore, of this route is that it states boldly that the church is doing something; the stance is confident; but unless it deals in the paradox of Christ's death, it lays itself open to criticism from some Churches of the Reformation.

The second route is exemplified by the English Anglican rite of 1980: "With this bread and cup . . . we remember." Many modern anaphoras of the Reformation traditions employ this model, with or without qualifications. Instead of starting with the sacrifice of the church, this prayer by contrast points to the

One Sacrifice of Christ. It is indubitably Reformation. But is it not, in its own way, as exaggerated as it claims (in another direction) the old Roman Canon was, with the piety that lay behind it? Is it really helpful to read a prayer which hits you with Calvary with the subtlety of a sledgehammer? For some it might, but I doubt if it makes for a healthy piety. It could seem to some to be made up of negatives, rather than paradoxes, all the time implying that if you think (and pray) otherwise, you are wrong! Its lasting weakness, surely, lies in its certainty about Calvary, and its glaring vagueness about what it says the bread and wine are there for.

The third route is exemplified by the United Methodist rite, and, to a greater extent, by the *Lima* liturgy. The formulation which expresses this most aptly is "in union with Christ we offer . . ." Such an approach may well have High Calvinism behind it, stressing the eternal sacrifice of Christ, and not fearing any abuse of that eternal character that might seem to place too much weight on the eucharist. From a literary point of view, this is the formula which moves on farthest from the first two routes, because it relies so heavily on what Christ is doing now, in his intercession, rather than on what the church is doing now in remembering and offering (the first route), or what Christ did once and for all on the cross (the second route). Its disadvantage is that in being so Christocentric, it may well place an inadequate emphasis on the paradox we have already seen inherent in the eucharist, namely, that it is not just *Christ's* action, but the *church's*. That, however, is a small Christological price to pay for a balanced theology.

The fourth route is a variant of the preceding one and is exemplified by the Church of Scotland. It may be characterized by the language of "pleading the eternal sacrifice." Unlike the preceding route, which may well stress the eternal sacrifice of Christ with his eternal self-offering, this approach links the eternal sacrifice with the spiritual sacrifice of the church, and with the invocation of the Spirit on the eucharist. A modern text which adopts this approach runs thus:

Father, we plead with confidence his sacrifice
   made once for all upon the cross,
   we remember his dying and rising in glory,
   and we rejoice that he prays for us at your right hand:

Pour out your Holy Spirit over us and these your gifts,
    which we bring before you from your own creation;
show them to be for us the body and blood of your dear Son;
unite in his cross
all who share the food and drink
of his new unending life.[34]

The advantage of such an approach is that it faces fairly and squarely some of the more detailed Reformation sensitivities which the first route in its Anglican form does not manage to do (in the eyes of some) simply by adding reference to Christ's single offering of himself. The disadvantage is that the action of bringing the gifts is moved from its older position, in the anamnesis, to its new position, in the epiclesis. That could be taken to imply that the remembering does not have much to do with bread and wine. But that, once more, is a small point, since the whole formulation is shot through with paradox and that is a necessary feature of any liturgical text that is to stand up to theological scrutiny.

If two rites deserve most criticism, it is the missed opportunities of the Roman Catholic and English Anglican texts. Both show signs of theological legacies from the sixteenth century that could well be shed without prejudicing the integrity of the tradition. On the other hand, if two rites deserve credit, it is the Scottish Presbyterian and American Episcopalian formulations, since they give the eucharist a dynamic that does not compromise the essential feature of Calvin's insistence on the drastic character of the work of Christ (on the one hand) and the traditional reappraisal of sacrifice that has been a feature of much Anglicanism from the seventeenth century (on the other). But yet more needs to be said in relation to our three criteria.

The "story" shows how essential it is to relate the recounting of salvation history not just to *what* the church prays when the anaphora moves from thanksgiving to supplication, but *how* it prays it. The "story" needs to have a balance of vertical and horizontal language,[35] so that what God is supposed to have done engages with how human beings are involved. This becomes clear when one looks at the way many modern thanksgiving-series have been written, in imagery that resounds for people today and yet also suggests an eternal dimension that is concerned with other ages as well.

Second, the "response" element needs to spread through the anaphora, but it is finely focused at the anamnesis-epiclesis, because that is where, in traditional style texts, the church says what it thinks it is doing. Theologically, some link needs to be made between the church as celebrant, and Christ who is both the subject and the object of the celebration. If the link is too strong, the church takes on the role of Christ, or else (like Roman EP IV) it appears to re-offer Christ, which is unacceptable in post-sixteenth-century Christianity. If, on the other hand, the link is too weak (as in the First EP of the English Anglican 1980 book), the prayer commits the opposite fault, of nailing Christ so firmly to the cross that he does not appear to be doing anything at the eucharist. But the "response" carries on through the epiclesis, and that should be an area where greater flexibility is permitted, so that after praying for the consecration of the bread and wine, the prayer for the communicants can alter from one set of circumstances (e.g., the liturgical season) to another.

Third, "gift" is perhaps the criterion that needs most careful handling. We have said little about the offertory, partly because many modern liturgies seem to have to admit its existence and yet slightly shun this action. Robert Taft[36] has shown how the Great Entrance, so far from being an Oriental offertory procession, is in origin a simple transfer of the gifts from the prothesis to the altar; and he goes on to show that the pre-anaphoral prayer, so far from being an "offertory prayer," points forward to the anaphora, and is in essence a preparatory prayer, no more. And yet the subsequent tale of the Great Entrance in the east is one of exaggeration, perhaps because it is a liturgical action which, unlike the recitation of the anaphora in a low voice, actually engages with the faithful on the hither side of the iconostasis. That development does illuminate our western problem, complete with the self-conscious bidding, *Orate fratres*, with its neat definition of roles between priest and people.

But problematical as the offertory continues to be, the way in which "gift" is expressed in the anaphora is to some extent equally difficult if the Roman and the English Anglican ways of handling it are to be regarded as solutions. Far more consistent are the other texts mentioned earlier, for the simple reason that they make a link between the eucharistic celebration and the bread and wine without (on the one hand) being over-precise and definite about what that link might be, or (on the other hand) being over-sensitive and vague. Perhaps Lutherans need to be a bit more bolder than they have been. One suspects that there may be more rhetorical ways of renewing the liturgy at this point, as witness the new Swedish Lutheran rite.[37]

* * * * * *

In conclusion, therefore, it must now be asked, is the eucharistic sacrifice an insoluble liturgical problem? Ever since Martin Luther (as the story goes) nailed his arguments to the door of his University Church in 1517, we have, as Colin Buchanan repeatedly reminds us, lost our innocence.[38] But the problem is not one confined to conservative Roman Catholics and Evangelical Anglicans of the English variety, however much it appears to be focused there. The problem belongs to all of us, for the moment we study history or cross the threshold into another ecclesiology where we might find ourselves praying something different from what we are accustomed to, then we enter the debate, willingly or not.

It should not, ultimately, worry us, because liturgy needs a rich ambiguity to survive. Many of us who live in the western tradition see around us signs of the collapse of Christendom and with that, perhaps, the death of many tired ideas. Liturgical history tells us two lessons here: first, ghettos can be mightily powerful affairs, but, second, new ideas have a habit of rising from dust and ashes. Meanwhile, we should, perhaps, beware of what all these many eucharistic prayers are doing to ordinary people, for whom much of the debate matters very little. For them, differences will be more about identity than that someone else who does something different is actually wrong. Style, rather than substance, is often the medium of distinctiveness. And yet the discussion *is* crucial, even more important than any discussions about eucharistic presence, because it has much more to do with what we think the eucharist does. In our own day, as I have argued elsewhere,[39] we need eucharistic sacrifice as a basic feature of ordinary eucharistic spirituality, to offset the frequency of the eucharist in many people's spiritual diets, and to bring home to people (presbyters included) that the *mysterium* is not just *fascinans* but also *tremendum*.[40]

Meanwhile, prayers develop as much by choice as by those seemingly mindless organic growths that are discernible in local rites down the ages. Much as we may pride ourselves on celebrating the eucharist with reverence, dignity, and well-written new liturgies, it is not so much that we own the Lord's Supper as that the Supper owns us. If solutions are needed for the way in which we link the Supper with Calvary, then we could do a lot worse than follow the simplicity of the Reformed patristic pattern exemplified in the American Episcopalian tradition, or the Christologically sensitive road struck by the High Calvinists of Scotland and Taizé. Whatever we pray is open to misunderstanding and misinterpretation. That is the nature of liturgy, for its purpose is to resound and evoke, rather than to define language and conceptualize symbols. After all, however, the twentieth-century *rapprochement* and *retour aux sources* may have left a few marks from the past that show the scars of old battles which are not quite so necessary to fight any more. They also show us, at root, how sacrifice keeps returning to give us new perspectives on that feast on which we shall endeavor to feed until the end of time.

Notes

1. ". . . in spite of a proper caution about speaking too loosely of the elements as 'offered' to God in the eucharist, we still need to say that the moment of *relinquishing what is ours* is crucial in the eucharistic process": quoted from Rowan Williams, *Resurrection-Interpreting the Easter Gospel* (London: Darton, Longman and Todd, 1982) 111. I owe a great deal to the "broadened" view of the eucharist expounded in this book.

2. *Vejledning i Den Danske Folkekirkes Gudstjenesteordning* (Copenhagen: Haase, 1955) 70-76 (the 1912 rite). For a collection of Lutheran texts of the sixteenth and seventeenth centuries, see Irmgard Pahl, ed., *Coena Domini*, vol. 1, *Die Abendmahlsliturgie der Reformationskirchen im 16/17 Jahrhundert*, Spicilegium Friburgense, vol. 29 (Freiburg: Universitätsverlag, 1983). The Grundtvig hymn, "i al sin glans nu stråler solen," is to be found in *Den Danske Salmebog* (Copenhagen: Haase, 1953) no. 247, where in stanza 5 there is reference to the eucharist as "thanksong's drink-offering." On Grundtvig's theology,

see A.M. Allchin, *The Kingdom of Love and Knowledge* (London: D.L.T., 1979, 71-89.

3. Text, with comparative notes, in Pahl, *Coena* 472-478.

4. *The Book of Common Order* (Oxford: University Press/Humphrey Milford, 1940) 119. This rite also includes two preparatory prayers before the eucharistic rite, one of approach, another offering the bread and cup, 117. Both of these are borrowed from the Catholic Apostolic rite, mediated through the *Euchologion* books of the Scottish Church Service Society. See the important essay by J.M. Barkley, "'Pleading His Eternal Sacrifice' in the Reformed Liturgy," in B.D. Spinks, ed., *The Sacrifice of Praise: Studies on the Themes of Thanksgiving and Redemption in the Central Prayers of the Eucharistic and Baptismal Liturgies in Honour of Arthur Hubert Couratin*, Ephemerides Liturgicae "Subsidia," vol. 18 (Rome: Edizioni Liturgiche, 1981) 123-140, especially 136ff, with discussion on the theology behind "plead," including William Milligan's contribution.

5. Kenneth W. Stevenson, *Eucharist and Offering* (New York: Pueblo Publishing Co., 1986) 149ff.

6. See ibid 167ff. For the quoted text, see J. Ernest Rattenbury, *The Eucharistic Hymns of John and Charles Wesley* (London: Epworth, 1948) 233 (number 121, second part of stanza 2).

7. English translation contained in R.C.D. Jasper and G.J. Cuming, eds., *The Prayers of the Eucharist, Early and Reformed*, 2d ed. (New York: Oxford University Press, 1980) 119-122.

8. *Lutheran Book of Worship* (Minneapolis: Augsburg Publishing House; Philadelphia: Board of Publication, Lutheran Church in America, 1978) 109ff.

9. *The Book of Common Order (1979)* (Edinburgh: St. Andrew Press) 7ff., 22ff., 36.

10. See Stevenson, *Eucharist and Offering* 183ff. and notes.

11. *The Book of Common Prayer* (New York: Seabury, 1979) 361ff. See also H.B. Porter, "An American Assembly of Anaphoral Prayers," in Spinks, *The Sacrifice* 181-196.

12. On the background of this prayer, see Leonel L. Mitchell, "The Alexandrian Anaphora of St. Basil of Caesarea: Ancient Source of 'A Common Eucharistic Prayer'," *Anglican Theological Review* 58 (1976) 194-206.

13. *The Alternative Service Book (1980)* (London: Clowes/SPCK/Cambridge University Press, 1980) 132; for the offertory section, see 129f.

14. See Richard F. Buxton, *Eucharist and Institution Narrative*, Alcuin Club Collections, vol. 58 (Great Wakering: Mayhew-McCrimmon, 1976) 110-132, 145-176.

15. *At the Lord's Table: A Communion Service Book for Use by the Minister*, Supplemental Worship Resources, vol. 9 (Nashville: Abingdon, 1981) 24; *The Book of Services* (Nashville: United Methodist Publishing House, 1986) 16f.

16. See Stevenson, *Eucharist and Offering* 198ff.

17. *Eucharistic Prayer of Hippolytus: Text for Consultation* (Washington, D.C.: International Commission on English in the Liturgy, 1983); see also *Eucharistic Prayer of Saint Basil: Text for Consultation* (Washington, D.C.: International Commission on English in the Liturgy, 1985).

18. See discussion in R.P.C. Hanson, *Eucharistic Offering in the Early Church*, Grove Liturgical Study, vol. 19 (Bramcote: Grove, 1979).

19. "This is novel and can hardly be said to retain "a most definitely traditional character." One who has some acquaintance with the medieval and reformation history of eucharistic controversy will recognize the inadequacy of such a position, and may be forgiven his disappointment that its tendentiousness has got into a Catholic formulary precisely at a time when it could have been diagnosed and avoided most easily." "Thoughts on the New Eucharistic Prayers," *Worship* 43 (1969) 9 (whole article 2-12).

20. *Baptism, Eucharist and Ministry*, Faith and Order Paper, vol. 111 (Geneva: World Council of Churches, 1982) 11-12.

21. See Max Thurian, ed., *Ecumenical Perspectives on Baptism, Eucharist and Ministry*, Faith and Order Paper, vol. 116 (Geneva: World Council of Churches, 1983) 241ff.

22. F. Schulz, *Die Lima Liturgie* (Kassel: Stauda, 1983), and "Zur Rezeption der 'Lima-Liturgie'," *Studia Liturgica* 17 (1987) 151-156.

23. Max Thurian, *L'Eucharistie: Mémorial de Seigneur, sacrifice d'action de grâce et d'intercession* (Neuchâtel: Delachaux/Niestlé, 1959).

24. See *Eucharistie à Taizé* (Taizé: Presses de Taizé, 1963).

25. See note 5 above.

26. David N. Power, *The Sacrifice We Offer: The Tridentine Dogma and Its Reinterpretation* (Edinburgh: T. and T. Clark, 1987).

27. Ibid. 43. Power also criticizes the offending part of Roman Eucharistic Prayer IV: "The Roman Church . . . indulges in a misinterpretation of its own earliest traditions when in the composition of new eucharistic prayers it presents the section after the supper narrative as an offering of Christ himself, or of his body and blood" (p. 180).

28. Ibid. 182. By no coincidence (?), this anaphora is the earliest to contain a prayer for the celebrant himself, in the first person singular, noted in Stevenson, *Eucharist and Offering* 44.

29. Ibid., passim, but see pp. 92f. This distinction of the role of

priest and congregation is a feature of the teaching of Pope John Paul II (pp. 21-23).

30. B.D. Spinks, *From the Lord and "The Best Reformed Churches": A Study of the Eucharistic Liturgy in the English Puritan and Separatist Traditions 1550-1633*, Ephemerides Liturgicae "Subsidia," vol. 33 (Rome: Edizioni Liturgiche, 1984); and *Freedom or Order: The Eucharistic Liturgy in English Congregationalism 1645-1980*, Pittsburgh Theological Monographs, New Series, vol. 8 (Allison Park: Pickwick Publications, 1984). Review of the former, by the writer, in *Journal of Theological Studies* 39:1 (1988) 312-314. Review of the latter, by the writer, in *Scottish Journal of Theology* 39 (1986) 418-421. Spinks has also since written on this theme in the Talley *Festschrift*, "The Ascension and the Vicarious Humanity of Christ in the Christology and Soteriology behind the Church of England's Anamnesis and Epiklesis," in J. Neil Alexander, ed., *Time and Community* (Washington, D.C.: The Pastoral Press, 1990) 185-201.

31. B.D. Spinks, "Eucharistic Offering in the East Syrian Anaphoras," *Orientalia Christiana Periodica* 50 (1984) 347-371.

32. B.D. Spinks, *News of Liturgy* 130 (October 1985) 7-8. See also Alasdair Heron, *Table and Tradition: Towards an Ecumenical Understanding of the Eucharist* (Edinburgh: Handsel Press, 1983) 168ff., where Heron questions Calvin. See review, by the writer, in *Scottish Journal of Theology* 38 (1985) 244-246.

33. See Stevenson, *Eucharist and Offering*, passim.

34. Text drafted for the Church of England Liturgical Commission. See Power's treatment of this theme: "the prayer of remembrance, which is known as a prayer of thanksgiving and praise, is also a prayer for forgiveness, reconciliation, and nourishment. It is the *pleading* (my italics) of the blood of Christ for mercy, the church's part in the intercession that Christ makes at God's right hand" (*The Sacrifice We Offer* 185).

35. See the important discussion of this theme by J.M. Sánchez, *Eucaristía e Historia de la Salvación* (Madrid: La Editorial Catolica, 1983).

36. See Robert F. Taft, *The Great Entrance: A History of the Transfer of Gifts and Other Preanaphoral Rites of the Liturgy of St. John Chrysostom*, Orientalia Christiana Analecta, vol. 200 (Rome: Pontificium Institutum Studiorum Orientalium, 1975); see also Stevenson, *Eucharist and Offering* 222ff.

37. See *Gudtjänstording: I Ritual* (Lund: Berlingska Bokytryckeriet, 1976) 25ff.; see, especially the anamnesis of the first eucharistic prayer (p. 28), "Se till det fullkomliga och eviga offer med vilket du i Kristus har försonat oss med dig själv" (= "Look on the perfect and

eternal sacrifice with which you in Christ have brought us together in unity with yourself.") This clause is part of the anamnesis.

38. For example, in the review of Stevenson, *Eucharist and Offering*, in *News of Liturgy* 147 (March 1987) 4-6.

39. See Stevenson, *Eucharist and Offering* 218-236. See also Kenneth Stevenson, *Accept This Offering: The Eucharist as Sacrifice Today* (London: SPCK, 1989).

40. See Reginald H. Fuller, *Preaching the New Lectionary: The Word of God for the Church Today* (Collegeville: The Liturgical Press, 1982) 154.

4

A Theological Reflection on the Experience of Inclusion/Exclusion at the Eucharist

THERE ARE MANY WAYS IN WHICH ONE MAY DISTINGUISH BETWEEN when a person is "included" in the eucharist and when "excluded." For example, when I go to a celebration of the eucharist in a Greek Orthodox cathedral, I participate in a way comparable to many of the other worshipers (given that I arrive with the considerable handicap of being a liturgist), simply because only a small minority actually receive the eucharistic bread and wine. On the other hand, when I attend (as I once did) a eucharist according to the Byzantine rite in a small Melkite church, I am ushered up to take my place in line with the other communicants, as a genuine ecumenical gesture from the Roman Catholic Church to a visiting Anglican. All this is to say the obvious: the revival of eucharistic faith and practice in the twentieth century places us in a context, and the context is that, when we consider the admission of children to communion, we are indeed doing so at a particular time when they *feel excluded* in a way which would not have been true, say, in seventeenth-century baroque Catholicism, or eighteenth-century Evangelicalism.

I have been asked to offer a "theological reflection," but I would like to stress at the outset that what follows is really a "theological reflection upon another theological reflection," and that primary reflection was going on inside me as a child.

THREE CHRISTIAN TRADITIONS

What I am about to describe is part travelography, part family history, part liturgical variety. It is about the experience of the interaction of three Christian traditions in the eucharistic life of a growing child. Because I was that child, I shall do my best not to be sentimental, not to lay it on too thick. There is no element of tragedy in it, because I enjoyed those three traditions and did not regret their separation. And I suppose it partly stems from the fact that I have a vivid mind, a wild imagination, an eye for beautiful things, an ear for good music. Not to put too fine a point on it, I have always enjoyed going to church. Moreover, as I try to put together my thoughts in some sort of not too jumbled order, I cast my mind back to the recent past, to 1979, the International Year of the Child, when many of us were reminded, sometimes somewhat forcibly, that children are *not* small adults, but are people in their own right. Such, I think, is the basis on which the patristic church could dare to give communion to young persons.

I was born in 1949. My parents met just after the Second World War, in Denmark. My father, himself half-Danish, had been drafted into MI6 in 1940 because he spoke Danish (his mother had brought him up virtually bilingual). But my father's family had roots in the Catholic Apostolic Church. His father had been an "angel" (or bishop) in the congregation in Edinburgh, and his mother's family was involved in many ways in that church in Denmark. Then along comes my mother, a "war-bride," the daughter of the Lutheran bishop of Århus, just to add another flavor to this rich religious cocktail.

While the Catholic Apostolic Church was at its strongest in Denmark and in Lutheran parts of Germany, it was relatively weak in the British Isles, even though it started its life in England in the 1830s.[1] By an early stage, probably while its liturgy was becoming increasingly enriched, children were admitted to communion on the following terms. First communion came soon after baptism, when the celebrant gave the baby the species with the aid of a spoon. Thereafter, children received communion on special occasions (the main festivals of Christmas, Easter, Pentecost, and All Saints) from an early age, depending on circumstances. Children were received into regular communion by the local angel (bishop) at the age of eleven, after which they could receive communion at any service.[2] The final stage in Catholic Apostolic initiation was "sealing," with the laying on of hands by the Apostle, a rite which included anointing with chrism. This took place at the age of eighteen, after a course of instruction. The last Apostle died in 1901, terminating ordinations, and signalling the eventual demise of the church. "Sealing" made no difference to receiving communion, but I mention it in passing as yet one more variant in the way the Western Churches have responded to historical inquiry and new patterns of religious experience and sacramental life.[3]

From the late 1840s and 1850s, such a scheme operated in Catholic Apostolic congregations, so that by the 1950s it was unquestioned—*de rigeur* in fact—that babies and small children should receive communion wherever manpower allowed the eucharist to be celebrated. In fact, I was lucky, because the Edinburgh church had a priest right through to Easter 1958, when he died at the age of 89. Because of his advanced age and the length of the liturgy, he only celebrated the eucharist (latterly) once a month, then only at festivals. I cannot recall a eucharist in that church when I did *not* receive communion. I can also remember one occasion when we attended the eucharist in the little church in Århus on a family Christmas holiday in 1954; there must have been others as well.

"Ambience" has a great effect on a child, and I was no exception. The Edinburgh church was a large Victorian building, designed by Rowand Anderson. It was neo-romanesque in style, with open space to make visibility as good as possible. The acoustics were terrible, but since the liturgy was usually intoned, that didn't matter. We would walk in through the vestibule, get our books from one of the doorkeepers or underdeacons, and we would go halfway up the left-hand side and occupy a (relatively) comfortable pew.

I don't remember all the details of the liturgy itself, but certain things stick in my mind, built up from this intermittent experience of the church. The entry of the ministers made quite an impression; it would consist of a small group of acolytes, and they would be followed by a group of elderly underdeacons, and at the end, in increasing old age, one could hear the shuffling feet of the celebrant. (I do vaguely remember a deacon.) All these ministers wore what we would call cassock and surplice, except the celebrant, who wore an alb, stole, and chasuble (the latter two invariably white, and cut in the gothic style).

Other parts that stick in my mind are the presentation of the tithes and offerings, because that involved more movement, this time from the rear of the church (the introit was from the side), and the Great Entrance, when the vessels were moved from the Table of Prothesis (in the upper choir) to the altar. But the climax always came when the family received communion together. Playing it by the book, the Edinburgh congregation restricted administration to the priest and the deacon.[4] When the old deacon died, it meant that only the priest administered to a congregation of about a hundred. Underdeacons hovered, replenishing the chalice from a large flagon (I remember once when this happened just before I communicated) and keeping an eye on the priest who right at the end of his life gave communion seated, so that we came up in pairs. Once (so I was told by someone in the congregation whom we knew well), I responded to the eucharistic gifts with the expression "Ta" instead of the any rebuff! Children were not given communion with any special motives or conditions. It was expected, natural, right. The liturgy, with its strong ecclesiology, and no doubt strengthened by the heightened atmosphere of a church getting ready to disappear, was enough of a binding force to what went on. I think what I remember most was the way my parents just let us experience this liturgy, with a bit of explanation here and there.

I have dwelt on this at some length, because it is the most unfamiliar of the three traditions. But let me now come to the second. Catholic Apostolics were usually told to become Anglicans. That held good of soldiers going to the front in the two World Wars, and also of those families that belonged to the church towards the end of its life. This meant that my intermittent experience of a long, late morning liturgy, in the Edinburgh Catholic Apostolic Church, was supplemented by a weekly attendance at the local Episcopal church at 8:00 in the morning. (In those days, matins was the normal service at 11:00 in the country churches.) The Episcopal Church in Scotland has a peculiar ambience. It is made up of two strands, the old Scottish "strict" tradition, which still has in its corporate memory Jacobite loyalties and persecution under the Hanoverians, together with its High theology of the eucharist from the seventeenth- and eighteenth-century divines. The other strand is the English "liberal" tradition, breathing the atmosphere of the English abroad, using the 1662 liturgy (*not* the Scottish 1929).[5] I was lucky in experiencing both these strands in two different congregations for the 8:00 eucharist. I was certainly not aware of all these hidden skeletons, but they were definitely in the background.

At this 8:00 eucharist, attended by only a small number, I soon realized both the *differences* from and the *similarities* to the Catholic Apostolic Service. The priest was considerably younger. The service was part of a regular diet which the congregation could (in the best sense) "take for granted." I remember the colors of the vestments changing and that the service was always *said*. The genuflection of the celebrant (and one or two of the congregation) during the Nicene Creed was another thing that was noticeable to the wandering eye. But one thing I could not fail to notice: I never, *ever* went up to the altar rail because I was not allowed to receive communion.

I didn't question this rule—one didn't in those days. In retrospect, it now seems clear that the reason my parents had me confirmed at Christmas 1958 was that my brother and I had been deprived of the eucharist altogether since the death, that Easter, of the last Catholic Apostolic priest. I remember the friendliness of the Episcopal clergy to me, since I seemed to take an interest in religious things. After confirmation, I became an acolyte, then a choir-boy, and so on up the ranks. I was soon caught up in many of the activities of a local congregation. But I looked back, and still do, to my earlier experiences, and informed myself better on the how and why, which became quite a mystagogical experience, perhaps even therapeutic. That all became a Ph.D. thesis in 1975.[6]

The third tradition stemmed from the family holidays. Each summer we would spend a month in Denmark with my mother's relations. My grandfather was interested in much of what we did, and, insofar as one can take seriously the decision of a boy of four years to be ordained, he was proud of the fact that *one* of his offspring wanted to follow what for him was the family trade (he was the sixth consecutive Lutheran pastor in his family). Every Sunday we would attend a Lutheran church, whether the cathedral in Århus or a local village church. But we would also go to special occasions, such as the diocesan synod service, which usually coincided with the holiday in early August, and ordinations. My grandfather really had to act as a double, because my father's father had died long before I was born. He was a towering, noisy, flamboyant Dane, with an active interest in English philosophical theology (my parents frowned on that interest!), entomology, and his vast rural diocese, which he seemed to know like the back of his hand.

I emphasize these family claims because they provided my *entrée* into this very *national* of Western Churches. The buildings remain vivid in my mind, because they were so different: whitewashed inside, usually with a lot of medieval art surviving, an organ in the west gallery, pastor in cassock and ruff, and alb and chasuble atop when at the altar. The liturgical movement was just stirring in Denmark through the 1950s, building up to what it is now, with ever-increasing numbers of communicants.[7] Wherever possible, my parents took us to communion. I remember occasions when we children remained in our seats. I also remember occasions when we went to the altar-rail, enjoying the Lutheran practice there of holding out a small silver cup, while the celebrant poured the wine from a large chalice equipped with a spout. Again, similarities and differences occurred to me, other than the language. I remember enjoying the solemnity of Lutheran worship, and the organ interludes always added something of a bonus, especially in Århus cathedral (whose organ was restored along neo-baroque lines in 1927 partly through my grandfather's friendship with Albert Schweitzer). The visual aspects of worship made considerable impact. Word and sacrament belonged together, but they had different symbolisms, as the pastor wore vestments at the altar, but stripped down to cassock and ruff for the sermon and intercessions at the pulpit. Although we often left the church for the sermon (for understandable reasons), I remember the feeling of expectation by the congregation when the sermon began. A good Danish Lutheran congregation expects a decent sermon. That was *not* something I had experienced before. The Catholic Apostolic priest was too aged (although in its halcyon days that church would have had a homily at every Sunday morning eucharist) and the Episcopalians never preached at the early service, though they did at matins, but I regarded that strange post-monastic office as something to endure rather than enjoy, so it didn't begin to compete with Danish delights. I referred to the "solemnity" of the Lutheran service; this was heightened at the communion, where each row of communicants was dismissed by a prayer, and the choir would halt during their communion hymn while the organ would improvise. Unlike the Anglican mini-sermon ("Take and eat this in remembrance that Christ died for thee, and feed on him in thy heart by faith, with thanksgiving" and "Drink this in remembrance that Christ's blood was shed for thee, and be thankful"), the Danish celebrant would declare the fact of redemption in this short prayer, which ended with the peace, and the sign of the cross made with the chalice. Once more, the symbolism and the context made a great impression on me. It was part of the holiday.

The three traditions, then, were a varied eucharistic diet on which I fed at various stages for family reasons. Each had its own context, and there was never any sense of clash. The Catholic Apostolic eucharist was what I experienced on special occasions. I was welcome at its altar. The Episcopal eucharist was the regular Sunday 8:00 celebration. I was only welcome there after confirmation, which, in a largely Presbyterian country, was felt very strongly as a social and religious boundary. Then, every summer, the Danish Lutheran Church impinged on my religious experience in a big way. Sometimes we took communion, sometimes not; after confirmation, we always did. As I grew up, I began to realize how strongly my parents felt that we should receive communion. The Catholic Apostolics, with their single corporate Sunday eucharist at which everyone took communion (including—if they wished—visitors from other churches), had got it right, whereas the Anglicans had got it wrong. I remember, too, at a later age, learning that the first Lutheran Bishop of Sjaelland, Peder Palladius, wanted children to receive communion from the age of six or seven.[8] His High Lutheranism didn't survive later Lutheran so-called "orthodoxy," but there is now pressure for children to receive before Lutheran confirmation, and any antecedents, however anomalous, are grist to the mill of those championing the cause. Professor Christian Thodberg of Århus University tells me that the controversy began as far back as 1880.[9] In view of the fact that Catholic Apostolic congregations existed in many parts of Denmark, I should not be at all surprised if there were not some indirect feedback from the new church to the old folk-church. History is full of ironies.

A SYNTHESIS

As I try to put these three strands together, I must begin by saying, without any qualification whatever, that I never felt that any one of the three churches was considered "wrong" by us, except on the question of admission to communion. I regarded, as did my parents, the three churches as three different, overlapping experiences. They helped me to enjoy the matter of *choice* and *option*. It was later on that I was to discover the fullness of the riches of the Catholic Apostolic heritage. I think that this is an important point to make, particularly when we consider today the question of children from what the latest jargon calls, in its inevitably clinical manner, an "inter-church marriage." Children are not fools. They don't necessarily think that if something happens in one way in one place, it's wrong if it doesn't happen in another. We live in a world full of choices and options. It should come as no surprise that the Christian Churches should express these things as well.

Second, I did feel committed to all three of those churches, and still do, because I arrived on three different kinds of church door-steps as a direct result of family commitment. In later years this helped me to range further afield, and as a student who was also an ordinand, I often surprised local clergy by spending a lot of time being a spiritual nomad, moving from church to church, to see what it was like. The conviction that spiritual nomadry is right for many students was strengthened after I became a university chaplain. I remember hearing of Archbishop Michael Ramsey's reaction to a particularly complex report on theological education: "The best thing you can do with ordinands is to leave them alone." But I still harbored in my underlying attitudes the feeling that there were some churches where I was a welcome communicant, some where I was tolerated, others where I should stay in my place, though this latter category diminished somewhat after Vatican II, as I became a regular communicant at Roman Catholic altars when on holiday in France, Belgium, and Germany. Communion *does* involve commitment, but some of the mistakes of the eucharistic revival in the western churches have been that it has sharpened the boundaries between "regular" and "occasional," to such a degree that the "occasional" feels cut off, whether the "occasional" is a visitor from another church (even another country), or is someone who only comes to church at Christmas.

Third, we adults continue to underestimate the importance for children of the visual and the significant role played by context, rather than text, in the celebration of the liturgy. The Catholic Apostolic experience was a drama in itself. We entered through the west door; we sat in our pews; we went up to the altar; then, after the service, we were allowed to walk round the building and become used to it, meeting people, seeing carvings, passages, light-switches, vestments. For me, all this was of vital importance, and I suppose it built up within me a healthy suspicion of that type of Western Protestantism and Tridentine Catholicism that seeks to impose on the liturgy what people are *supposed* to believe—what Aidan Kavanagh has referred to as "secondary theology."[10] I once talked to an upright and pious student who was thinking about being ordained. Part of his problem was that he way trying to think, all the time, about what God was teaching him, at any given moment. "The trouble with some of you Evangelicals," I replied, "is that you are so determined that God is *teaching* you, when in fact God might be loving you, affirming you, even enjoying you."

Fourth, as we embark nowadays on admitting children to communion, I think there is a grave danger in trying to predetermine what they will experience. It was obviously a joy for

my parents to take me to a church where I would be a welcome and natural communicant. But the catechesis I received
was the liturgy itself, with snatches here and there of explanation and back-up.[11] Later on, as a teenager, I rebelled and
argued and quarrelled and sifted through the family corporate
memory and identified myself with those parts of my own
contemporary Christianity which fed me. We all have to move
on. But predetermination is not something you will find in the
baptismal pro-catechesis of the fourth-century Fathers. I remember Father Ted Yarnold once addressing a gathering in
London on his beloved fourth-century homilists and ending
the answer to a penetrating question with the throw-away,
"Someone really ought to analyze these baptismal catechists
from the point of view of modern educational psychology.[12]
My experience was my experience was my experience, and it
was different when I could take communion. I knew it was important, for the liturgy led up to it, deliberately, with its
rhythms and changes. I am not arguing for obscurantism. But
I am pleading for a basic *trust* in the liturgy to do its own job.

Fifth, the experience of exclusion is a painful one, whether
or not that exclusion is questioned, whether or not it is explained.[13] But the exclusion was not just me, at the Episcopalian services, before I was confirmed. It divides families. The
eucharist, we keep telling ourselves, is a corporate activity of
the whole church. When families are divided within themselves, whether because one or two children are not confirmed, or because in other instances husband or wife belongs
to another church, exclusion is a form of spiritual blackmail. I
do not wish to seem to argue the case for admitting children
to communion.[14] This is another's task. But the case rears its
head when the child in question knows both inclusion and exclusion. To put it bluntly, I identified with the Catholic Apostolic eucharist, for all its length and my impatience with a
protracted communion due to the age of the priest that forced
him to administer the elements sitting in his chair. The sacred
was allowed me there, in that strange, nineteenth-century
church which has so much else to teach Christianity, whereas
the sacred was *not* given me, down the road, at the local Episcopalian tabernacle.

Sixth, for a child word and symbol go closely together. That is something which many modern educational approaches are building upon, and rightly so. That makes me ask myself, in retrospect, why it was that I could "hear" the word preached Episcopalian-style (for all that it was usually done at matins), and yet I was not able to "hear" the sacrament by partaking of the bread and wine. Perhaps multiple printing and trivializing of preaching have made us lose out on the real purpose of the ministry of the word to such a degree that all we have left is the eucharist.[15] As we rediscover the interaction of words and symbolism, of children and older people, of community and individual, in ways that are appropriate for *our* century, so we may also rediscover the inevitable interaction and inseparable nature of word and sacrament at the Table of the Lord.

Seventh, and finally, for me, living with three churches at a time, age meant very little. Confirmation at the age of nine was a means of receiving communion. The Spirit had already been given at baptism, as my own baptismal liturgy taught me. The Spirit was also being given and experienced in a whole series of intermeshing activities and reflections on life and faith. I have grave doubts about the popularity today of the age limit of six or seven. It's arbitrary, adultist, and in no sense an important age *for the child* as the child experiences it. Let me end with one more anecdote, to illustrate. The last diocese in which I was a presbyter has recently embarked on a controlled experiment, which allows for congregations, with the agreement of the parents, to admit children to communion from the age of seven; confirmation would then, it is half-expected, be delayed until the mid/late teens.[16] Before this was formally passed by our Diocesan Synod, two local Ecumenical Projects in the diocese went ahead with their own experiments, one of which was the Higher Education Chaplaincy, where I was to work and serve. I therefore arrived on the scene after my congregation had agreed to move forward, but before the diocese had debated and agreed on the issue. We were as a family happy with this innovation. In due course, both my daughters became regular communicants. But what of my son? Technically, the answer was "no" until he reached the magic age. He, therefore, was excluded. And, of course, when I was a visiting preacher in other parishes which have *not* taken up the new option, technically my daughters should not be communicants either. However, in 1984 my family holidayed in Denmark and stayed with various relations and friends. On the Sunday, we all went to the morning eucharist at Århus cathedral, a building full of family memories, and where my grandfather is still remembered. James was five that summer. He announced, "I want communion." He remembered being in Århus two years earlier, so it was for him a special occasion, returning to the familiar. For all sorts of reasons, I decided to throw my Anglican loyalties to the winds, and I made a gut-reaction, back to my own experience as a child; and up he came. Just to add a piquant note, the long communion hymn was one of Nikolai Grundtvig's compositions, "Rejs op dit hoved, al kristenhed"[17] ("Lift up your heads, all Christianity"), a hymn that rejoices in the nearness of the Kingdom, the fullness of Christian hope. It all seemed the most natural thing in the world.

Notes

1. See K.W. Stevenson, "The Catholic Apostolic Church—Its History and Its Eucharist," *Studia Liturgica* 13 (1979) 21-45.
2. See *Book of Regulations* (London: Strangeways, 1878) 15ff. The recommendation is that children should be "phased" into regular communion, starting with the main festivals, then monthly, then the blessing and reception into regular communion. Local ministers and parents played a significant role in the formal and informal catechesis.
3. See Paul J. Roberts, "The Pattern of Initiation: Sacrament and Experience in the Catholic Apostolic Church and Its Implications for Modern Liturgical and Theological Debate," Manchester University Ph.D. dissertation, 1990.
4. Other congregations employed underdeacons for the administration of the chalice in later years.
5. For these two strands, see Marion Lochhead, *Episcopalian Scotland in the Nineteenth Century* (London: Murray, 1966).
6. K.W. Stevenson, "The Catholic Apostolic Eucharist," Ph.D. dissertation, Southampton University, 1975. See section on this liturgy forthcoming in *Coena Domini* II.
7. Much of the liturgical movement in Denmark has been marked by recovery of classical Lutheran features in worship, rather than by

the adoption of new liturgical texts; hymnody and music have played an important role. See Christian Thodberg, "Grundtvig the Hymn-writer," in *N.F.S. Grundtvig: Tradition and Renewal*, eds. Chr. Thodberg and A. Thyssen (Copenhagen: Den Danske Selskab, 1983) 160ff.

8. See H. Haar, ed., *Peder Palladius; En Visitatsbog* (Copenhagen: Haase, 1940) 68, where Palladius uses Mark 10:14 in support of children coming early to communion. The Visitation Book dates from September 1541; see p. 52, where Palladius stresses the need for parents to take young children to church, and for them to walk up and down the aisles to keep them quiet; the editor notes the demise of Palladius' recommendations about early communion (168, n. 11).

9. Conversation with Christian Thodberg, Århus, during August 1984.

10. Aidan Kavanagh, *On Liturgical Theology* (New York: Pueblo Publishing Co., 1984).

11. See *Book of Regulations* 16 (sections 535f).

12. See. E.J. Yarnold, "Initiation: Sacrament and Experience," in *Liturgy Reshaped*, ed., Kenneth Stevenson (London: SPCK, 1982) 17-31.

13. See D.R. Holeton, "The Communion of Infants and Younger Children," in *And Do Not Hinder Them*, ed., G. Müller-Fahrenholz, Faith and Order Paper, vol. 109 (Geneva: World Council of Churches, 1982) 68, where Holeton recounts my experience from which this paper developed.

14. See D.R. Holeton, *Infant Communion—Then and Now*, Grove Liturgical Study, vol. 27 (Bramcote: Grove, 1981).

15. See, for example, Kavanagh, *On Liturgical Theology* 103ff, for a discussion of the not always beneficial effect of the invention of printing on worship.

16. A Pastoral Letter from the Diocesan Bishop to All Clergy, Diocese of Manchester, May 1983. This followed a debate at Diocesan Synod, December 1982, at which a report was discussed, prepared by a committee under the chair of the Right Rev. Prof. R.P.C. Hanson.

17. *Den Danske Salmebog* (Copenhagen: Haase, 1985) n. 229.

MARRIAGE

5

Origins of
the Nuptial Blessing

IN ONE OF HIS MORE ADVENTUROUS MOMENTS, THE LATE ANTON
Baumstark suggested that prayers beginning with the word
eulogetos were in origin inspired by Jewish models, and one of
the examples given by him is the blessing *eulogetos ei Kyrie*
from the Byzantine marriage service.[1] This particular prayer,
however, does not appear in the earliest manuscript (*Barberini
336*), and when it first does appear, the pseudo-Jewish opening is sometimes lacking.[2] However, his suggestion about Jewish inspiration has provoked the tentative ideas which follow,
in which we shall attempt to chart a course through Jewish
blessings, the blessings from the book of Tobit, spasmodic references among the Fathers, and Latin and Greek blessings
from the period of later liturgical texts, in order to take us
from the marriage in Cana of Galilee to the Gregorian Sacramentary—and beyond.

Jewish Blessings

The Old Testament sees marriage in a domestic setting, as
the accounts demonstrate, where marriage is a sacred covenant, worked out between the bride's father and the groom.[3]
The actual texts of the Seven Marriage Blessings as are to be
found in various Jewish prayerbooks show a common struc-

ture, with set themes, but a certain degree of variety in the phraseology and in some of the subject matter.[4] This bears out Heinemann's contention that Jewish prayers at the time of Christ were not the set texts which we once supposed them to be.[5] Moreover, among the blessings which a regular rabbi had to know, we find the benedictions of the marriage ceremony, and one rabbinical source affirms that "from the manner in which a man recites the benedictions, we can discern whether he is a boor or a scholar."[6]

What do we find in these benedictions? After the opening vine-blessing, there are blessings for creation, the creation of humankind, and for human destiny; supplication for Zion, the barren one; supplication for the couple, with reference to the Garden of Eden; blessing for the joy of the couple; and a long blessing and supplication for the qualities of married life, with reference to the marriage feast. The progression of ideas is, in fact, very close to that found in the Gregorian Sacramentary's nuptial blessing, *deus qui potestate*, which we shall look at later.

If Heinemann is right, there would have been an agreed structure and basic content for the Seven Benedictions, but the details would vary from place to place, and from one tradition to another. It is only in the fourth and fifth blessings that he demonstrates the truth of this theory,[7] but we can assume that it applies to the rest of the sequence.

Tobit

The Book of Tobit is a charming example of late Jewish pious literature. No one is sure as to its date or place of origin, and there are many textual difficulties; long ago Charles was convinced that it emanated from late-second-century Egyptian Judaism.[8] In this book there are no fewer than three marriage blessings, although there are many other (purely conversational) ones.

The first is Raguel's blessing of Sarah and Tobias as they join hands, just before the marriage contract is made, *deus Abraham . . . ipse vos conjungat . . .*[9] It is this blessing which reappears in the eleventh-century Sacramentary of Vich (Spain), during the *dexterarum junctio* at the end of Mass, an obvious use of a biblical source for a comparatively new liturgical ceremony.[10]

The second is of more interest, put into the mouth of Tobias himself, in the marriage chamber; an opening bidding, a blessing of the whole of creation, creation of Adam and Eve (one manuscript actually quotes the Genesis account),[11] affirmation by Tobias that he wants marriage for children only and not for lust, so that God may be glorified by more people.[12] This prayer can be compared for its domestic setting and its structure with the Seven Benedictions; and for its structure and content with one very long blessing which appears in manuscript A of the eleventh-century Visigothic *Liber Ordinum*, the prayer *deus qui in principio hominum*;[13] but it also has structural affinities with the Gregorian prayer mentioned earlier.

The third blessing need not detain us. On the morning after the night before, Raguel blesses Sarah "through" Tobias, *benedictio . . . sit super uxorem tuam*.[14] We next encounter this prayer in the tenth-century Pontifical of Egbert (another domestic rite), but never again.[15] Before leaving Tobit, it is worth noting that the first and second blessings, like the Jewish, are of both bride and groom, and also that the presence of Raphael and other protecting angels, though not mentioned in these blessings, occurs earlier in the book, and is a theme taken up by the later prayers of the Visigothic and Anglo-Norman families.[16]

Early Quotations

Most references in the early patristic writers simply state that marriage happened, and very little else. Thus, the oft-quoted dictum of Ignatius about the local church and its bishop being involved in Christian marriages is evidence that at Antioch, at least, the question of who married whom was one which the local church deemed to be important, and, we may conclude, a matter over which the bishop presided, when he probably gave a blessing.[17] Whereas heretical groups are marked by rigorism, orthodox writers clearly favor letting men marry young.[18] In the late New Testament period, we have evidence about the role of bishops as guardians of morality,[19] which leads one to assume that Ignatius was not inventing something new. But whether marriage was purely domestic or *in facie ecclesiae* is hard to tell.

Tertullian is the writer to whom we can easily turn, but his directions may only reflect North African rigorism of the time; the church founds (*conciliat*), the eucharist confirms (*confirmat*), the blessing seals (*obsignat*), the angels proclaim (*renuntiant*), and the Father ratifies (*rato habet*).[20] Does this mean a nuptial eucharist? And a nuptial blessing? On balance, it seems doubtful that the eucharist was celebrated at home, though possible; on the other hand, there is evidence of a nuptial eucharist in a domestic setting at Alexandria during the time of Timotheus.[21] Certainly, Tertullian envisages a marriage *in facie ecclesiae*, and with a special blessing; but whether the angelic presence is patristic oratory or liturgical allusion is uncertain. In one of his sermons Tertullian insists on the propagation of children as the prime reason for marriage,[22] like Tobias in his blessing. Moreover, we have Clement of Alexandria's amusing warning against bridal wigs, couched in such terms as would suggest a nuptial blessing with the laying on of hands[23]—it is the bride's own hair, not the false stuff, that gets blessed, he insists.

Ritzer, in his study of the marriage liturgy, is ready to minimize the evidence of Ignatius and Tertullian, but he shows a surprising degree of indulgence in interpreting the marriage blessing in the apocryphal *Acts of Thomas*, where the apostle happens upon a domestic wedding scene, and a blessing is prized from him.[24] The blessing itself is lengthy, and the majority of its periods are invocations to the Most High; only in the very last section is blessing and prayer actually besought for the couple. Ritzer goes on to say: "a bishop or a presbyter of the second or third century could well have blessed a young couple with this formula."[25] If it does indicate second- or third-century liturgical usage, it is certainly wordy and foreign to the structure of the Jewish *berakot* which we looked at earlier; but, of course, this need not be important.

When we move into the fourth century, we are on surer ground. Chrysostom refers to *euchai* and *eulogiai* at weddings, possibly echoing the diaconal biddings and priestly blessings in the Byzantine rite.[26] And Jerome attains the height of presbyteral bigotry when he warns priests to keep well away from marriages,[27] which suggests that they took place at home, and that they had a ritual (and, surely, Christian) form.

Among the writings of Paulinus of Nola, there is a full account of the marriage of Julian, son of the Bishop of Benevento, to the daughter of the Bishop of Capua. Of course, it cannot be said to typify late fourth-century practice, as anyone who has taken part in a wedding which involves two clerical families will know well. In the relevant section of *Carmen XXV* are expressions suggesting that we are in church, the bishop blesses with his hand, bestowing the grace of Christ, with angelic help, giving justice and peace; and, in the recognized manner, he places a veil over the shoulders of *both* the man and the woman, and blesses them, and Christ gives them reverent hearts through the chaste hands (of the bishop).[28] Thus the nuptial blessing is given by a bishop, with a veil over both the man and the woman, and there are hints of what the blessing might contain.

Liturgical Texts

The two classic forms of the nuptial blessing in the west are to be found in the *Leonianum-Gelasianum* (*Le/Ge*) and the *Gregorianum Hadrianum* (*Gr*).[29] Although they are different in content, their structure is identical, which suggests that the latter is a thorough reworking of the former. *Pater mundi conditor* (*Le/Ge*) appears in a few of the later medieval books, but *deus qui potestate* (*Gr*) wins the day.[30] Each prayer starts not with a blessing, but with a conventional collect-type opening. The themes, however, are surprisingly similar, even familiar; creation, creation of man, creation of woman, marriage (*Gr* inserts the unity between Christ and the church); then prayer for the bride, marital virtues, her life with husband, eternity, and children. (One section of *Gr* is slightly reminiscent of Paulinus' *Carmen*—"May her yoke be one of love and peace. May she marry in Christ as one faithful and chaste.")

Both prayers take place during the nuptial Mass, after the Canon, and both bless the bride only—in common with the pagan Roman tradition, where the ceremonies emphasize the bride's change of state.[31] It is remotely possible that the short blessing, *benedictio . . . super uxorem tuam* in Tobit could be an influence. This blessing of only the bride is a quite novel feature so far: it is a significant step away from Paulinus' unequivocal blessing *amborum*, and all the evidence in the subsequent development of the nuptial blessing prayers in the west (both variants of this prayer, and entirely new compositions

placed here or elsewhere in the rite) points to a universal dis-
satisfaction with this Roman peculiarity as the Middle Ages
progressed. All other prayers bless the bride and groom without exception.[32]

In the Byzantine rite, the earliest known text (*Barberini 336*)[33]
is from the eighth century, and the main blessing is *ho Theos ho
hagios ho plasas*, which has an engaging simplicity and theological content; creation of man, creation of woman, prayer for
their married life together, and for children. The later Byzantine prayers follow a similar pattern, as do the other eastern
rites, but they are, on the whole, longer and more manneredly
biblical.[34]

* * * * * *

Where does this leave us? Not with very much, but the following conclusions can be drawn, some with much qualification, others with some probability.

(1) An obvious but gradual shift from domestic marriage
paternally/clerically blessed, to a proper nuptial liturgy, with
blessing by bishop or presbyter.

(2) The blessing could have been adapted from the Jewish
pattern at an early stage, since there is so much in common in
the domestic setting; but the influence of this pattern on the
set texts of the western and eastern books is clear.

(3) The blessing is improvised at first, and could have been
improvised according to set norms, as in other services, as
convention took over gradually.

(4) The Jewish influence is discernible in that
    (a) the nuptial blessing is related to the Seven Benedic-
        tions, with the same structure;
    (b) but the development of *both* traditions continues;
    (c) and the use of Tobit for actual *texts* does not occur
        until much later.

(5) The pagan influence is to be seen in the survival (?) at
Rome of the exclusively bridal blessing.

(6) So that the early pattern for nuptial blessing indicated by
the central portion of the Seven Benedictions, the long blessing
in Tobit, the formulas in *Le/Ge, Gr*, and *Barberini 336*, backed
up by hints from Paulinus and elsewhere, could have been as
follows:

Creation
Creation of man, creation of woman
Marriage
Supplication for the married couple: their life together (angelic protection?), marital virtues (exemplified by biblical characters?), children (and children's children), and life to come, in eternity.

Notes

1. A. Baumstark, *Liturgie comparée* (Chevetogne: Editions de Chevetogne, 1955) 72, n. 3.

2. J. Goar, *Euchologion* (Venice: Javarina, 1730) 320; K. Ritzer, *Formen, Riten und religiöses Brauchtum der Eheschliessung in den christlichen Kirchen des ersten Jahrhunderts*, Liturgiewissenschaftliche Quellen und Forschungen, vol. 38 (Münster: Aschendorff, 1962) 135ff. (= Ritzer)

3. Genesis 24:3, 26:34f, 27:46, 38:6.

4. For example, *The Authorised Daily Prayer-Book* (London: Bloch, 1908); see Ritzer 12.

5. J. Heinemann, *Prayer in the Talmud* (Berlin-New York: De Gruyter, 1977) 37ff.

6. Ibid. 47.

7. Heinemann, *Prayer* 74ff.

8. R.H. Charles, *The Apocrypha and Pseudepigrapha of the Old Testament*, vol. 1 (Oxford: University Press, 1913) 174ff.

9. Tobit 7:15 (Vulgate).

10. Ritzer 192ff.

11. Charles, *The Apocrypha* 223.

12. Tobit 8:7-10 (Vulgate).

13. M. Férotin, *Le Liber Ordinum en usage dans l'église wisigothique et mozarabe d'Espagne du cinquième au onzième siècle*, Monumenta Ecclesiae Liturgica, vol. 5 (Paris: Didot, 1904) 436-437.

14. Tobit 8:10-12 (Vulgate).

15. W. Greenwell, ed., *The Pontifical of Egbert*, Surtees Society, vol. 27 (1853) 126.

16. For example, Tobit 6:16ff (Vulgate); see J.-B. Molin and P. Mutembe, *Le Rituel du mariage en France du XIIè au XVIè siècle* (Paris: Beauchesne, 1973) 324, 326, 327.

17. Ignatius, *Ad Polycarpum* 5:2.

18. *Did. Ap.*, Cap. 22.

19. 1 Timothy 3:4f, 12f, 5:4,10; Titus 1:6, 2:3-5.

20. Tertullian, *Ad Uxorem* 2:8; see Ritzer 57ff.

21. Timotheus, *Resp.* 11.

22. Tertullian, *Adv. Marc* 1-29.

23. Clement of Alexandria, *Paed.* III, 11, 63, 1.

24. Ritzer 55ff.

25. Ibid. 56.

26. Chrysostom, *In Gen. Hom.* 48 (at Antioch).

27. Jerome, *Epistola* 52:16.

28. Ritzer 343; see "ante altaria, sanctificante manu, Christi gratia, benedicta cohors . . . angelici agminis, justitia et pax, ordine recto," and then "jugans capita amborum sub pace jugali velat eos dextra quos prece sanctificat," and "perque manus castas corda pudica juva."

29. L.C. Mohlberg, L. Eizenhöfer, P. Siffrin, *Sacramentarium Veronense* (Rome: Herder, 1956) no. 1110; L. Eizenhöfer, P. Siffrin, L.C. Mohlberg, *Liber Sacramentorum* (Rome: Herder, 1960) no. 1453; J. Deshusses, *Le Sacramentarium grégorien*, Spicilegium Friburgense, vol. 16 (Fribourg: Presses Universitaires, 1971) no. 858.

30. See K.W. Stevenson, "Benedictio Nuptialis—Reflections on the Blessing of the Bride and Groom in Some Western Mediaeval Rites," *Ephemerides Liturgicae* 93 (1979) 457-478: reprinted as Chapter 6 of this volume.

31. See J.-P. De Jong, "Brautsegen und Jungfrauenweihe," *Zeitschrift für katholische Theologie* 84 (1962) 300-322, where De Jong tries to show a greater linkage between the pagan Roman and sacramentary traditions than the evidence will permit.

32. See Stevenson, "Benedictio Nuptialis."

33. Goar, *Euchologion* 321 (see 317 for full text).

34. For other Oriental rites, see H. Denzinger, *Ritus Orientalium*, vol. 2 (Würzburg: Stahl, 1864) 373-374 ("Domine Deus noster, creator omnium": Coptic); 390 ("Deus magnus, qui per Christum": Syrian); 417 ("Domine Deus noster": Maronite); 461f. ("Domine Deus exercituum": Armenian).

6

"Benedictio Nuptialis": Reflections on the Blessing of Bride and Groom in Some Western Medieval Rites

THE MARRIAGE RITES OF THE WESTERN MIDDLE AGES ARE DERIVED from two main sources—the nuptial Mass formularies of the early sacramentaries and the domestic rites of Western Europe.[1] In our overall understanding of the evolution of the marriage liturgy, we are much indebted to the work of Ritzer,[2] and Molin and Mutembe,[3] especially in the latters' study of the French rites. The purpose of this inquiry is to look into one element in all these rites—the blessing of the bride, or of the bridal pair—and to trace its rather nervous development through our period. Throughout the inquiry, attention will be drawn to the position of the blessing in the rite, and to the question whether it is directed exclusively to the bride, or both the man and woman.[4]

The Sacramentaries

In the *Sacramentarium Leonianum* (*Le*), the *Gelasianum* (*Ge*), and the *Hadrianum* (*Gr*) we encounter the nuptial blessing set within the proper for a Mass. *Le* gives the somewhat obtuse[5] *pater mundi conditor*,[6] as does *Ge*, but prefixing it with a preparatory prayer, *ds q mundi crescentis*,[7] and adding a postcommunion prayer, *dne sancte pater*,[8] which blesses both bride and groom. In *Gr*, however, the formulas are different and, as one would expect, they predominate in the later books; the preparatory prayer is *propitiare dne*,[9] and the nuptial blessing is *ds q potestate*,[10] a much finer composition, the result of a thorough reworking of the earlier *pater mundi conditor*.[11] What we have in all these books is a nuptial blessing which has as its main themes the thanksgiving for creation,[12] and supplication for the bride, that she may be a good wife, and follow the example of the holy women of the Bible.[13] It is inserted at a conventional but climactic point in the eucharist, between the Canon and the Pax.[14] The other prayers refer in part to both bride and groom, but only in *Ge*'s postcommunion is there a blessing of both.

Anglo-Saxon and Anglo-Norman Books

When we come to the Anglo-Saxon and Anglo-Norman books, there is much more variety. The Pontifical of Egbert (a "domestic" and therefore noneucharistic rite) has a final blessing which is immediately addressed to the man, but for his wife—*benedictio dni sit super uxorem tuam*,[15] (Raguel's blessing in Tobit) and prays for the continuation of family-life, similar to the concluding portion of the *Gr* nuptial blessing.[16] It also has two earlier prayers which are found in the Ritual of Durham, *benedicat vos dnus, et custodiat vos Xtus* and *benedic, dne, istos adolescentulos*,[17] and both of these prayers become common coin in later books.[18] Subsequent formularies give only a pontifical blessing, to follow the nuptial blessing before communion.[19] Both Claudius and Lanalet give the prayer *omnipotens ds q primos parentes*;[20] this appears in other benedictionals and similar books,[21] and a shorter version occurs in the later Pontifical of Lyre, given by Martène.[22] Lyre also has *benedicat ds corpora vestra*,[23] which Evesham (both versions) makes pontifical, and places before the Pax.[24] The Canterbury Benedictional has perhaps the most interesting composition, full of Scripture and angelic imagery, *ds q non solum*, and this is its only occurrence.[25] Westminster and John Longlande both give *summa providentia*, a distinctly heavy prayer.[26] All these blessings are of both bride and groom, and their themes are varied in expression but common in base—God's strength in their married life together.

An Opposition?

Thus we have what appears to be an opposition in an important part of the rite, between a blessing of the bride (before communion) in the sacramentaries, and blessing both bride and groom in other sources, including the pontificals. Although these latter will have been given in conjunction with a nuptial Mass (with the exception of the Pontifical of Egbert),[27] it is nonetheless a curious fact that *the* "nuptial blessing" should originally be directed exclusively to the bride. De Jong has attempted to show that the earlier Latin tradition anterior to the sacramentaries was one of blessing both the bridal pair,[28] but there is no concrete evidence, and Metz's thorough study of the rite of consecration of virgins has demonstrated that the blessing of virgin during the Mass with the veil arose out of the corresponding blessing of the bride, and not *vice versa*.[29]

Pluralizing the Verbs

But is the "opposition" so simple? The evidence points otherwise, and in two different quarters.

First, there is a tendency to pluralize the verbs at the end of the prayer *ds q potestate*. This does not alter the basic sense of the nuptial blessing, but it shifts the direction of the sense, and the development of this tendency is worth tracing.

The earliest verified occurrence of this is Cambrai 159, dated 812 in Lietzmann's edition of the Gregorian Sacramentary.[30] The next appearances are in some manuscripts of *Gr*, all in the group described by Deshusses as "Hadrianum authentique corrigé," but none in the more numerous groups described as "Grégorien d'Aniane" and "Grégorien d'Aniane corrigé."[31] In those which opt for the plural verb, the last two verbs become *videant* and *perveniant*, and in a few, the antepenultimate verb is also pluralized—another *perveniant*.[32] It is interesting to note the drift in the later manuscripts away from the plural ending, back to the more authentic singular reading. The next appearance is in the Sacramentary of Vich, which is two centuries later, but which in all probability contains Visigothic material of a much earlier date; all three verbs appear in the plural, *perveniant, videant,* and *perveniant.*[33] The *Liber Ordinum* ms B does not contain this item at all, but has a new and lengthy blessing of both the bridal pair, *ds q ad propagandum.*[34] These Visigothic blessings occur at the end of the Mass, a feature of this rite.[35] On the other hand, the Sacramentary of Fulda (which is noted for its Visigothic material) not only has the singular form, and also the *Ge* prayer, but follows them with a blessing "super utrumque," *dne ds noster q purum hominem.*[36]

We next encounter the plural ending in a much more important variant of *ds q potestate,* the eleventh-century *Cologne 141* manuscript. The precatory section, in all other manuscripts exclusively bridal, is adapted as follows: "Look with kindness upon your manservant and maidservant, who are to be joined in the relationship of marriage, as they ask to be strengthened with your protection."[37] This is no longer a blessing of the bride, nor yet a blessing of the bride with bridegroom implicated at the end, but rather a blessing of both bride and bridegroom. But it is a short-lived experiment, and we only encounter plural endings thereafter, in different places and in different ways. *Bamberg 53,* also of the eleventh century, uses this ending, from which (?) it secured inclusion in mss B and O of the twelfth-century Roman Pontifical (using Andrieu's edition).[38] Another and perhaps surprising twelfth-century witness is the Irish Missal; here the preparatory prayer, *propitiare . . .* is lacking,[39] but *pariter* is added before the first *perveniant;*[40] this latter is an obvious amplification of sense. Following the prayer comes *ds q crescentis* (as *Ge*) and *omnip semp ds q primos parentes.*[41] The absence of *propitiare* thus cannot be taken as indicating an under-developed rite—these three prayers suggest rather the reverse.

Thereafter, in the British Isles, we only come across the plural form in the thirteenth-century Pontifical of Anianus of Bangor, which has *et ambo . . . perveniant*[42] (another obviously conscious elaboration), and the fourteenth-century Evesham Book, which reads *pariter,* as the Irish Missal.[43] In France, the only ordos given by Martène or Molin-Mutembe are both North French and thirteenth century—Rouen, with *ambo*[44], and St. Vedast of Arras[45]—a minority.

In Scandinavia, however, the fashion for the plural ending was popular. Ms O of the *Manuale Norvegicum* has the plural ending, with *ambo,* and also adds the prayer *ds Abraham . . . impleat benedictionem.*[46] The Manual from Notmark also contains the plural ending, but with a small gap in the manuscript at this point,[47] and the Skara and Hemsjö books have the same, but with *uterque perveniat et videat . . .*[48] In the *Manuale Rosckildense* we find *utrique permaneant et videant,*[49] a clear re-editing and possibly an improvement, which has reappeared in the new Roman ordo.[50] The Slesvig Agenda has the plural verbs,[51] as also Linköping, with *ambo.*[52] Åbo and Uppsala, on the other hand, hold out in isolation, with the singular form.[53]

Apart from the thirteenth-century *Manuale Norvegicum,* it is conceivable that all these books were influenced by the 1481 Venice edition of the *Missale Romanum,*[54] through which the plural ending, with *ambo,* got into the Tridentine Missal.[55] However, the interesting feature about the 1481 book is that it prefixes the final section of the blessing with the words "super utrosque oratio."[56] This is a far cry from the "velatio nuptialis" of *Le* and other such exclusively bridal titles in earlier rites.[57] We will return to this question later on in our inquiry.

Two Bridal Prayers in the "Liber Ordinum"

The other route which may bring evidence is less circuitous. Among the various blessings given in the supplement of the *Liber Ordinum* there are two which are directed to the bride. The first (*LO 440*) is called *ordo ad benedicendum eos qui noviter nubunt,* but the "weight" is decidedly on the bride—*concede, dne, huic famulae ILL.*—although towards the end the man is implicitly mentioned, but after the fashion (though less guardedly) of the plural ending *ds q potestate* prayers, *ita carne uterque fructificent.*[58] Moeller suggests that it may be a survival of the ancient blessing before communion, as the prayer shows features different from the more systematic prayers in the rest of his collection.[59]

The other prayer, however, is the *benedictio solius puellae,* and it comes again from the supplement (*LO 439*), and begins *ds qui tegi Rebeccam.*[60] Once again Moeller is intrigued, and suggests an ancient tradition behind the prayer.[61] As they stand, the prayers do not appear to have been used in isolation, but as for what was the original Visigothic tradition (if such a thing there was), this is an open question. Could *LO 440* be "an original" nuptial blessing, modelled on *Ge* or *Gr*? The outline of the prayer might suggest this, although there are no marks indicating linguistic common ground, or even source-use.[62] On the other hand, could *LO 439* be "an original" nuptial blessing, subsequently subsumed by prayers of blessing for both bride and groom?[63] More likely, however, is the conclusion that the Visigothic tradition originally blessed both the bridal pair, and that *LO 440* is a subsequent reworking of *ds q potestate*, with the basic sense and structure of the plural ending version, but with new material (the heavy opening), and stronger accent on sexuality (on which *ds q potestate* is restrained). *LO 439* would seem to be another (but more distant) reworking of the Roman original, but written specifically for use with the bridal veil.

Some Conclusions

Thus far, we can make the following conclusions:

1. The early prayers *pater mundi conditor* and *ds q potestate* were both written as exclusively bridal, in line with the ancient Roman tradition;

2. Subsequently, *ds q potestate*, by far the more predominant of the two, developed a plural ending;

3. This plural ending developed either in North Europe, in the Aachen tradition (as the manuscripts indicate), or possibly in Spain (if the Vich reading antedates and is the source for Cambrai 159);

4. The plural ending never won universal acceptance, nor a uniform pattern, but gained enough in Germany to ensure inclusion in the Missal of Pius V, and in one noble case even altered the middle of the prayer (Cologne 141).

5. The Spanish contribution included:

a) *either* an important parallel to the Roman tradition of blessing the bride only, if *LO 440/439* are "original";

b) *or* an important variant from the Roman tradition, in blessing both the bridal pair, if *LO 440/439* are witnesses to borrowing from a Roman liturgical principle, and adapting from the same Roman liturgical source.

6. But, already, the nuptial Mass was developing other blessings, of both bride and groom.

It is to these that we must now turn.

Positions of the Blessings

There are two main positions where blessing occur. The first is at the end of the Mass, and the second is in that part of the rite immediately preceding the Mass, Molin-Mutembe's section F.[64] Durham has *benedicat vos ds et custodiat*, as in the Pontifical of Egbert.[65] In the twelfth-century Roman Pontifical tradition, there is a threefold episcopal blessing, *omnip dei et dni*, where B and O prescribe, peculiarly, in *sabbato sancto*,[66] clearly an error, even an impossibility. In the Appendix of Andrieu's edition, however, appear both a lengthy formula *benedicere dne hunc fam tm N et hanc fam tm N* and the short *benedicat vos pater . . . q trinus*.[67] The York Manual has another special blessing, *dne sanc pater . . . ut coniunctionem . . . coniungi meruerunt*,[68] whereas the Hereford gives the short *benedicat vos divina*, but preceded by *adiutorium*, and with the chalice.[69] Manuscript O of the *Manuale Norvegicum* prescribes the short *benedicti sitis a dno*,[70] and in Notmark, we find the ingenious use of *ds humilium visitator* to which Ottosen draws attention in his edition.[71] Even though this list is selective, it is indicative of a lack of concern to encumber the rite at this point, and only in the twelfth-century Roman Pontifical and the York Manual do we find a prayer of substance which is specifically marital in its content.

The blessings before the introit of the Mass are more numerous and more complex. This does not surprise us because there is no Mass-structure to operate as a conditioning influence, as is the case between the Canon and the Peace.

Since no one rite is identical in the prayers chosen and the order in which they appear, a synthetical approach serves our purpose best. By far the commonest is *ds Abraham . . . ipse vos conjungat . . . impleatque*, the "blessing of Tobit,"[72] which occurs in virtually every rite in which the ring-giving comes before the Mass, and also in those rites which place the giving-away at the end of the Mass.[73] The force of the prayer is to *join* the couple in wedlock, and it has only one variant.[74] Another very common prayer is *respice . . . super conventionem*, which comes in two main forms, the later and longer amplifying the angelology and the intention of the prayer, which is for peaceable life together.[75] Very few rites have both the shorter and the longer versions, and never side by side, except in one case, clearly the result of accumulation.[76] *Benedic dne adolescentulos* is also a popular prayer, both in its earlier form,[77] as in the Red Book of Darley and the Magdalen Pontifical,[78] and also in its much more popular later form, prefixed by *ds Abraham;*[79] in this prayer the main petition is for the married couple to *learn* about living under God's sight. These are the main prayers used at this point in the rite.

Others include *omn (semp) ds q parentes*, the earliest examples of which (in this position) are Lyre,[80] and the Magdalen Pontifical,[81] taken from earlier benedictionals, and later appearing in the presbyteral books.[82] Then there is the Trinitarian *benedicat vos ds pater, custodiat vos Xtus . . .*, which, while often lush in language, is not specifically marital.[83] Similarly, the slightly less fulsome *benedicat vos dnus omni benedictione* occurs first at Lyre, and occasionally thereafter.[84] The principle idea in this prayer is that the couple should please God in body and mind. Another infrequent prayer is *benedicti sitis,*[85] Trinitarian and unmarital. *Benedicat vos dnus ex Sion* is a late English composition and very Jewish-sounding,[86] with the prayer that the couple may see their children's children and peace on Israel— another theme in common with the ending of *ds q potestate.*[87] A similar theme occurs in a variant of *respice dne*, which first appears in the twelfth-century Bury St. Edmunds book, and thereafter occasionally;[88] the ending is even more similar to that of *ds q potestate.*[89] Two rarities are *ds q mundi crescentis* (from *Ge*), which also appears in the Bury book, and thereafter in the thirteenth century, in the Missal of Hanley Castle and MS O of the *Manuale Norvegicum;*[90] and *dns sancte pater . . . te supplices*, which is to be found in the Hanley Missal and the fourteenth-century Evesham book.[91]

One provision which is pastorally of great importance is occasionally made, namely, optional blessing prayers for older couples. The earliest (and fullest) appears in the early twelfth-century Bury St. Edmunds book. Here the "oratio super illos quo maioris aetatis sunt" is the earlier version of *respice . . . su-*

per conventionem: another prayer is *da qs dne benedictionem,* followed by *benedic clementissime,* all of which are given at the end of this section of the rite.[92] *Da qs . . .* simply prays that they may be subservient to each other, and *benedic . . .* prays that they may be preserved from evil and live in perfect love together. None of the French books makes this sort of provision, and it only occurs in a few later rites—in England, in the fourteenth-century Westminster Pontifical,[93] and in the sixteenth-century Westminster Missal,[94] clearly a local peculiarity, which in Scandinavia appears in the 1535 Linköping Manual.[95] But in all three it consists only in the two prayers *da qs* and *benedic clementissime.* Do either of these prayers appear in other rites, in which they are definitely not restricted to elderly couples? Apart from the Norwegian Manual, the only example seems to be the fifteenth-century Harleian 2860 MS, which gives *da qs* only after *ds Abraham . . . ipse vos* in an unusually austere rite.[96]

So much for the prayers and their content. Three important questions must now be asked.

National/Local Characteristics?

First, are there any national/local characteristics discernible from the manuscripts? The answer is a qualified "yes." The French books are on the whole simpler and give fewer blessings than the English and Scandinavian books. With the exception of Lyre,[97] the *Codex Victorinus,*[98] Rouen,[99] and Amiens,[100] very few prayers are given even in those rites in which the giving-away comes at the end of the Mass. Since Lyre and *Victorinus* are both in the Anglo-Norman orbit, it is not surprising when we find similarities between these and the English books of the same time. And unlike the French books, which simplify this section of the rite as time goes on, the English books do precisely the reverse. In the twelfth-century, the prayers number four-five, as in the Irish Missal, and the manuscripts of the Magdalen Pontifical.[101] Elaboration continues in the next century, with Hanley Castle adding somewhat grotesquely to *ds q primos parentes* and *ds q mundi crescentis,*[102] and Anianus of Bangor giving a balance which is similar to those found two centuries later in the Welsh Manual[103] and the Rathen Manual.[104] The York Manual keeps a simplicity, with six prayers, while Westminster[105] has eight, and Hereford and Sarum have nine each.[106] The Scandinavian books vary, but they resemble more the English than the French, as would be expected. The Roskilde Manual has only three,[107] while MS O of the Norwegian Manual has nine,[108] but if the last three prayers were meant for elderly couples (they are the same as those noted before), then this would become number six, which would be more in tune with MS B and the period.

A Structure?

The second question is, can a structure be discerned in this section of the service? (At this point we are speaking only of those rites which place these blessing prayers immediately before the Mass.) The answer is a qualified "no." The overall pattern is to have *ds Abraham . . . ipse vos* immediately after the giving of the ring, or very soon indeed afterwards. French books are more uniform in this than the others.[109] The English books vary more; most of them have the prayer straight away, or more or less so, but some (e.g., Magdalen and Sarum)[110] work up to it with a few preceding blessings and some *preces*. But whatever other variations there may be, this prayer is by far and away the commonest in this part of the rite. As for the other prayers, *benedicti sitis* tends to come either right at the beginning (before *ds Ab ipse . . .*), as in Anianus of Bangor and the Rathen Manual,[111] or right at the end, as in Linköping and Skara.[112] Similarly, *omn ds q primos parentes* nearly always comes last or second last, except for MS O of the Norwegian Manual.[113] *Ds Ab . . . benedic adolescentulos* tends to come in the middle of the section, in England,[114] but at the beginning or the very end in Scandinavia,[115] and *benedicat vos ds pater* usually appears at or just before the end of the section, or at the end of a little group, just before a set of *preces*.[116]

The Preces

The third question to be asked concerns the *preces* (responsive prayers for the couple), which we have only touched upon in our inquiry. Is there a pattern? The answer is a very qualified "yes." In the English books they appear about halfway through the section, except in the Magdalen Pontifical, where they do not occur at all.[117] In two cases there are two sets of *preces*, and both are noted for having no fewer than nine prayers in this entire section; the Hereford Manual appears to position them in such a way as to give climactic place to the prayer *benedicat vos dnus ex Sion*[118] (a prayer confined to England anyway[119]), but the Sarum Manual does not seem to have any particular reason for two sets of *preces*, other than length.[120] However, the Bury St. Edmunds book gives the *preces* immediately after *ds Ab . . . ipse vos . . .*—the only case—and this would seem to enhance this one further as "the" prayer which joins the couple together.[121] Of the French books which have a fully developed section at this point, Lyre, *Victorinus*, and both Rouen[122] put the *preces* immediately before *ds Ab . . . benedic*, and this appears deliberate (only *Victorinus* has two sets of *preces*). The Scandinavian books show no special characteristics, although they have much in common with England.[123] All that can be said, therefore, about the *preces* is that they break up the section into sub-groups, a welcome development in a fast-growing part of the rite, and that in so doing, they can give prominence to certain prayers.

Conclusions

From our discussion of these short blessing prayers, the following conclusions can be drawn:

1. Throughout the later Middle Ages the concluding section of the rite before Mass continues to develop blessings;

2. The difference between them and the nuptial blessing is that these former vary to a very great extent, so that only in exceptional cases does one rite resemble another in the order and content of the prayers;[124]

3. The English family of rites is by far the richest, probably a mixture of local tastes, and the fact that these rites are more uniform in the structure of the whole service than, say, the French, with the nuptial blessing invariably before communion, and the giving-away nearly always before the Mass;[125]

4. The common denominator in the series of blessing prayers is *ds Ab . . . ipse vos conjungat*, which should not surprise because of its growing association with the giving away and the legal aspect of marriage;[126]

5. In liturgical style, some prayers (e.g., *respice dne super hanc
. . .*)[127] can easily be distinguished from later ones (e.g., *benedic,
dne . . .*);[128] the former tend to be shorter than the latter, patristic and not medieval in their absence of the *"benedic"* formulas;

6. Often the later prayers form at the very beginning or the
end of the section, a further indication of age of composition;[129]

7. Some of the prayers contain echoes of ideas from the nuptial blessing, which include creation,[130] Old Testament characters,[131] moral virtues in marriage,[132] and the continuation of
family life;[133]

8. Other prayers are distinguished by their allusions to angelology,[134] protection from evil,[135] and the life of the world to
come;[136]

9. But *all* these blessings refer to both bride and groom.

Development of the Nuptial Blessing

As these many and varied short blessing prayers developed
in number and importance, the nuptial blessing itself was developing as peculiarly distinctive, in three ways, which we
must now examine.

The first way is by far the most important from the liturgical, theological, and pastoral point of view. It is to restrict the
nuptial blessing to those who are being married for the first
time. Martène quotes a catalogue of early Fathers who shun
second marriages, and his list includes Ambrose, Theophilus
of Antioch, and Irenaeus.[137] But it is not until later that the
nuptial blessing becomes denied specifically to such cases, and
the line of evidence contains the names of Caesarius of Arles,
Theodore of Canterbury, and Urban II.[138] Gradually the nuptial blessing comes to be regarded as specifically sacramental,
and both Hildbert of Tours (d. 1133) and Hugh of Amiens,
Archbishop of Rouen (d. 1164) interpret the blessing as privileged and priestly.[139] The liturgical books do not mention any
restriction until later. The Norwegian Manual (MS O) singles
out the *ds q tam excellenti* paragraph of the nuptial blessing as
the "oratio virginum."[140] On the other hand, a few other Scandinavian books go further and deny the whole prayer to wom-
en previously married (Linköping, Skara, Hemsjö).[141] Herein

lies the key to a basic difference of opinion, between those who would focus the sacramental blessing on a few words near the beginning of the prayer, and those who would regard the entire prayer as the sacramental blessing. Some French books restrict the whole prayer, including Avignon[142] and Cambrai,[143] and we may assume that this was the norm.[144] It is, furthermore, interesting to note that the *Liber Ordinum* has a special blessing for widows,[145] similar to the pastoral principle observed before.[146] On the other hand, it is the English books, particularly the printed ones, which make a meal of the restriction. Evesham states categorically that the blessing cannot be repeated.[147] The Hereford, York, and Sarum Manuals all locate the blessing formula in the clause *ds q tam excellenti*, and justify the restriction by citing Ps-Ambrose and Aquinas.[148] Moreover, they agree that there are three places in the rite where blessing is given, before the Mass, during the Mass, and after Mass, but they insist that the second is the most important, and is therefore restricted.[149] We have already seen how much more complex was the pre-Mass set of blessings in England, and so such an explanation was obviously necessary. But it was not necessary in the more austere French rites.[150]

The second mark of distinction for the nuptial blessing is the use of a veil or pall, extended over the bridal pair.[151] It is by far the most common in France, although the directions vary considerably. At Lyre, four men hold the pall over the prostrated couple,[152] whereas at Arles the priest veils the couple, over the bride's head, but only over the shoulders of the groom.[153] At St. Maur the couple kneel,[154] but at Rouen they prostrate themselves,[155] as also at Lyon.[156] Mateus of Braga has the couple covered in linen, a survival of the ancient "velamen."[157] In England and Scandinavia the custom is not universally popular. England gives late instances, probably the result of French influences, with the Welsh, Hereford, York, and Sarum Manuals, and the Westminster Missal making the necessary directions for the pall to be extended over the bridal pair, sometimes held by four clerks (Welsh and Sarum), one by two clerks (York),[158] the others not defining this aspect of the ceremonial. In Scandinavia, the Norwegian Manual (MS O) once again betrays maturity of development, with the pall and the prostration.[159] Notmark mentions the pall "super capita,"[160]

Åbo has the pall held at four corners,[161] while Linköping merely prescribes the pall and the prostration.[162] Clearly, the veil/
pall has a dramatic effect on the service, which would very obviously be missed when the nuptial blessing was not given. It
would have helped to give the blessing a sacramental "feel,"
and so its somewhat quaint use to legitimize children born before the marriage need not surprise us.[163]

The third mark of distinction is more specifically liturgical—make *ds q potestate* into a preface, preceded by *sursum corda*. The earliest example is in the *Vich Sacramentary*,[164] after
which we meet it at Albi,[165] and thereafter increasingly in the
north, at St. Vedast, St. Maur, and St. Victor.[166] It survives into
many of the "Neo-Gallican" rituals,[167] in defiance of Tridentine austerity. We do not find it in any of the English books, although it does appear in a few Scandinavian, including Skara,
Hemsjö, Åbo, and Linköping.[168] Some of the books, including
those which do not go in for the preface introduction, give directions for chanting the nuptial blessing, sometimes "sub
tono lectionis" (as in England in all the Manuals),[169] and sometimes as a preface (as Meaux, Barbeau, and Paris).[170]

Neither the preface addition nor the method of chanting is of
great importance, although they both would serve to enhance
the nuptial blessing as a liturgical climax in the whole service.
However, the combination of the three distinctive features—
restriction, the veil, and the preface—would serve to mark off
this blessing as that which makes a nuptial Mass peculiarly
nuptial.[171] In this process we see, once again, the Visigothic tradition of elaboration, and the English tendency to overload the
service through a somewhat indiscriminate eclecticism.

* * * * * *

What, then, of the nuptial blessing in the later middle ages
in North and West Europe? From our investigation, the following points emerge:

1. The formative influences are the Gregorian Sacramentary
and the *Liber Ordinum*, in both of which can be seen the tendencies to bless the bride only, and the bride with the groom
at the conclusions of the prayer. We have suggested the possibility that the two traditions originally differed, and that *Gr*

blessed only the bride, whereas *LO* blessed both. This is con-clusive in the case of *Gr*, for we know its manuscript tradition; it is only an hypothesis with regard to *LO*, but a very strong one at that.[172]

2. From our examination of the blessing prayers which de-veloped later, the structure and themes of the *Gr* nuptial bless-ing continue to influence other more local compositions, some-times to the point of direct verbal parallel.[173]

3. These other blessings continue to develop throughout the middle ages, France being the country where Visigothic, Ro-man, and Anglo-Norman traditions meet and diffuse. The va-riety leads to apparent confusion in England, as witness the question whether the whole nuptial blessing or the Christolog-ical clause only constitutes *the blessing*.[174]

4. The profusion of these blessings witnesses to the impor-tant pastoral principle that the married couple require *interces-sion* in their liturgy, so that as the Mass propers become re-mote from them, with the decline in communion and general participation, so the prayers over them by the priest increase in importance.[175]

5. As their development and variety continue, and indicate further the story of medieval liturgical accumulation, through local experiment and cross-fertilization of different rites, so they all point to the fact that matrimony is a sacrament of hus-band and wife together, and that both man and woman stand equally before God for the divine blessing.

6. The persistence of *ds q potestate* as basically a blessing of bride only demonstrates the influence of *Gr* in the medieval west, even when later strata of prayers bless both bride and groom; even when the ending verbs are pluralized; and even when the later middle ages supplies its own liturgical-ceremonial differentials for this prayer, with pall, preface, chant, and restriction.

7. Obscure as the restriction debate may be, it could none-theless suggest the reason why the original version of *ds q pot-estate* was exclusively bridal, in the Christological section which mentions the love between Christ and his church. The church is loved by Christ, the bride is loved by the groom, therefore the church gives the bride her special blessing. This theory would, perhaps, explain why every other theme in *ds q*

potestate is taken up by later prayers, *except this specifically Christological* one.

* * * * * *

By way of postscript, we must take a brief look at some rites which have been compiled since.

The 1549 Prayer Book[176] of the Church of England reduces on the English Manuals, although it still has no fewer than six prayers of blessing, each related in some degree to a Latin original; the longest one is a reworking of *ds q potestate*, but is related to both man and woman throughout, "look mercifully upon these thy servants."[177] This remains part of the Anglican tradition in the successive Prayer Books, although a certain variety in the prayers continues.[178] The *Rituale Romanum* of 1614, on the other hand, is austere to the point of bareness,[179] with the prayer *respice . . . super hanc* (only) at the end of the pre-Mass section, but the nuptial blessing of the missal in its traditional place.[180] How paradoxical to find Anglican elaboration in the face of Roman simplicity in this particular service! And yet, it could be argued that it is a continuation (albeit under a different guise) of medieval English enrichment and patristic Roman sobriety.

More recently, Anglican and Roman have begun to work along parallel lines. The Church of England and American Episcopal rites provide for both eucharistic and non-eucharistic services, with the blessing located in the second part of the liturgy, at the end of what is an intercessory section.[181] Although neither has the nuptial blessing in its traditional place, even when the eucharist is celebrated, each contains a full blessing prayer, which is obviously inspired by *ds q potestate*. Moreover, each maintains the Anglican tradition of blessing both the bridal pair, but they improve considerably upon 1549 and 1662 in that they begin on a note of thanksgiving.[182]

In the new Roman rite, the balance has been redressed in both directions—there are more blessing prayers after the marriage itself, with a proper intercessory section (analogous to the *oratio fidelium*),[183] and the nuptial blessings refer to both bride and groom explicitly throughout. Of these latter, there are no fewer than three. The first is an adaptation of *ds q potes-*

tate,[184] and the other two are new compositions, one elaborating on the covenant theme,[185] the other more overtly contemporary, stressing such features as mutual support for each other in married life.[186]

In this sacrament of matrimony, in which all Christians may share, and in which we witness to a common tradition of married life experienced down the ages and prayed about in the liturgy, we can observe with much thanksgiving how in our generation the riches of the past have been used creatively in revising our marriage rites. But this has happened without subjecting ourselves to those areas of Christian tradition which we find hard to explain or understand, into which category we would place the bridal nuptial blessing of old. What we now have are rites which retain the beauty, dignity, and order of what we understand to have been the Christian medieval west, but which at the same time make sense of what Edward King, sometime bishop of Lincoln, described as "one of God's greatest gifts, one of the closest symbols of what He is, and of the union between Himself and us."[187]

Notes

1. J.-B. Molin and P. Mutembe, *Le Rituel du mariage en France du XIIe au XVIe siècle* (Paris: Beauchesne, 1974); preface by P.-M. Gy, 5. (= Molin-Mutembe)

2. K. Ritzer, *Formen, Riten und religiöses Brauchtum der Eheschliessung in den christlichen Kirchen des ersten Jahrtausend*, Liturgiewissenschaftliche Quellen und Forschungen, vol. 38 (Münster: Aschendorff, 1962).

3. See note 1: explanation of the origin of the work in the preface by Gy, 5-6.

4. On the origin of the nuptial blessing, see Ritzer 159ff., Molin-Mutembe 223ff.; see K.W. Stevenson, "The Origins of the Nuptial Blessing," *Heythrop Journal* 21 (1980) 412-414 (reprinted as Chapter 5 of this volume).

5. Ritzer 174ff.

6. L.C. Mohlberg, L. Eizenhöfer, P. Siffrin, *Sacramentarium Veronense* (Rome: Herder, 1956) no. 1110.

7. L. Eizenhöfer, P. Siffrin, L.C. Mohlberg, *Liber Sacramentorum* (Rome: Herder, 1960) no. 1453.

8. Ibid. no. 1451.

9. H. Lietzmann, *Das Sacramentarium Gregorianum nach dem Aachener Urexemplar* (Münster, Aschendorff, 1921) 111.

10. Ibid. 111.

11. A. Chavasse, *Le Sacramentaire Gélasien* (Tournai: Desclée, 1958), 485f.

12. See the first clause, *ds q potestate . . . licere disiungi*.

13. See the third and following clauses, *respice propitius . . . perveniat senectutem*.

14. J.-A. Jungmann, *Missarum Sollemnia*, vol. 3 (Paris: Aubier, 1953) 182-185.

15. W. Greenwell, *The Pontifical of Egbert*, Surtees Society, vol. 27 (1853) 126. See Chapter 5 for discussion of Tobit prayers.

16. See *ut videas . . . generationem* (Egbert) with *ut videat . . . perveniat senectutem* (*Gr*).

17. Greenwell, *The Pontifical of Egbert* 126; see W.G. Henderson and U. Lindeloff, *The Durham Collectar* (2d edition), Surtees Society, vol. 140 (1927) 110f.

18. Molin-Mutembe 322 (no. 14), 326 (no. 36).

19. For example, H.A. Wilson, *The Benedictional of Archbishop Robert*, Henry Bradshaw Society, vol. 24 (London, 1903) 55 (see 150f); R.M. Woolley, *The Canterbury Benedictional*, Henry Bradshaw Society, vol. 51 (London, 1937) 126; G.H. Doble, *The Lanalet Pontifical*, The Henry Bradshaw Society, vol. 74 (London, 1937) 65; W.G. Henderson, *The Pontifical of Christopher Bainbridge*, Surtees Society, vol. 61 (1875) 182; R.M. Woolley, *The Benedictional of John Longlande*, Henry Bradshaw Society, vol. 64 (London, 1927) 72; see also E.-E. Moeller, *Corpus Benedictionum Pontificalium*, Corpus Christianorum, vol. 162 (Turnholti-Brepols, 1971), vol. 1, nos. 83, 115, 163, 169, 349, 450, 639; vol. 2, nos. 1020, 1153, 1657, 1739, 1798, 2005. It is interesting to note that Moeller is intrigued by the possible origin of nos. 639 and 1135; we shall return to this later.

20. D.H. Turner, *The Claudius Pontificals*, Henry Bradshaw Society, vol. 97 (London, 1971) 82; see *The Lanalet Pontifical* 65.

21. Moeller, *Corpus Benedictionum* nos. 1798 and 1657; and also *The Pontifical of Christopher Bainbridge* 182 (not mentioned by Moeller).

22. E. Martène, *De Antiquis Ecclesiae Ritibus* (Antwerp, 1763), Lib. I, Cap. IX, Art. V, Ordo III, p. 128 (= Martène); the short version here does not appear earlier, though it is tempting to suggest that it antedates the longer pontifical form: this needs to be used with A.-G. Martimort, *La Documentation liturgique de Dom Edmond Martène*, Studi e Testi, vol. 279 (Vatican: Biblioteca Apostolica Vaticana, 1978).

23. Martène 129 (blessing at home).

24. H.A. Wilson, *Liber Evesham*, Henry Bradshaw Society, vol. 6 (London, 1893) 37 (long version), 40 (short version).

25. *The Canterbury Benedictional* 126: "I cannot find this elsewhere," p. 163 (= Moeller, *Corpus Benedictionum* no. 416).

26. Moeller, *Corpus Benedictionum* no. 2005.

27. See note 17.

28. J.-P. De Jong, "Brautsegen und Jungfrauenweihe," *Zeitschrift für katholische Theologie* 84 (1962) 300-322.

29. R. Metz, *La Consécration des vièrges dans l'église romaine* (Paris: Presses Universitaires, 1954) 366ff.

30. P. Bruylants, *Les Oraisons du missel romain*, vol. 2 (Louvain: Abbaye du Mont César, 1952) 120 (no. 434) and Lietzmann, *Das Sacramentarium Gregorianum* 111.

31. J. Deshusses, *Le Sacramentaire grégorien*, Spicilegium Friburgense, vol. 16 (Freiburg: Press Universitaires, 1971) 310f (no. 838).

32. See ibid. 31, with "table des sigles" and *apparatus criticus*.

33. Ritzer 362.

34. M. Férotin, *Liber Ordinum en usage dans l'église wisigothique et mozarabe d'Espagne du cinquième au onzième siècle*, Monumenta Ecclesiae Liturgica, vol. 5 (Paris: Didot, 1904) 438-439.

35. Ritzer 229ff.

36. Ibid. 372ff; see 292ff.

37. Ibid. 369.

38. M. Andrieu, *Les Ordines Romani du haut moyen âge*, vol. 1, Spicilegium Sacrum Lovaniense, vol. 11 (Louvain: Spicilegium Sacrum Lovaniense, 1931) 69; M. Andrieu, *Le Pontifical romain au moyen âge*, vol. 1, Studi e Testi, vol. 86 (Rome: Biblioteca Apostolica Vaticana, 1937) 262 (*v. apparatus criticus*).

39. F.E. Warren, *The MSS Irish Missal* (London, 1879) 82.

40. Ibid. 83.

41. Ibid. 83f.

42. W.G. Henderson, *The York Manual*, Surtees Society, vol. 63 (Durham/Edinburgh, 1875) 162*.

43. *Liber Evesham* 44.

44. Molin-Mutembe, *Le Rituel* 295.

45. Ibid. 298.

46. H. Faehn, *Manuale Norvegicum* (Oslo: University Press, 1962) 23.

47. K. Ottosen, *The Manual from Notmark*, Bibliotheca Liturgica Danica, S. Latina, vol. 1 (Copenhagen: Gad, 1970), 73, n. 12; see also Kenneth Stevenson, "The Marriage-Rites of Mediaeval Scandinavia," *Ephemerides Liturgicae* 97 (1983) 550-557.

48. J. Freisen, *Manuale Lincopense, Breviarium Scarense, Manuale Aboense* (Paderborn, 1904) 136; see H. Johansson, *Hemsjömanualet*, Acta Historico-Ecclesiastica Suecana, 1904, Lund 24 (Stockholm, 1950)

175. Hemsjö is identical to Skara, except for the opening directions and the *Dominus vobiscum* at the beginning (see Freisen, *Manuale* 131 and Johansson, *Hemsjömanualet* 171).

49. J. Freisen, *Manuale Roskildense* (Paderborn, 1898) 21.

50. *Missale Romanum* (Vatican: Typis Polyglottis Vaticanis, 1969) 744.

51. F. Freisen, *Liber Agendarum Ecclesiae et Dioecesis Sleswicensis* (Paderborn, 1898) 67 (but after communion).

52. Ibid. 177; I. Collijn, *Manuale Upsalense* (Stockholm, 1918).

53. Freisen, *Liber Agendarum* 177; Collijn, *Manuale Upsalense* 30.

54. R. Lippe, *Missale Romanum 1474*, Henry Bradshaw Society, vol. 33 (London, 1927) 278.

55. *Missale Romanum* (Antwerp, 1682) XCVIII; see also, e.g., *Rituale Parisiense* (Paris, 1697) 383; *Rituale Bejocense* (Paris, 1744) 278; *Rituel de Lodève* (Avignon, 1773) 188; *Rituale Catalaunense*, vol. 2 (Châlons, 1776) 331; *Rituale Parisiense* (Paris, 1839) 391; *Rituale Romanum* (Arhas, 1854) 187.

56. *Missale Romanum 1474* 278.

57. See "velatio nuptialis" in *Le*, "oratio ad sponsas velandas" in *Gr*.

58. Moeller, *Corpus Benedictionum* no. 639, p. 253.

59. See ibid.: he ends his note "cette question mériterait une étude."

60. Moeller, *Corpus Benedictionum* no. 439, p.473.

61. See ibid.; once more he ends his note, "ce point mériterait une étude."

62. The structures are identical:

Both open on the theme of creation:

LO 440 "q primordialia humani generis incrementa . . ."

Gr "q potestate virtutis tuae de nihilo cuncta fecisti, q dispositis . . ."

LO locks the allusion in Gr to the unity between Christ and the church and to original sin.

Both continue on the virtues of marriage:

LO 440 "concede . . . q novello nectitur vinculo coniugali, sinceram . . ."

Gr "respice propitius . . . qae maritali iungenda est consortio . . ."

Both then allude to the need for protection:

LO 440 "ita eius inhaeret populo, ne tuo recedat ullatenus a praecepto"

Gr "tua se expetit protectione"; see later "doctrinis caelestibus erudita."

Both then refer to children:

LO 440 "ita carne uterque fructificent, ut spiritu . . . ita munere filiorum"

GR "sit fecunda . . . et videat filios filiorum."

And both conclude on an eschatological note:

LO 440 "ut post felicia longioris vitae curricula ad regna mereantur pervenire"

Gr "et ad beatorum requiem atque ad caelestia regna perveniat . . ."

63. *LO 439* is a more even prayer in structure, being distributed into three clauses. In the first, Rebecca and her veil are mention, leading on to the allusion to the "velamen" of marriage; in the second, a reference to chastity and the marriage virtues; in the third, a reference to Abraham and Sarah, and the gift of children. All these three themes could be the result of a rewording of *Gr*.

64. Molin-Mutembe 283; this section is dealt with in chapter VIII, pp. 295-305; it is the least full of the chapters in the book, because the French rites tend to be brief at this point in the service.

65. See note 15 above.

66. Andrieu, *Le Pontifical* 262.

67. Ibid. 301.

68. Henderson, *The York Manual* 39.

69. Ibid. 120*.

70. Faehn, *Manuale Norvegicum* 23.

71. Ottosen, *The Manual from Notmark* 74; see 22f.

72. Molin-Mutembe 323, no. 21; see full discussion, 131f.

73. For example, the Ambrosian Ritual, in Martène, Ordo XV, p. 140.

74. See note 72 above; the only variant is the omission in some earlier versions of the words "ipse vos coniungit."

75. Molin-Mutembe 324, nos. 24, 25.

76. Among those which have both separately, *The Irish Missal* 81; *Manuale Norvegicum* 21; Slesvig, *Liber Agendarum* 64, 65; Metz 1543, Molin-Mutembe 318; Amiens 15th century is the only example with the two prayers side-by side, Martène, Ordo IX, p. 134.

77. Molin-Mutembe 327, no. 39.

78. The Red Book of Darley, in W.G. Henderson, *The York Manual* 158*; H.A. Wilson, *The Pontifical of Magdalen College*, Henry Bradshaw Society, vol. 39 (London, 1910) 203.

79. See note 77 above.

80. Martène, Ordo III, p. 128.

81. H.A. Wilson, *The Pontifical of Magdalen* 223 (later MS).

82. These include The Missal of Hanley Castle, The Welsh Manual, the Hereford Manual, and The York Manual, in W.G. Henderson, *The York Manual* 163*, 168*, 29; also in *Liber Evesham* 40; A. Jeffries Collins, *The Sarum Manual*, Henry Bradshaw Society, 91 (London, 1960), 50; J.

Wickham Legg, *The Westminster Missal*, vol. 3, Henry Bradshaw Society, vol. 11 (London, 1897) col. 1238; D. MacGregor, *The Rathen Manual*, Aberdeen Ecclesiological Society (1905) 3/2; *Manuale Norvegicum* 21; *The Manual from Notmark* 71; *Manuale Lincopense* 41; *Breviarium Scarense* 133; *Manuale Aboense* 174f.; *Hemsjömanualet* 172.

83. Molin-Mutembe, 322, no. 14.

84. Ibid. 322, no. 15; among those in which it is found are Rouen 15th century, Martène, Ordo VII, p. 132; Metz 1543, in Molin-Mutembe 318; and from the British Isles, The Pontifical of Anianus and the Hereford Manual, in Henderson, *The York Manual* 163*, 119, and MacGregor, *The Rathen Manual* 3/2.

85. Molin-Mutembe 323, no. 19; see also the Trinitarian *benedicat vos . . . q. trinus*, ibid. 322, no. 17.

86. Found in the Welsh and Hereford Manuals, Henderson, *The York Manual* 168*, 118*, and also in Collins, *The Sarum Manual* 50.

87. "Et videatis filios filiorum vestrorum et pacem super Israel"; see "et videat filios filiorum suorum . . ." (*Gr*).

88. Molin-Mutembe 324, no. 26; among those in which it appears are Rouen, 13th century, Molin-Mutembe 295; Rouen, 14th century, Martène, Ordo VII, p. 132; Cambrai, 14th century, Molin-Mutembe 313; Ely, Anianus, Welsh, and Hereford, all in Henderson, *The York Manual* 162*, 163*, 169*, 118*; also in Collins, *The Sarum Manual* 50, MacGregor, *The Rathen Manual* 3/1, and (perhaps the only example in Scandinavia) Freisen, *Manuale Aboense* 174.

89. "Et filios filiorum suorum usque in tertiam et quartam generationem incolumes videant, et in tua fidelitate semper perseverent et in futuro ad coelestia regna perveniant." The resemblance is too great to be coincidental.

90. Molin-Mutembe 323, no. 22 (see p. 201); Bury St. Edmunds, ibid. 290, Hanley Castle, in Henderson, *The York Manual* 165*; *Liber Evesham* 40; *Manuale Norvegicum* 20; and also Amiens 1509 (as Molin-Mutembe).

91. Hanley Castle, in *The York Manual* 165*, and *Liber Evesham* 40; the prayer occurs at the end of the Mass in *Codex Victorinus*, Martène, Ordo IV, p. 130; and also *The York Manual* 39 (see also Ritzer 349). That Hanley Castle and Evesham should both use it in this position suggests a local peculiarity.

92. Molin-Mutembe 290, and *Liber Evesham* 39.

93. Pontifical of Westminster, in *The York Manual* 165*.

94. *The Westminster Missal*, vol. 3, col. 1237.

95. *Manuale Lincopense* 41.

96. *The York Manual* 167*.

97. Martène, Ordo III, p. 128.

98. Martène, Ordo IV, p. 130. Martimort suggests this comes from Mont Saint Michel.

99. Rouen 13th century, Molin-Mutembe 294-295; Rouen 14th century, Martène, Ordo VII, p. 132.

100. Amiens 15th century, Martène, Ordo IX, p. 132.

101. *The Irish Missal*, 81; *The Pontifical of Magdalen College*, 203 and 222-224.

102. Hanley Castle and Anianus of Bangor, in *The York Manual*, 164*f., 162*.

103. Welsh Manual, in *The York Manual*, 168*.

104. *The Rathen Manual* 2/2-3/2.

105. *The Westminster Missal* coll. 1235-1238.

106. Hereford Manual, in *The York Manual* 118*f.; *The Sarum Manual* 49f.

107. *Manuale Rosckildense*, 17f.

108. *Manuale Norvegicum* 20f.

109. For example, Bayeux 12th century, Molin-Mutembe 284; Auxerre 14th century, Martène, Ordo VI, p.131; Rouen 13th century, Molin-Mutembe 294f.; St. Vedast, 13th century, Ibid. 298; Avignon 14th century, Ibid. 309f.

110. *The Pontifical of Magdalen College* 203, 222; *The Sarum Manual* 49.

111. Anianus of Bangor, in *The York Manual* 162*; *The Rathen Manual* 2/2.

112. *Manuale Lincopense* 41, 133.

113. *Manuale Norvegicum* 20f.

114. For example, Ely, Anianus, Hanley, Hereford, and York, in *The York Manual* 161*, 163*, 164*, 118*, and 28.

115. *The Manual from Notmark* 70; *Breviarium Scarense* 132; *Hemsjömanualet* 171 (at beginning); *Manuale Rosckildense* 18; *Liber Agendarum* (Slesvig) 65 (at end).

116. The Red Book of Darley, The Ely Pontifical, in *The York Manual* 159*, 162*; *The Irish Missal* 81; *The Pontifical of Magdalen College* 203, 222; *Le Pontifical romain* 301 (at or near the end); the Welsh and Hereford Manuals, in *The York Manual* 168*, 118*; *The Sarum Manual* 49; *The Westminster Missal*, vol. 3, col. 1236; *The Rathen Manual* 2/2; *Manuale Aboense* 173f. (at end of a group of prayers before the *preces*).

117. *The Pontifical of Magdalen College* 203ff., 222ff.

118. *The York Manual* 118*.

119. See note 86 above.

120. *The Sarum Manual* 49f.; a reason for the first set may be that *ds Abraham . . . ipse vos* comes later than usual.

121. Molin-Mutembe 290.

122. Martène, Ordo III, p. 128; Ordo IV, p. 129; Molin-Mutembe 294f.; Martène, Ordo VII, p. 132.

123. See Ritzer 310ff. See also note 47 above.

124. For example, Skara and Hemsjö.

125. See Leofric and Cotton Claudius A III, and the Red Book of Darley, in *The York Manual* 158*f., for early English rites with marriage formulas at the end of Mass.

126. Molin-Mutembe 202-204.

127. Ibid. 324, no. 24.

128. Ibid. 321, no. 13.

129. See the 13th and 14th century Rouen Ordos, with identical structure, except for the addition of *benedicat ds omn*, Molin-Mutembe 295; Martène, Ordo VII, p. 132.

130. For example, *omn semp ds, ds q mundi*, Molin-Mutembe 323, nos. 23, 22.

131. For example, *ds Abraham . . . ipse vos, benedic dne hunc famulum*, ibid. 323, 321, nos. 21, 13.

132. For example, *respice dne super hanc conventionem* (shorter version), *benedic clementissime*, ibid. 324, 321, nos. 24, 12.

133. For example, *respice dne . . . ut sicut* (longer version), *respice dne propitius*, ibid., 324, nos. 25, 26.

134. For example, *omn semp ds* (pontifical version), *ds q non solum*, Moeller, *Corpus Benedictionum* 735, 416, nos. 1798, 1020.

135. For example, *omn dnus huis receptaculo*, Moeller, ibid. 712, no. 1739, *benedic clementissime*, Molin-Mutembe 321, no. 12.

136. For example, *benedicere, dne, hunc famulum*, ibid. 323, no. 18.

137. Martène, Art. I., sec. IV, p. 121; Ambrose, *De Viduis*, 11; Theophilus of Antioch, *Ad Autolycum*, lib. 3; Irenaeus, *Adv. Haereses*, 3, cap. 19.

138. Martène, Art. I, sec. VII, p. 121; Caesarius, *Sermo* 289; Theodore of Canterbury, *Capitula Selecta*, no. 16; Urban II, *Epist. ad Rainoldum*.

139. Molin-Mutembe 384ff.

140. *Manuale Norvegicum* 23.

141. *Manuale Lincopense* 44, 135; *Hemsjömanualet* 174.

142. Molin-Mutembe 310.

143. Ibid. 314.

144. Ibid. 236f.

145. Ritzer 236.

146. See the earlier discussion of special provision in blessings prayers for older couples.

147. *Liber Evesham*, col. 43 n 2 (by a later hand).

148. Hereford and York, in *The York Manual* 117*f., 35ff.; *The Sarum Manual* 53ff.

149. "Sed quia plures benedictiones sunt in nuptiis celebrandis, scilicet in introitu ecclesie, et super pallium, et post missas, et super thorum in sero . . .," *The Sarum Manual* 56.

150. Molin-Mutembe 237.

151. Ibid. 228ff.

152. Martène, Ordo III, p. 128.

153. Ibid., Ordo V, p. 131.

154. Molin-Mutembe 300.

155. Ibid. 295; see Martène, Ordo VII, p. 132.

156. Ibid., Ordo VIII, p. 133.

157. Molin-Mutembe 292.

158. Welsh and York, in *The York Manual* 169*, 35; *The Sarum Manual* 53.

159. *Manuale Norvegicum* 26, 22 (N.B. both MSS B and O).

160. *The Manual from Notmark* 73.

161. *Manuale Lincopense* 176.

162. Ibid. 44.

163. Molin-Mutembe 232f.

164. Ritzer 362.

165. Molin-Mutembe 293.

166. Ibid. 298, 300, 303.

167. For example, *Rituel de la province de Reims*, Paris, 1677, p. 277 (post-communion, with pall); *Rituel de Toul*, Toul, 1700, p. 377 (post-communion, with pall); *Rituale Parisiense*, Paris, 1839, p. 391.

168. *Manuale Lincopense* 135 (Skara), 176 (Åbo), 46 (Linköping); *Hemsjömanualet* 174.

169. Welsh, Hereford, in *The York Manual* 169*, 120*, but not explicit in York itself; *The Sarum Manual* 53.

170. Molin-Mutembe 297, 307; Martène, Ordo X, 135.

171. See Ottosen's introduction in *The Manual from Notmark* 21.

172. See above.

173. See note 89 above.

174. See above.

175. On the new Roman rite, see below.

176. *The First Prayer-Book of King Edward VI, 1549*, The Ancient and Modern Library of Theological Literature (London: Griffith Farran, n.d.) 235ff.; on the sources, see W.K. Lowther Clarke, ed., *Liturgy and Worship* (London: SPCK, 1932) 467, and F.E. Brightman, *The English Rite* (London: Rivingtons, 1915) 800ff., and Kenneth Stevenson, *Nuptial Blessing: A Study of Christian Marriage Rites* (London: SPCK, 1982; New York: Oxford University Press, 1983) 134ff., the study written since.

177. *The First Prayer-Book* 237f.; J.H. Blunt, ed., *The Annotated Book*

of Common Prayer (London: Longmans, 1882) 457f. (juxtaposition of 1662 text and Latin).

178. See Clarke, *Liturgy and Worship* 467f.

179. Molin-Mutembe 271ff.

180. *Rituale Romanum* (Antwerp, 1826) 234.

181. See *Alternative Service Book* (London: SPCK, 1980) 296ff.; and *The Book of Common Prayer . . . according to the Episcopal Church* (New York: Seabury, 1979) 430f.

182. *The Alternative Service Book* 299; *The Book of Common Prayer* 431.

183. *Ordo Celebrandi Matrimonium* (Vatican: Typis Polyglottis Vaticanis, 1972) 14.

184. *Missale Romanum*, 1969, pp. 743ff.; see P.-M. Gy, "Le nouveau rituel du mariage," *La Maison-Dieu* 99 (1969) 127, 137-138. See also my discussion, since written, Kenneth Stevenson, *To Join Together: The Rite of Marriage*, Studies in the Reformed Rites of the Catholic Church, vol. 5 (New York: Pueblo Publishing co., 1987) 113-161.

185. *Missale Romanum* 748f.

186. Ibid. 752f.

187. B.W. Randolph, ed., *The Spiritual Letters of Edward King* (London: Mowbray, 1910) 48.

7

Van Gennep and Marriage—
Strange Bedfellows:
A Fresh Look at
the Rites of Marriage

IN 1908 ARNOLD VAN GENNEP PUBLISHED HIS MAJOR WORK, *LES RITES de passage*, which was a landmark in the development of what we nowadays call social anthropology. In the first chapter, the reader is introduced to various types of passage, among which figures the important sequence:

rites *préliminaires* (séparation)
    liminaires (marge)
et   *postliminaires* (agrégation).[1]

These are normally translated as rites of separation, liminality, and incorporation. Later on, the author surveys various types of marriage rites, although (for obvious reasons), he does not pay great attention to Christianity.[2] The axe he has to grind is the way in which primitive societies cope with the disturbance to individuals and communities as important relationships change during the life-cycle; he is, for example, aware that the rites of marriage and initiation partially overlap.

So far, however, liturgists have shown some reluctance in working out Van Gennep's hypothesis in relation to marriage.

Yet the paradigm is there, if we know where to look for it. It is a truism to observe that his threefold schema fits what we are all telling ourselves about Christian initiation.[3] Here, the preliminary rites correspond to enrolling for the catechumenate; the period of preliminary is the final stages of the catechumenate (or even the entirety?); and the incorporation finds supreme expression in the Easter sacraments of baptism, confirmation (if it must be so-called!), and eucharist. If Van Gennep's scheme is to be applied to marriage, it must take into account betrothal (rite of separation), time of engagement (liminality), and the celebration of marriage (rite of incorporation). Because for most of us, our liturgical context is a western one, such a division *may* reflect that of the real world, but it impinges little on the worshiping life of the church.

I have attempted to write a history of the main themes of the rites of marriage in the western churches.[4] I started with the early sources and continued with the nuptial Mass in the Roman sacramentaries, the Anglo-Norman "rite of consent" at the church-door before the Mass; and history seemed to work to a high point in the elaborate rite of the *Sarum Manual* and in Cranmer's *Book of Common Prayer*. And yet the western tale is, for the most part, a story in which the church takes over the domestic rite of consent, at betrothal, and prefixes it to the marriage celebration, so that what we are left with at the end of the Middle Ages is a single (if complex) liturgy, which by Van Gennep's reckoning would correspond *only* with the third stage, the rite of incorporation at the end. The logical conclusion to this is to be found in John Wesley's 1784 *Sunday Service*, which proved to be the foundation for North American Methodist liturgy. Here, Cranmer's rite is stripped down further; the ring (originally a sign of *betrothal*) disappears because the Puritans regarded it as popish, and the psalm which so neatly divides the marriage service into two parts disappears because Methodist architecture involves no long walk of bride and groom to the altar up through a medieval chancel.[5]

In our own century, the new rites of Western Christianity have included an unprecedented recovery of features which were lost. Thus in the 1969 *Ordo Celebrandi Matrimonium*,[6] consent and the nuptial blessing are the two central and most significant features, and the whole liturgy has been enriched by a fuller euchology, including the old Visigothic-type blessings at the end. (Cultural adaptation is officially encouraged in the *Praenotanda*, although there is little evidence of it happening where it is most needed.) Moreover, the 1979 American Episcopal *Book of Common Prayer*[7] sets the rite in the context of the eucharist, perhaps stressing something Cranmer knew would never take on as the norm, that those joined together as man and woman should partake of the holy supper as an integral part of their marriage celebration.

So much for the history of the attenuation of marriage rites in the Christian West. But what of Van Gennep's three stages? Before discussing how they appear in the Eastern Churches, and how they once appeared in the medieval west, it is necessary to examine more closely these stages in the light of Victor Turner's more elaborate clarification,[8] particularly with regard to the middle phase, that of liminality.

Turner identifies the sense of *communitas* as that which is established during the time of liminality, and this can be shown up in three ways. First, the initiates find themselves in a situation of *powerlessness*, because many things are expected of them, but they have no rights. Second, while they are undergoing a change of station, there is also a *cultural inversion*, as those about to be honored are humiliated. Third, the cultural *mores* are for a time *suspended*.

Many couples go through precisely these phases before marriage, and they even do so when they do not intend to get married at all. Powerlessness is a genuine phase of engagement, because the couple may be baffled by the feeling of being looked at by the wider family, the local community, and yet they are not left alone (except if they deliberately seek to do so!). Second, many local customs in connection with engagement parties (and jollifications immediately prior to marriage) are set out to humiliate the partners, even down to the crude jokes that may embarrass (or, to the contrary, amuse) either partner. Third, many couples start living together before marriage, and may even regard this as a "trial" experience, without any definite commitment to marry; such a phenomenon of cohabitation has a long history, and is nothing new to the so-called "permissive society." Indeed, as we shall see, rites of betrothal in the late Middle Ages frequently started (whether by accident or design) such relationships. In such ways liminality is a time of confusion and adjustment. And the churches of the west do little (if anything) to ritualize this process. Indeed, it is arguable that "liminality" is an experience Christian couples experience *after* marriage, if they take modern rites seriously.

Much is being written about liminality in relationship to the catechumenate, but it is surprising that nothing has so far been written about marriage as a rite of passage through which many couples go on their own, unsupported by the very community which is taking the RCIA so seriously at the moment. Indeed, I would go so far as to say that Van Gennep's three stages and Turner's explanation of liminality are real experiences for the majority of couples who come to the church to ask for its blessing. At a time when marriage is under severe pressure throughout western society, it is hardly to be expected that an attenuated marriage celebration which lasts little more than thirty minutes is really enough. Nor will it really do to regard pre-Cana weekends as adequate preparation, because that hands everything over to the therapists and educationalists. We need to *ritualize reality*, even if it means rethinking what we mean by marriage, and thereby asking some searching and uncomfortable questions of our respective churches.

In order to get a full picture of betrothal and marriage, let us now look at various eastern and medieval western rites, in order to see how rich antiquity was (and still is!) over this essentially pastoral liturgy of matrimony.

SYRIAN AND ARMENIAN

Gabriele Winkler has taught liturgists to take the Armenian rite[9] more seriously, and to regard it as no mere eccentric appendage to Byzantium, but rather as a serious cousin of the Syrian rites.[10] In all four of these liturgical families (Maronite, Armenian, Syrian, Jacobite, and East Syrian) there are clear traces of a fundamental desire to ritualize the preliminary (i.e., "separation") as well as the marriage (i.e., "incorporation"). Whereas the Maronite and Armenian rites (this latter, in the early texts collected by Conybeare[11]) have only two services, of betrothal and marriage, the Syrian Jacobites and East Syrians include others, such as the "joining of the right hands," and (East Syrian only) the blessing of the robes and the making of the bed-chamber. But it must be noted that later Armenian texts add robe-blessings and a domestic rite after the marriage services.

The Maronite rite betrays Latin influence, in the consent, hand-joining, and stole-wrapping in the marriage proper. But all four make the crowning of *both* partners the central focus of the marriage celebration, which is heightened in the fact that all four *bless* the crowns (which the Byzantines do not). It would appear that the removal of the crowns originally took place some time after the marriage celebration, to ritualize the consummation of the marriage. Moreover, whereas all four share a basic common core (separate rites for betrothal and marriage, and a marriage rite introduced by lessons from Ephesians 5:21ff. and Matthew 19, and clothed with chants and rich euchology), each set of rites has its own style, and each betrothal rite has a peculiarity.

Armenians exchange crosses at the betrothal. The Syrian Jacobite priest goes to the home of each partner at betrothal to act as a sort of intermediary. The Maronites include an anointing of the couple at betrothal, which they probably took from the Copts,[12] but worked into its use the symbolism of the anointing at Bethany (hardly a winner for marriage!), whereas the origin of the Coptic usage of oil appears to be baptismal. Finally, the East Syrian rite of betrothal ends with the *henana*,[13] when the priest places the rings into a chalice filled with wine, into which he places some ashes and water (the *henana* itself), a mixture which the couple drink. The symbolism appears to be that of dying to the old relationships in order to live to the new, a rich expression of the transitional character of betrothal. The Chaldean chants are particularly rich in the imagery of Ephesians 5, Christ and the church, his spouse.[14] It is significant that the peculiarities occur in the *betrothal* rites, as if there was a need to clothe them with something special and important, in order to make this rite have as much impact as possible.

COPTIC AND ETHIOPIC

The Coptic and Ethiopic rites are basically similar.[15] The Coptic rite, unlike all the other eastern rites (except the Armenian), bases the betrothal liturgy round a synaxis, with readings and prayers. Whereas the Armenian lessons relate directly to marriage, the Coptic ones (1 Cor 1:1-10 and Jn 1:1-17) only do so indirectly. The betrothal rite begins with a thanksgiving prayer and censing of the couple, which lead into the readings just mentioned. Then follow the betrothal prayers, which are of considerable beauty, and which Raes suspected of being very ancient.[16] (The offering of incense at the beginning as a symbol of prayer is entirely in accord with the use of incense in the Coptic rite.[17]) The second part of the betrothal liturgy centers round the blessing of the bridal robes, and it ends with the veiling of the couple.

The Coptic marriage rite once ended with a eucharist, and like the betrothal, it has a threefold shape of thanksgiving with incensations, readings, and solemn prayer for the couple. The service, however, begins with the consent of the couple, and ends with the anointing and crowning. The anointing, which began to disappear in the nineteenth century, is still common. Van Overstraeten has studied the Coptic sources and has concluded that the origin of the Coptic anointing lies in the notion of baptism as a marriage, and therefore of marriage as a way of sharing in the kingdom of God.[18]

BYZANTINE

Like the other eastern rites, the Byzantine services of betrothal (*arrabôn* = "pledges") and marriage (*stephanôma* = "crowning") are normally celebrated in sequence, but however close together they occur, separate origin is apparent in the texts as they have come down to us.[19] The earliest manuscript (*Barberini 336*), as Ritzer has shown,[20] embodies the essential ingredients, which later texts clothe round with enrichments. Thus, the betrothal rite is celebrated at the door of the church, as in the Anglo-Norman West, but it is a full liturgy, with diaconal biddings and prayers, and (from the twelfth century at least) prefixed by short questions on consent.[21]

The marriage rite itself, like the other eastern services, is embodied in a liturgy of lessons, marriage prayers, and crowning. The readings are Ephesians 5:20-33 and John 2:1-11; the former is universally used in the other eastern rites, but the Cana-reading only occurs in the Armenian rite of robe-blessing,[22] which is not entirely surprising, in view of the strong "Cana spirituality" which undergirds all the eastern marriage liturgies. Passarelli[23] has recently studied the manuscripts in detail, and has shown how three traditions shaped their marriage rites differently. First, the "Metropolitan" (Constantinople) incorporates the service within the liturgy of the presanctified, which began to replace the eucharist, from the eleventh century, at marriage. Second, the Italo-Greek tradition places the readings *after* the crowning (where it is today in the Byzantine rite). Third, the "Greek-Eastern" tradition (probably more anciently) places the readings *before* the crowning, as in all the other eastern rites. The crowning is followed by the "dance of Isaiah," where the priest walks the couple in a circle, to symbolize their union, whereupon the crowns are removed.[24] But the betrothal rite is, by comparison, a simple affair, and develops little from *Barberinii 336*.

VISIGOTHIC

The Visigothic (or old Spanish) tradition[25] is represented by two sets of manuscripts which are contained in Férotin's edition of the *Liber Ordinum*, which were compiled in the eleventh century, but which are generally regarded to be considerably earlier (probably fifth or sixth century), and which typify the old Castilian rite of central Spain.[26] LO has two rites: MS A has a betrothal and a nuptial Mass, whereas MS B has both these, but also contains a blessing of the bed-chamber and a proper for vespers before betrothal and the Mass. The domestic rite in B begins with the sprinkling of salt (a sure sign of fertility) and moves on to an *oratio* and a *benedictio*, the latter punctuated by Visigothic "Amens." The vesper-proper is incomplete in the manuscript; but it shows how the liturgy of the hours was once part of the ritual process of marriage, in which the community identified itself with the couple preparing for marriage. In both A and B the betrothal rite and the nuptial Mass are very similar. The betrothal is called *Ordo Arrarum* (= "order of pledges," cf. Byzantine terminology). It is a brief service and in the prayers, the blessing given is not of the *arras* but rather of the *giving* of the *arras*, which curiously deals with the later Reformation controversy about blessing inanimate objects, rings at marriage included.[27]

Both A and B follow this with the Mass.[28] Each causes the priest to "hand over" the bride to the groom. There may well be signs of romanization in the prayer, *ds q tegi Rebeccam*, which blesses the bride only, whereas all the other Visigothic blessings bless *both* partners.[29] But both bride and groom are covered with a pall or veil, and a marriage stole (Isidore of Seville's *vitta* or garland) is also placed round them, binding them together as man and wife. This latter custom was taken by the Spaniards on their imperial expeditions, and it is a common folk rite among both Hispanics and Filipinos today, where it resembles a lasso.

John Brooks-Leonard[30] has drawn attention to three features of these rites, which could also be applied to the eastern liturgies just looked at. First, the blessing of the chamber and the offering of *arras* are domestic rites that were celebrated with a rich euchology. Second, the community appears to be involved in the interim and preparatory rites, and not just in the nuptial Mass. Third, the connection between baptism and marriage is implicit throughout; just as the Fathers preached the importance of preserving and holding on to baptism, so these venerable prayers speak of the importance of preserving and holding on to marriage.

LATE WEST

The western medieval rites of Northern Europe arise from two main sources. The first is the nuptial Mass contained in the sacramentaries. The second is the domestic rite in which the couple, the bed-chamber, and (eventually) the ring were blessed. Gradually the two were fused together, as consent took on crucial importance. This resulted in the distinction between consent at betrothal ("verba de *futuro*") and consent at marriage ("verba de *praesenti*"). The liturgical legacy of this arrangement was that the nuptial Mass came to be preceded by a short rite of consent and ring-giving, which in the Anglo-Norman tradition took place at the door of the church, to stress its preliminary character. The English rite of Bury St. Edmunds (c.1125-1135)[31] is the first to provide a text for consent and ring-giving. In the preceding century there is a rite from Reims[32] which shows vestiges of the earlier tradition whereby betrothal was distanced by some space of time from the marriage Mass.

Western scholasticism placed increasing emphasis on the contractual aspect of marriage, which eventually resulted in the identification of the consent of the partners as the irreducible minimum required for a valid marriage. But in practice, western rites of the later Middle Ages show remarkable variety over what the priest is there to do.[33] Spanish (and Southern French) rites direct that the priest "hands the woman over" to the man, as we saw in the old Visigothic rites. Germany, however, tended to see the priest as the one who witnesses the consent. England, on the other hand, gave the priest nothing whatever to say or do, thereby showing that the priest is the president of the liturgical assembly, not the performer of sacraments. (Such an understanding underlies Cranmer's reformed rites in the 1549 and 1552 Prayer Books.) It is left to Normandy, in the fourteenth century, to go over the top with the priestly formula *ego vos in matrimonium conjungo* (= "I join you together in marriage"), which was agreed at the Council of Trent and which appeared in the 1614 *Rituale Romanum*. The 1969 *Ordo Celebrandi Matrimonium* has a more balanced view, requiring *two* essential ingredients in the service, the consent of the partners and the nuptial blessing, so that the priest's role is clearer and less self-conscious.

But separate rites of betrothal begin to appear again in the later Middle Ages which are different from the short set of prayers which we saw in the old Visigothic rites. Indeed, it is clear that such betrothal rites were used to start trial marriages; some rites give in to this tendency (or else to the common custom of straight cohabitation) by directing that children born before marriage are legitimized if they are placed under the canopy which was often used during the nuptial blessing of their parents.[34] French rites abounded in betrothal liturgies as well as domestic rites after the nuptial Mass. Neo-Gallican rites sometimes have prayers to deal (somehow) with infertility.[35] These later betrothal rites, however, reflect the scholastic distinction noted earlier in their structure. For just as consent at marriage consisted of interrogatives by the priest, consent of the individual partners, and the priestly formula, so did the betrothal rites usually have questions by the priest, followed by consent, and concluded by the formula *et ego affido vos* (= "I betroth you"). We are well into the era which is almost obsessed by intentionality.

* * * * * *

What, then, can history teach us about the three stages?

First of all, it is clear that—once upon a time—betrothal was an essential part in the process of getting married as a Christian. Indeed, the way in which betrothal was ritualized shows with what care such separate rites were developed, not as mere preliminaries, but as liturgies in their own right. In the east, each rite has a special symbolism: Armenian crosses, Syrian Jacobite presbyteral wandering, Maronite anointing, East Syrian *henana*, Coptic veiling, and Byzantine use of the church door for betrothal.[36]

Second, some rites went even further, and did not only ritualize betrothal, but also the period of liminality. These include the blessing of the robes (Coptic and Armenian), as well as the blessing of the chamber before the wedding and the use of the liturgy of the hours (Visigothic).

Third, it is the western emphasis on consent that eventually spells doom for betrothal because consent has to precede marriage immediately as a legal requirement. This means that the ring has to become part of marriage, instead of being a token of betrothal. (Today's "engagement rings" are thus the result of a duplication.)

Fourth, where betrothal rites did survive in the west, they express a direct and legal relation with consent at marriage, and therefore are formed in the same liturgical structure, consisting of the "unit" of questions, consent, priestly formula. But there is little or no euchology to "carry" such a rite of separation, and none to look forward to the period of liminality.

Fifth, a tension develops between "church" and "home" which is common to both Protestants and Catholics from the sixteenth century onwards, so that any domestic rites (whether before marriage or at home afterwards) are exceptional.[37] Only among special groups do these survive as, for example, among Hispanics today.[38] As we seek to help modern secularized Christians understand that prayer is not something only done in church, we can see that we are heirs of this tradition that excludes family prayer from the home even in the marriage liturgy.

Sixth, the eastern rites have a more tenuous relationship with the eucharist, although their whole *ambience* and use of symbolism is considerably richer than anything in the west, with the exception of the old Visigothic traditions. On the other hand, the western rites, by placing the marriage liturgy within the celebration of the eucharist, have the undoubted advantage of bringing marriage to the table of the Lord, but this becomes problematic (for some Catholics) when one of the partners is not a Roman Catholic. In this connection, the enthusiasm for the nuptial eucharist in such circumstances to the extent of refusing the bread and wine to the non-Catholic partner is to be deplored, even when it is backed up by the self-righteous rhetoric about "the pain of division." Marriage is not the occasion to flaunt variations of ecclesiology, since the connection between marriage and eucharist is intimate and personal, not automatic and routine.

Seventh, the lessons of the Christian East and the older west could help us to ritualize the reality felt by many couples who want to be married in church. The situation facing us today is, by any standards, a grave one, with a high divorce rate that will not diminish by well-intentioned male celibates preaching indissolubility. What we have inherited in marriage done instantly on Friday and Saturday evenings in short liturgical bursts, isolated from the Christian community, is comparable to what we have inherited in baptism at three o'clock on Sunday afternoons. The difference is that Vatican II agreed about the catechumenate; and even though it took a much greater (and deeper) interest in marriage through its conciliar documents, modern marriage liturgies fail to meet what pastoral jargon describes as "felt needs" by providing full rites which reflect what the liturgist would describe as marriage's "deep structures."

Past models do exist for rites of betrothal as well as ways of ritualizing liminality.[39] It is not here proposed that we should commit ourselves to yet one more example of western, legalistic rigorism. What we need is a richer liturgy that matches up to our renewed theology of marriage. Among the most captivating of all the liturgical symbolisms are the eastern crowning-rites, which speak of the presence of God on the couple; and the Coptic rite of anointing, which points to marriage as an extension of baptism, a true vocation in the Christian life. It strikes me as not without significance that in the "spiritual Gospel" (i.e., St. John), the Master performed his first "sign" at a wedding, in Cana of Galilee.

Notes

1. Arnold Van Gennep, *Les Rites de passage* (Paris: Librairie Critique, Emile Nourry, 1909) 14.

2. Ibid. 165-207.

3. Aidan Kavanagh, *The Shape of Baptism: The Rite of Christian Initiation* (New York: Pueblo Publishing Co., 1978) passim; see, e.g., 199ff., where Kavanagh discusses "liminality" of the catechumenate.

4. Kenneth W. Stevenson, *Nuptial Blessing: A Study of Christian Marriage Rites*, Alcuin Club Collections, vol. 64 (London: SPCK, 1982; New York: Oxford University Press, 1983).

5. See ibid. 155ff. on Methodist rites. Wesley's omission of the psalm follows the proposals of Lindsey, see G.J. Cuming, *A History of Anglican Liturgy* (London: Macmillan, 1982) 137, 139; see also Stevenson, *Nuptial Blessing*, (New York edition, 259, for list of *addenda/ corrigenda*).

6. *Ordo Celebrandi Matrimonium* (Vatican City: Typis Polyglottis, 1969); see also Stevenson, *Nuptial Blessing* 182-189.

7. *The Book of Common Prayer* (New York: Seabury, 1979) 422-432; for a discussion of its adaptation of the "Metz" order, see Stevenson, *Nuptial Blessing* 192ff.

8. Victor Turner, *The Ritual Process* (London: Routledge and Kegan Paul, 1969) 94-165.

9. For texts, see H. Denzinger, *Ritual Orientalium*, vol. 2 (Würzburg: Stahl, 1864) 451ff. (Armenian), 385ff. (Syrian Jacobite), 419ff. (East Syrian); see also French translation in A. Raes, *Le Mariage dans les églises d'orient* (Editions de Chevetogne, 1958) 69ff. (Armenian), 103ff. (Syrian Jacobite), 135ff. (Maronite), and 153ff. (East Syrian). See also Stevenson, *Nuptial Blessing* 113ff.

10. Gabriele Winkler, *Das Armenische Initiationsrituale: Entwicklungsgeschichte und liturgievergleichende Untersuchung der Quellen des 3. bis 10. Jahrhunderts*, Orientalia Christiana Analecta, vol. 217 (Rome: Pontificium Institutum Orientalium Studiorum, 1982).

11. F.C. Conybeare, *Rituale Armenorum* (Oxford: University Press, 1905) 109-114.

12. Jeanne-Ghislane Van Overstraeten, "Le rite de l'onction des époux dans la liturgie copte du mariage," *Parole d'Orient* 5 (1974) 83-84.

13. G.P. Badger, *The Nestorians and Their Rituals*, vol. 2 (London: Masters, 1852) 244-281, for English text of the whole rite; see ibid 137, note: "The original word is *hnana*, and is now applied to the clay or dust taken from the tombs of respected saints, to be used as a charm, or given as medicine to the sick. It is also mixed with the wine which is given to bridegrooms and brides when married."

14. Jeanne-Ghislane Van Overstraeten, "Les liturgies nuptiales des églises de langue syriaque et le mystère de l'église-épouse," *Parole d'Orient* 8 (1977/1978) 235-310.

15. For texts, see Denzinger, *Ritus Orientalium* 364ff., and Raes, *Le Mariage* 21ff. See also Stevenson, *Nuptial Blessing* 108ff.

16. Raes, *Le Mariage* 24.

17. See Robert F. Taft, "Praise in the Desert: The Coptic Monastic Office Yesterday and Today," *Worship* 56 (1982) 513-536; see also Taft, *The Liturgy of the Hours in the Christian East and West* (Collegeville: The Liturgical Press, 1986) 249ff.

18. See Van Overstraeten, "Le rite de l'onction" in note 12 above, full text of the article, pp. 49-93: if this analysis is correct, then my suggestion of a later date (*Nuptial Blessing* 111) is wrong.

19. For texts, see J. Goar, *Euchologium sive Rituale Graecorum* (Venice: Javarini, 1730) 310-326 (early texts), and Raes, *Le Mariage* 49ff. See also Stevenson, *Nuptial Blessing* 97-104.

20. Korbinian Ritzer, *Formen, Riten und religiöses Brauchtum der Eheschliessung in den christlichen Kirchen des ersten Jahrhunderts*, Liturgiewissenschaftliche Quellen und Forschungen, vol. 38 (Münster: Aschendorf, 1962) 133ff. (= Ritzer)

21. See chart showing the evolution of the Byzantine rite in Stevenson, *Nuptial Blessing* 251: the procession from the narthex takes place during the *psalm* (and *not* at the start of the betrothal rite, as indicated).

22. John 2:1-11 appears in the early Armenian marriage rite (see Conybeare, *Rituale Armenorum* 109), but later is part of the rite of blessing robes (Denzinger, *Ritus Orientalium* 456). The robe-blessing does dot appear in the Conybeare collection; it would seem that the Johannine lesson has a preliminary and domestic association in the Armenian tradition.

23. Gaetano Passarelli, "Stato della ricerca sul formulario dei riti matrimoniali," *Studi Bizantini et Neogreci* (Galatina: Congedo, 1983)

241-248; Passarelli, "La cerimonia dello Stefanoma (Incoronazione nei riti matrimoniali bizantini secondo il Codice Cryptense G.b. VII (X sec.)," *Ephemerides Liturgicae* 93 (1979) 381-391; see also the articles cited in Stevenson, *Nuptial Blessing* 228, note 1.

24. The crowns were originally left on the heads of the couple, and removed after the feast and consummation of the marriage, as in the other eastern rites.

25. Texts in M. Férotin, *Le Liber Ordinum en usage dans l'église wisig-othique et mozarabe d'Espagne du cinquième au onzième siècle*, Monumenta Ecclesiae Liturgica, vol. 5 (Paris: Firmin-Didot, 1904) 433-439 (MS B in main text, MS A in footnotes).

26. See Stevenson, *Nuptial Blessing* 48ff.

27. On this very western problem, see Stevenson, *Nuptial Blessing* 126 (Luther), 136 (Cranmer); the British Methodist rite (1975) follows this Visigothic rationale, and blesses not the ring, but the giving of it (see ibid 201).

28. See note 26 above.

29. See Kenneth W. Stevenson, "Benedictio Nuptialis: Reflections on the Blessing of Bride and Groom in Some Western Mediaeval Rites," *Ephemerides Liturgicae* 93 (1979) 462ff. and notes. Reprinted as Chapter 6 of this volume.

30. See John Brooks-Leonard, "Another Look at the Visigothic Marriage Rite," unpublished paper presented to graduate seminar, University of Notre Dame, Indiana, Spring Semester, 1983.

31. J.-B. Molin and P. Mutembe, *Le Rituel du mariage en France du XIè au XVIè siècle*, Théologie Historique, vol. 26 (Paris: Beauchesne, 1973) 289-291 (Ordo V). (= Molin-Mutembe)

32. See Ritzer, *Formen* 369f.

33. See Stevenson, *Nuptial Blessing* 51 (Visigothic "handing over"), 75 (later Norman "joining"), and 90 (German "confirming"); see also my "The Marriage Rites of Mediaeval Scandinavia: A Fresh Look," *Ephemerides Liturgicae* 97 (1983) 550-557, and Joanne Pierce, "A Note on the *Ego vos conjungo* in Medieval French Liturgy," paper presented to graduate seminar, University of Notre Dame, Indiana, Spring Semester, 1983, and published in *Ephemerides Liturgicae* 99 (1985) 290-299.

34. See Molin-Mutembe 306 (Ordo XV, Barbeau, 14th century), 311f. (Ordo XVII, Cambrai, 14th century), and 316 (Ordo XIX, Metz, 16th century). "Legitimizing" was known in France from the twelfth century (and in England); some French dioceses added a special prayer, from the seventeenth century; see ibid 232f.

35. John Brooks-Leonard, "Another Look at Neo-Gallican Reform: A Comparison of Marriage Rites in Coutances," *Ephemerides Liturgicae* 98 (1984) 458-485.

36. See the following chapter for discussion of this issue.

37. For the domestic rites, see Ritzer 353ff. and Molin-Mutembe 284ff. (texts of complete marriage rites). See also Stevenson, *Nuptial Blessing*, passim.

38. Salvador Aguilera, "Mexican American Nuptial Tradition," unpublished paper presented to graduate seminar, University of Notre Dame, Indiana, Spring Semester, 1983.

39. Betrothal could be incorporated into the eucharist or the liturgy of the hours; or else it could be celebrated at home. The rite itself could stress preparation for marriage, and the grace of God; there is no need for a stress on intentionality. The period of engagement could be ritualized in a similar way, with intercession for the couples preparing for marriage in the eucharist and other liturgies.

8

Marriage Liturgy: Lessons from History

MARRIAGE IS DEFINITELY "IN" AT THE MOMENT. MANY REASONS CAN be given, such as the crisis over divorce and family life in western society, the growth of human sciences and their application to social patterns, and, as far as liturgical studies are concerned, marriage is one of those areas where the relationship between official text and local application can be at its most tantalizing. Here is a case in point: compare the elaborate provisions for consent and vow in the Sarum Manual with the silence of some late medieval Scandinavian rites over the matter of consent, for of all the rites in the latter family that are available to us today, only the Norwegian Manual of the thirteenth century gives us anything approaching a truly vernacular tradition.[1]

As a result of writing a monograph on the liturgy of Christian marriage down the ages,[2] I want to address some issues which history raises and which are also raised by the contemporary situation. For the purposes of ease in handling the material, I will divide these issues into (1) "domestic" versus "ecclesial"; (2) the role of the priest versus the role of the partners; (3) the relationship with the eucharist and the place of the word; and (4) the "unity" of the rite.

"DOMESTIC" VERSUS "ECCLESIAL"

In surveying some of the early material, it is not clear in what context the liturgy was celebrated. Writers such as Clement of Alexandria and Tertullian do speak of betrothal and marriage as two separate stages, and there seems to be an increasing tendency as time goes on to refer to the marriage celebration in specifically liturgical terms, as witness a definition of marriage by Basil of Caesarea, where *eulogia* and *hagiazo* are juxtaposed in a manner that recalls the anaphora bearing his name.[3] Jewish roots are obvious, whether from the variegated corpus of the Old Testament traditions (the J and P narratives of Genesis), the domestic setting for the marriage in Tobit, or the equally domestic (but obviously "corporate") rites of the Talmud. When we find patristic homilies for baptism using marital imagery, they are, arguably, quoting some kind of liturgical procedure, but the starting point appears to be the "enlarged family" of the local Christian community.[4]

The charming feature of this domestic rite phenomenon is that it never really dies, at least until the western Reformation. Whether or not the domestic rite prayers contained in the ninth-century Pontifical of Egbert are supposed to be used in addition to a nuptial Mass in the church, or exclusively without it (and it does seem that both these options were actually employed), the relatively short series of marriage prayers for use at home and in the marriage-chamber persists throughout Western Europe in a manner that is, to us at least, remarkable.[5] Moreover, the domestic rite affects the "church" rite by the appearance of the blessing of the (non-eucharistic) common cup, and here comparative liturgy comes to our aid. The earliest Byzantine text, *Barberini 336*, contains a "Cana" prayer, which has been variously interpreted, usually as a eucharistic substitute, and yet the "Cana spirituality" that lies at the roots of the Byzantine rite seems to suggest a Jewish origin.[6] Further, although subsequent Byzantine texts clearly posit the whole rite in church and, one assumes, around the eucharist, there is nothing in the *Barberini 336* text to suggest that it must take place in church, which gives further plausibility to the argument that the background of this rite is domestic.[7]

On the other hand, when we encounter the common cup in

the west for the first time in the important twelfth-century Bury St. Edmunds rite,[8] the background seems less clear. Is it a eucharistic substitute? Is it Jewish? Is it "Cana-adapted"? The origin seems to be a desire to "domesticate" the public liturgy, which in the twelfth century shows signs of the church's taking over, for it is also in the Bury St. Edmunds order that we find for the first time a proper rite of consent before the Mass. Moreover, the subsequent development of prayers at the end of Mass, and their relation to prayers at home afterwards, shows that the domestic rite is having an indirect influence on the church rite.[9] In the east, the signs are slightly different, for the old Byzantine "Cana" cup is immediately absorbed into the developing "public" liturgy, to the extent that modern Byzantine commentators want to keep it if the rite is to be reformed and the eucharist reintroduced.[10]

Another example of the domestic rite's treatment in the eastern books is over what to do with the crowns. They are formally removed at the end of the marriage liturgy (having originally been allowed to remain on the couple's heads and *later* removed after an interval in earlier customs). But the East Syrian rite, which is the most complex of all, has no formula for removing them, and ends with the rite for making the bedchamber,[11] which suggests that they were removed at home.

The west, for a variety of possible reasons, opted out of domestic rites as ancillary to the "church" rite. None of the Reformers makes any provision for them, not even the most conservative, Thomas Cranmer.[12] One can surmise their motives. Having the minister at home might be taken to imply a sacramental understanding of marriage, or at any rate might suggest that what has gone on in the church is in some sense insufficient; and their knowledge of late medieval history perhaps encouraged them to discourage by such a lack of provision the undesirable "clandestine marriages" that were so much part and parcel of their social heritage. What perhaps clinches this last reason is that Roman Catholic rites after Trent similarly tend to opt out of the home rite, with the glorious exception of Neo-Gallican books,[13] which go their own way, building upon medieval foundations, and doing this in the face of the most austere marriage rite that history had ever produced, the "irreducible minimum" of the 1614 *Rituale Romanum*. The subsequent missionary efforts of European Catholic countries in Latin America and elsewhere show that this minimalism was combined with an acute suspicion of local pre-Christian customs, as witness the question about what to do with contemporary Hispanic "para-liturgies."[14]

So we come full circle today. Many North American churches have known domestic rites of marriage, which consist of the entire church-rite conducted "in some proper house," as the first American Episcopal Prayer Book puts it,[15] and the English continue to watch American television with some surprise when they see such exclusively domestic liturgies, even in the somewhat unsacralized contexts of soap-operas like *Dallas*. The domestic setting of many of these marriages may well be the reason for the Episcopal and Methodist Churches' enthusiasm at the end of the eighteenth century for abbreviating Cranmer's much fuller form.[16] But celebrating the whole liturgy in a domestic context, as the early Christians did, is a different exercise from celebrating the nuptial eucharist in church and continuing the celebration at home, at the feast, perhaps with the "Cana" cup and the blessing of the bed-chamber afterwards. Nonetheless, the Roman Catholic *Ordo Celebrandi Matrimonium* of 1969, so immeasurably richer and more pastoral than its predecessor of 1614, permits the entire celebration to take place outside the church,[17] which was no doubt a provision made with a view to countries and cultures where this is more appropriate.

So we have domestic origins in the patristic church, the lingering medieval domestic prayers, followed by an era of dissociation at the Reformation, culminating in (theoretical) flexibility today, which leaves us with a problem. Are the various modern rites, in their valiant efforts to restore a eucharistic context and a richer euchological tradition, running the risk of making the marriage liturgy so church-orientated that "domestic" prayer becomes nothing more than the grace, no doubt recited by the priest, at the marriage feast? There is much to be admired in such recent American rites as those of the United Methodist Church and the United Church of Christ,[18] with their solution to the problem of the pre-communion nuptial blessing by incorporating thanksgiving and supplication for the couple within the eucharistic prayer itself. But public liturgy has to carry far too much: unless it is built upon domestic prayer, with appropriate domestic rites, particularly at critical stages in our human development, then the public liturgy will not arise out of and lead back into a vibrant spirituality that is related to what that *rite de passage* actually is. I am not trying to suggest that we must all get marriage liturgies that involve the priest's coming home and blessing the couple in bed (perhaps together with that quaint warning to abstain for three nights, a custom some neo-Puritan era of the future might well welcome). By sealing the triumph of the "ecclesiastical" liturgy over the "domestic," we have solved some problems but exacerbated others, and we must await solutions.[19]

<h2 style="text-align:center">THE ROLE OF THE PRIEST
VERSUS
THE ROLE OF THE PARTNERS</h2>

It has been difficult for the Latin tradition to try to "un-live" its recent past, with the kind of minimalistic thinking which says that the couple "confect" the sacrament by their consent, especially as words like "confect" in the English-speaking world have overtones suggesting the mixing of a cocktail. Moreover, this tradition is all the more difficult to understand fully when one examines closely the 1614 *Rituale Romanum*[20] itself, for the "magic words" (if an Anglican may be allowed so to describe them) are quickly accompanied by the telling formula *ego vos in matrimonium conjungo*. Thus, whatever the canon lawyers may say,[21] the liturgy teaches something else—yes, the couple do make their consent, and this is central, but the priest is the person who actually "joins them together," before even the nuptial Mass has begun.

History has many surprises here. The early nuptial blessing, for all its exclusively bridal focus, at least implied that God joins the couple together, in the context of the eucharist, and the Gregorian and Gelasian sacramentary traditions[22] deliberately build up to the peace and the communion as the very first "acts" the couple perform as man and wife, in much the same way as Church of England priests have over the years told couples that the Psalm which links the first part of the rite

to the second includes a walk to the altar, "your first walk together as man and wife." Moreover, the later Middle Ages em-
brace so many different kinds of rites, all implying different
notions of what the priest is there to do, that we are left to
form the conclusion that different countries and cultures had
different understandings of this interrelation of couple and
priest, probably based on separate development and distinct
expectations. The Visigothic rites include a form of consent before the Mass, but the priest "hands the girl over" to the man
after the Mass, as the *paterfamilias* of the Christian family, a
role adopted in the North of France but placed instead immediately after the consent, and therefore before the Mass.[23] But
Rouen in the fourteenth or fifteenth century introduces what is
to be the rationale of the future—*ego vos conjungo*, "I join you
together"—and so the way is paved for Trent and after.[24]
Meanwhile German rites use *ego*-type formulas, but with different words, such as *solemnizo*. Only the British rites abstain
from any such language, finding the old Raguel prayer of Tobit
("May the God of Abraham . . . join you together") a sufficient
performative formula.

What lies behind these somewhat self-conscious priestly
formulas is an inner skepticism, it seems to me, as to what the
canon lawyers were saying. It reads to a twentieth-century
mind rather like the restrictive practices of a Trades Union:
"This is what you are here to do, and this is what I am here to
do, and it is all neatly expressed and defined in what we have
to say to each other." The compilers of the Rouen rite saw the
need to shift the role of the priest away from being a latter-day
paterfamilias so that he should stand there exercising a more
specifically sacramental role. However, across the English
Channel the priest has no performative formula, thus consti-
tuting, at least from a comparative view of liturgy, a stunning
silence, and a silence that is even more eloquent when we realize that the various eastern rites, notably the Byzantine, know
of no such priestly formulas, the Byzantine using the passive
voice ("The servant of God N. is *crowned* . . .") in a liturgical
convention that can be traced back to the Baptismal Homilies
of John Chrysostom.[25]

There do not seem to be "right" and "wrong" answers here,
though the twentieth century, in its general desire for a more

patristic ("presidential") role of the priest, will probably lean more in the direction of the Sarum Manual's view of the priest, a role Cranmer adapted in his own way. The liturgy is a public celebration, during which the spotlight falls on the couple, with the priest there as president of the assembly, leading them in prayer, sacred reading, homily, and eucharistic celebration. From a comparative point of view, what the priest "does" in the 1969 *Ordo* differs very little from the 1549 Prayer Book.[26] But it seems to me that the reason why the late medieval Northern French rites (followed by Trent) fastened onto this notion was that they wished to offset the exclusive emphasis on the couple with a formula that would, in a specific sense, represent the rest of the church.

But there is another side to the story, too, which may explain why the eastern rites (other than those churches in communion with Rome affected by the requirements of Trent) know of no confusion about roles. In the medieval west there was no specifically Christian rite of betrothal, at least not until just before the betrothal rite became the pre-Mass rite of consent. This means that when the pre-Mass consent forms were evolving, they could only be "directed" in the rubrics, and thereafter develop willy-nilly according to the availability of good vernacular traditions, in which contest the Sarum Manual probably wins the prize.[27] The eastern rites, however, at some early stage, *did* develop full rites of betrothal, which means that they required no self-conscious "christianization," since the prayer forms were there already. A good example of this is in the opening prayer of the Coptic rite, which lucidly and symbolically expresses the mind of the couple and the assembly in offering a resolve to rely upon the blessing and strength of God.[28] And the conservatism of the eastern rites in maintaining, at least in theory, a separate rite of betrothal in the context of a liturgy that was developing organically resulted in no need to "insert" role-defining formulas.

The role of the priest, therefore, is seen more theologically in patristic terms, according to twentieth-century views of ordained ministry, where priestly ministry arises out of the community, rather than is imposed upon it. Nevertheless, the need for performative language still lingers, and there are test cases for this in the study of English Free Church rites over how the

Matthean pronouncement ("those whom God has joined together . . ." Mt 19:6) is actually employed. Cranmer used this
formula as a comment on consent already having taken
place.[29] But it is clear that subsequent generations interpreted
it in a more priestly manner.[30]

So we encounter nineteenth-century Methodist rites that declare the couple married after their consent, and follow this
declaration with the pronouncement, a solution to the debate
on roles that first appears in the rite drawn up in England by
Richard Baxter at the Savoy Conference in 1661,[31] one of which
is also (paradoxically) enshrined in the corresponding part of
the 1969 Roman *Ordo*. Pastors will be familiar with the question, "When will we actually be married?" To which few will
have the courage to respond with a long and complex tutorial
along patristic (theological) and holistic (psychological) lines.
The debate about roles and "magic moments" reaches its climax when one watches a domestic wedding in a movie, where
the pastor, in black suit, recites the Matthean pronouncement
over the couple, with his right hand raised in priestly blessing.

Thus it seems that we can be as self-conscious about roles
these days as we are about the interpretation of symbolism.
One answer to the issue is that the consent and declaration
that the couple are married, which most modern rites do now
contain, should follow the ministry of the word (unlike the
Cranmerian shape, whether in its full or its reduced form),
and that this should lead into solemn prayer for the couple.[32] I
have suggested elsewhere[33] that the nuptial blessing really belongs in the intercession, and not before communion, partly
because it interrupts the flow of the eucharist in that position,
and also because by coming sooner in the service, the two basic "movements" of Christian marriage are at last united, offering to God a commitment in order to ask for blessing and
strength. (Here the American Episcopal Prayer Book points to
a clearer "shape" of the marriage liturgy.) Moreover, the nuptial blessing should refer to *both* partners throughout.[34]

We have by now long since gotten over the feminist debate
about whether or not "she" is to obey "him." Ironically, part of
the trouble was caused in the Cranmer-based rites by the sixteenth-century welcoming the full forms of vow in Sarum, for
all the fifteenth-century British Manuals included the promise

to obey. Luther did not, partly because the rite he inherited was a brief one.[35] The lesson of history is that, once you refer to one of the partners, whether in vow or prayer,[36] you start defining roles closely, and these may in a subsequent generation become quite outmoded. Medieval and post-Reformation chauvinism is not the same as the kind of obedience of which the Bible speaks, and those who have championed women's equal rights have some history to lean on; there are many medieval forms of consent (including the very first, directed in the rubrics) that imply no subservience. Again the American Episcopalians have led the way, in directing that the consent be asked first of the woman before the man, thus inverting the traditional order.[37]

RELATIONSHIP WITH THE EUCHARIST
AND THE PLACE OF THE "WORD"

One of the features of nearly all the new western rites is that there is now provision for the marriage rite to follow the ministry of the word, and for the eucharist to be celebrated afterwards, as an essential part of the whole service, and not "tagged on" at the end. Historically, the situation has been much more fluid, and the story is one where the ambivalence between the close-knit Christian family and the *rite de passage* of the nominally attached each fights for recognition. For example, the Byzantine rite shows signs of eucharistic context, and all the eastern rites are structured round a synaxis, with common liturgical units of introduction, lessons, crown-blessing, and crowning, surrounded by various kinds of intercessory and hymnic material.[38] The Byzantine rite alone shifts the readings until after the crowning, perhaps in order to view the readings as illuminating what has "happened," in a manner comparable to Cranmer's biblical catechesis after the marriage rite, which was originally intended as a homily at the eucharist.[39] In this respect, the various eastern rites show further signs of antiquity.[40]

When one compares the Tridentine rite with the 1969 *Ordo*, however, the structure is quite different. The Missal of 1570 and the Ritual of 1614 together provide a simplified version of what was going on at the end of the Middle Ages in the west, namely, a pre-Mass rite of consent, followed by a nuptial Mass, with the nuptial blessing now just before the *libera nos*, instead of between the Canon and the Lord's Prayer. The structure of consent and nuptial Mass developed with a certain unease: in the Evesham book (ca. 1300), the old Gregorian Sacramentary "secret," which speaks of marriage in legal terms and refers implicitly to the nuptial blessing to follow, is replaced by a version of the corresponding prayer in the Gelasian Sacramentaries (but reworked by Fulda in order to refer to both bride and groom throughout), which prays in general terms for the marriage couple. This substitution was followed in the British Manual traditions and also in parts of Scandinavia.[41]

My own theory for this development is theological. The old Gregorian "secret" prayer could be interpreted as downgrading the pre-Mass rite of consent, because it is part of a much earlier separate liturgical unit, namely a Mass-set that includes the nuptial blessing, all of which *antedates* the rite of consent by a few hundred years. It therefore had to give way to another prayer which was less specific in its ideas. Here we have medieval accumulation at its most profuse. But when the new Roman rite was put together after the Second Vatican Council, the edifice could be rebuilt,[42] taking materials from the old structure, but more critically, with an eye on our better knowledge of liturgical history. A synaxis proved the best and most flexible structure, even when the eucharist was not to be celebrated. This pattern finds itself repeated in various modern Anglican books, though the Church of England, carrying flexibility a little further in matters of liturgical structure than other branches of world-wide Anglicanism, allows for the "word" to follow the marriage, thus keeping Cranmer's scheme in its post-medieval entirety.[43]

Nuptial eucharists are much more common among the liturgical traditions of western Protestantism than they were, and the provision to allow the Lord's Supper made in the 1936 British Methodist *Book of Offices*[44] was a bold one, considering that this book sought to bring together various Methodist traditions that had splintered from each other during the great period of growth in the nineteenth century.

But where should the "word" be placed? There seems to be a trend towards the synaxis, but the Byzantine rite, together with Luther, Cranmer, and some of their modern derivatives, do place the "word" at the end. I wonder if the reason for this persistence, at least among some Lutherans and Anglicans, is a psychological one, to cater for an anxiety on the part of the couple to "get their bit over as soon as possible." Post-feudal England still produces hordes of couples who have only a marginal membership in the church (Gregory Dix's "amorphous mass of Pelagian good-will"),[45] and whose basic attitude is reflected in such a desire. One even hears of couples who want a nuptial eucharist, but who ask for the lessons and homily to follow the rite of consent. This is folk religion, and (as we all know), there are different attitudes as to how to deal with it. Perhaps Luther's rationale of "sacred reading" is what lies behind the gospel lesson at the altar at the end of his *Traubüchlein*.[46] What is interesting is that early Danish Lutheranism, because it inherited from the late medieval Catholic books a full nuptial Mass and Luther did not, immediately added a collect and readings, to follow a slightly expanded and euchologically richer version of Luther's bald marriage rite.[47]

But the relationship between word and eucharist and the form the prayers should take, regardless of whether a eucharist is in fact celebrated, is more subtle still. Reginald Fuller has commented on the lessons for use at marriages.[48] On the whole, they fall into two categories: biblical *stories* (whether the J or P creation narratives, Tobit, or Jesus at Cana) and biblical *reflections* (whether the virtuous woman of Proverbs 31, or the famous analogy in Ephesians 5). Some of them are easier to handle in the liturgy than others, and the tale of Cranmer's rite from 1549 down to the proposed revision of the English book in 1928 is one of the gradual elimination of biblical characters in the prayers he wrote from the Latin of the originals.[49] Many of us know today the problems of *alluding* to difficult ideas, and usually the first two on the list are Jesus at Cana and the Ephesians analogy. History has intermittently latched onto one or the other of these ideas in prayer-writing. For instance, the Byzantine rite is built upon a Cana spirituality, whereas the old Gregorian nuptial blessing includes the Ephesians analogy, an idea that subsequent medieval prayer-writing (a rich exercise by any standards)[50] studiously avoids;

but Cana comes back into popularity with some of the Reformers precisely because it is biblical.

The use of the Bible as a quarry for prayer-composition as well as a source for varied lessons at the marriage liturgy is a fascinating business. Today most rites tend to provide a wide range of options in the readings but less choice of biblical imagery in the prayers themselves, possibly in the hope that the twentieth century will in time produce its own kind of marriage prayers.[51] But even allowing for such flexibility in principle, I would argue for great care in the selection of appropriate lessons, and for prayers themselves being selected or written because they use imagery from those readings. Modern rites have difficulty in handling the biblical tradition in their opening exhortations, yet provide a rich catalogue of possible lessons from Scripture; the new Canadian Anglican book is a case in point.[52] Furthermore, when it comes to writing prayers, the strength of many of the biblical images is that they set the marriage within the wider context of creation and redemption (that particularly Christian insight), and thus act as a preventive to the somewhat pietistic and introverted aspirations of many prayers of a more "experiential" kind.

Kathleen Hughes' study of the Easter-cycle collects in the new Roman Mass amounts to a stimulating and original doctoral thesis,[53] in which the disciplines of linguistic structural analysis provide a useful critique of the images used in these prayers. A similar job needs to be done with marriage prayers, which may suggest that the *story* told or alluded to in the first part of the prayer should refer (directly or indirectly) to the petitions sought in the second part of the prayer. On this score, a prayer using the Ephesians analogy at the beginning should have something to say towards the end about the marriage of man and woman as a reflection of Jesus' love for redeemed humanity.

THE "UNITY" OF THE RITE

A common criticism of modern liturgies, especially for large occasions, is that they try to "say" too much. I have attended eucharistic celebrations in which children were baptized, special ministers of the sacrament given their "papers," as well as

other special features, and all within a liturgy peppered with
"introductory" formulas, explaining what we are about to do,
as if the congregation were illiterate. With the kind of flexibility now built into so many of the western liturgies, it is indeed
possible to overlay the menu, so that the congregation at the
end feels at saturation point. When I was a university chaplain, it was my salutary experience to sit in the pew rather
more frequently than I do as a parish priest. I have found that
I am critical about different things in the two circumstances. I
am constantly reminded of the motto used by Mervyn Stock-
wood when he was bishop of Southwark: "I don't care whether you are High Church or Low Church, as long as you are
Short Church."

Marriage liturgies are sometimes concocted with a similar
eye on packing so much into the allotted time that it all becomes much more hard work than it should be. There are a
number of ways of doing this. Music can take over, and it is a
good and joyful thing that we are employing well-trained local talent. Or the people taking part can involve, as we'd say
in England, "Uncle Tom Cobley and all." It may be genuine
"fun" on the occasion, but I really wonder if both this tendency and the general expectation of big public liturgies to "carry" too much do not implicitly ask rather more basic questions. Let me explain. Van Gennep's work on *rites de passage*[54]
is still far too neglected by liturgists, and those of our trade
who try to work out its basic insights in our teaching are, I
fear, a minority. In marriage, as a developing relationship
within a community, the three stages he describes are discernible: separation, liminality, and incorporation. It seems to me
that most modern western liturgies of marriage provide material for celebration simply and solely for the last of these three,
where the couple are "incorporated" into the community as a
married pair. And the weakness is that we have no means of
"ritualizing" these two other stages, which the vast majority of
couples really feel, but in the somewhat decayed and misera-
ble manner of privatized western society. The "separation" is
the private engagement in which the couple get accustomed to
each other, and then along comes the marriage liturgy. The
current practice of couples living together in a "trial marriage"
is another issue, but it is a phenomenon which probably lies

behind many of the medieval western rites which provide for
betrothal before marriage.

My work with the eastern and neo-Gallican rites convinced
me that here, at least, were attempts to ritualize these phases
in various ways. The Syriac rites (Syrian, Jacobite, Maronite)
involve more than just betrothal.[55] Some of the eastern rites,
too, sacralize the bed-chamber, and our current preoccupation with sex demonstrates, it seems to me, our inability as
Christians to cope with sexuality in liturgy. Most Christian
couples have some sort of "public" recognition of their engagement, which, after all, was what betrothal originally was,
and their "liminal" stage will consist of pre-marriage classes
of one sort or another, but neither of these phases is built into
the liturgy, with the result that neither will be ritualized, a
situation even more harmful when the engagement is broken
because things do not work out. I would like to see betrothal
and the stage of engagement in some way given liturgical expression. The former could take place after a synaxis, with a
prayer and blessing, and the latter could be similarly "prayed
through" in a series of word services, or even at the liturgy of
the hours, following the pattern that the *Liber Ordinum* provides,[56] but in a way appropriate to our culture. That quaint
English practice of calling the "Banns of Marriage" in church
may have its drawbacks, but it is, in its own way, a kind of
half-rite of engagement.

Moreover, a new symbolism could be introduced into our
liturgies. I remember giving a lecture on the three Syriac marriage rites and provoking a lengthy discussion on the East Syrian *henana*[57] (ash, placed in water, and drunk with wine). What
did it mean? Everyone came forward with an answer, until a
seminarian from Texas who is of Mexican origin offered the explanation that ash is still used among Hispanics at stages of
transition, expressing penitence and expectation, and was this
not a useful parallel? A priest from Sierra Leone gave this theory his wholehearted support. Now, I doubt if white Americans
(to say nothing of the tight-lipped English) would take kindly
to consuming ash at betrothal, but we would do well to have
appropriate means of ritualizing these important stages in our
lives. Our renewed understanding of baptism as the culmination of the catechumenate and leading into mystagogy should

help us here, and I rejoice at the increasing provision for celebrating anniversaries of marriage (as in the old sacramentaries) thereby "extending" the sacrament into a series of real life experiences, thus moving us away from viewing marriage in arid legalistic terms as something that "goes chink" in heaven.

So let me conclude on a symbolic note. It appears that, so far from reaching a destination, we have in fact arrived at another point of departure. We need to become less self-conscious about symbols in liturgy, and intellectualize less about them. Then we may be able to relate to them better and more effectively, so that we may come to *enjoy* the liturgy more. Marriage in Christian history has so much to offer us. Byzantine crowns and Coptic anointing[58] and Armenian crosses form as great an element in the whole picture as medieval western consent and signing those Reformation registers. For marriage is not just a matter of coupling partners publicly. It is a sacrament which is eucharistic and baptismal, redemptive and eschatological.

Notes

1. See Kenneth Stevenson, "The Marriage Rites of Mediaeval Scandinavia: A Fresh Look," *Ephemerides Liturgicae* 77 (1983) 550-557.

2. Kenneth Stevenson, *Nuptial Blessing: A Study of Christian Marriage Rites*, Alcuin Club Collections, vol. 64 (London: SPCK, 1982; New York: Oxford University Press, 1983).

3. See ibid 13-32; the reference in Basil is Canon 27 to Amphilochius of Iconium, *Ep. ad Amphilochium* 188, *eulogia gar hagiasmou metadôsis estô*("for by the blessing is there an imparting of consecration"). The words *eulogô* and *hagiazô* are juxtaposed in the early Coptic version of the Anaphora of Basil at the institution narrative (*eulogêsas. hagiasas*: see J. Doresse and E. Lanne, *Un Témoin archaïque de la liturgie copte de S. Basile*, Bibliothèque du Muséon, vol. 47 (Louvain: Publications Universitaires/Institut Orientaliste, 1960) 16f., and the same doublet occurs in the later Byzantine version at the epiclesis (see F.E. Brightman, *Liturgies Eastern and Western* [Oxford: Clarendon, 1896] 329).

4. For example, Cyril of Jerusalem, *Cat.* 17.

5. See W. Greenwell, *The Pontifical of Egbert*, Publications of the Surtees Society, vol. 27 (1853) 125f., 132. This rite is discussed in K.

Ritzer, *Formen, Riten und religiöses Brauchtum der Eheschliessung in den christlichen Kirchen des ersten Jahrtausends*, Liturgiewissenchaftliche Quellen und Forschungen, vol. 38 (Münster: Aschendorff, 1962) 209, 240 (= Ritzer); see Stevenson, *Nuptial Blessing* 63f. For domestic rite prayers, see the collection assembled in J.-B. Molin and P. Mutembe, *Le Rituel du mariage en France du XIIè au XVIè siècle* (Paris: Beauchesne, 1974) 325-327. (= Molin-Mutembe)

6. See G. Baldanza, "Il rito de matrimonio nel'Euchologio Barberini 336," *Ephemerides Liturgicae* 93 (1979) 316-351, for a discussion of this rite; see the treatment of the Greek Fathers in Stevenson, *Nuptial Blessing* 21-25.

7. Stevenson, *Nuptial Blessing* 97-104.

8. Text reproduced in Molin-Mutembe, Ordo V, pp. 289-291. I am inclined toward the view that it is a Christianized survival of a domestic rite, modeled on the marriage feast; the Bury prayer refers directly to the marriage at Cana (ibid. 325).

9. See note 5 above.

10. See J. Meyendorff, *Christian Marriage: An Orthodox Perspective* (Crestwood, NY: St. Vladimir's Seminary Press, 1975) 47f. But Meyendorff still regards the Cana-cup as a eucharistic substitute.

11. See charts in A. Raes, *Introductio in Liturgiam Orientalem* (Rome: Pontificium Institutum Studiorum Orientalium, 1946) 156-160.

12. On Cranmer and his use of sources from the Sarum (and the other Manuals), see Stevenson, *Nuptial Blessing* 134-140, and App. 2a, p. 250; see also F.E. Brightman, *The English Rite* (London: Rivingtons, 1915) 2:800-817.

13. See Molin-Mutembe. A detailed study of Neo-Gallican marriage rites has yet to be made; see Stevenson, *Nuptial Blessing* 173-175.

14. See Stevenson, *Nuptial Blessing* 176-178; see also R. Ramirez, "Reflections on the Hispanicization of the Liturgy," *Worship* 57 (1983) 26-34. I am indebted to Sal Aguilera, student at the University of Notre Dame, 1983, for discussions on this issue.

15. See W. McGarvey, *Liturgiae Americanae* (Philadelphia: Church Publishing Co., 1897) 312, together with comparable table of the early American Episcopal rite and its (draft) 1786 and later 1892 forms.

16. See Stevenson, *Nuptial Blessing* 147, 157ff.; see also the Oxford edition's appendix of addenda/corrigenda, p. 259. Robert Sanderson, who was deposed from his professorship at Oxford during the Commonwealth (and who became bishop of Lincoln at the Restoration in 1660), had an abbreviated marriage rite for "underground Anglicans" omitting the second part of Cranmer's service (*inter alia*)

in his *Liturgy in the Times of Rebellion and Usurpation*, which is in W. Jacobson, ed., *Fragmentary Illustrations of the History of the Book of Common Prayer* (London: Murray, 1874) 38-40. But Sanderson lost his enthusiasm for shortening marriage after 1660, because the Prayer Book became once again the established norm throughout the realm.

17. *Ordo Celebrandi Matrimonium* (Vatican: Typis Polyglottis, 1969) p. 10, n. 18. On the Roman Catholic rite, see G.S. Sloyan, "The New Rite for Celebrating Marriage," *Worship* 44 (1970) 258-267. In preparing my book I was allowed to use the files of Père P.-M. Gy, O.P., who was chairman of the Study Group that drew up the new rite; see Stevenson, *Nuptial Blessing* 181-189.

18. See *A Service of Christian Marriage*, Supplemental Worship Resources, vol. 5 (Nashville: United Methodist Publishing House, 1979) x-xii (compare with the "dry" eucharistic prayer, pp. viii-ix); and *Proposed Services of Marriage to be Included in a Book of Worship* (Office of Church Life and Leadership, United Church of Christ, 1982) 13-15 (compare "prayer of intercession and thanksgiving" where there is no eucharist, pp. 10f.). I am indebted to Professor James White for drawing my attention to these important new rites.

19. See below on the "unity" of the rite.

20. *Rituale Romanum* (Antwerp, 1824) 222-235.

21. See Molin-Mutembe 32-47.

22. See Kenneth Stevenson, "'Benedictio Nuptialis': Reflections on the Blessing of Bride and Groom in Some Western Mediaeval Rites," *Ephemerides Liturgicae* 93 (1979) 464ff. (reprinted as Chapter 6 in this volume). There are problems over the Leonine Sacramentary (see *Nuptial Blessing* 35-37) because the nuptial blessing comes last of six prayers, in which the initial sequence (collect, secret, *hanc igitur*) is clear; the fourth prayer reads *connectes* (future tense: "you will bring together," which is made into *connectis* in subsequent use by the Gregorian and Gelasian books); the fifth prayer repeats the themes of the occasion; the sixth prayer is the long nuptial blessing itself. (Ritzer wrongly reads *connectis* in his Leonine text, 346). I am inclined to the view that prayer 4 is for use after communion, as is 5, and that 6 may therefore be in the genre of *oratio super populum*, even though it is the nuptial blessing, but I am aware of the slippery nature of parts of this sacramentary.

23. See Stevenson, *Nuptial Blessing* 821ff., 93f.; see also Stevenson, "Marriage Rites of Mediaeval Scandinavia," where the dual influences of England and northern France on Scandinavia are to be seen.

24. See Stevenson, *Nuptial Blessing* 79. *Ego vos conjungo* appears in the late fifteenth-century Norman rites; see A. Duval, "La formule 'ego vos in matrimonium conjungo . . .' au concile de Trente," *La Mai-*

son-Dieu 99 (1969) 144-153; for text, see Molin-Mutembe 304. The verb "join" seems to be inspired by the "Raguel" prayer from Tobit; ibid. 323. Molin and Mutembe regard the "joining" formula as "absolument equivalente" to the earlier *ego trado eam tibi* ("I hand her over to you"), and Gy does not think that *ego vos conjungo* indicates a priestly sacramental role (ibid. 124, and Gy's preface, p. 6). I have reservations about both these interpretations; see *Nuptial Blessing* 225, n. 40. There are problems over the dating of the Roman *Ordo* reproduced by Molin and Mutembe. Molin follow Martène's date (fourteenth century), but the manuscript has been lost. I have followed Martimort's dating (1455); see *Nuptial Blessing* 75. Molin also reads *conjugo* instead of *conjungo*, which is the reading in Martène's text.

25. See Stevenson, *Nuptial Blessing* 101 and App. 2b (p. 251). There are two errors on this page: the procession into church does not take place until the Psalm, and what I have described as the "First marriage prayer" in fact comes immediately before the crowning, and after the two later marriage prayers. For the baptismal formula, see E.C. Whitaker, *Documents of the Baptismal Liturgy*, 2d edition (London: SPCK, 1970) 36, 40f.

26. The study-group was obviously concerned to clarify roles, and the fact that *ego vos conjungo* (or its cognates) does not appear is significant. On the whole question see Stevenson, *Nuptial Blessing*, passim.

27. See Molin-Mutembe 283-318, for a collection of texts. I have traced the British and Scandinavian development in *Nuptial Blessing* 68ff. The absence of any directions for the form of consent in some late medieval texts is tantalizing (see Stevenson, "The Marriage Rites of Mediaeval Scandinavia"); the fourteenth-century Hungarian *Missale Notatum Strigoniense ante 1341 in Posonio*, eds., Janka Szendrei and Richard Rybarie, Musicalia Danubiana, vol. 1 (Budapest: Magyar Tudományos Akadémia, Zenetudományi Intézet, 1982), lacks any form for or even reference to consent (f. 310 r), and yet has some interesting peculiarities, e.g., the absence of the "Raguel" prayer in the pre-Mass rite, but the inclusion of an adapted form of this prayer as the Introit to the nuptial Mass (f. 311 r), following the Roman pontifical tradition (and the eleventh-century Sacramentary of Vich). I hope to publish at some future date a study of the Hungarian rites.

28. The prayer "Deus, qui formasti . . ."; text in H. Denzinger, *Ritus Orientalium* (Würzburg: Stahel, 1864) 2:367.

29. See Ulrich Leupold, ed., *Luther's Works*, vol. 53, *Liturgy and Hymns* (Philadelphia: Fortress, 1965) 113. For Cranmer, see Stevenson, *Nuptial Blessing* 137. The use of Mt 19:6 was already in the Lyon 1498 rite, as well as in Hermann von Wied's Cologne rite. It also occurs (and to be said no less than *three* consecutive times, to the ap-

parent amusement of the editor) in a Premonstratensian rite in a mid-fifteenth-century *Breviarium* from the island of Csút (Bibl. Univ. Budapesti c.1.67), cited from P. Radó, *Libri Liturgici Manuscripti Bibliothecarum et Limitropharum Regionum* (Budapest: Akadémia Kiadó, 1973) 339.

30. See my discussion of nineteenth-century British Free Church rites in *Nuptial Blessing* 158ff., esp. p. 159 (1860 Primitive Methodist rite, which omits it, and they were hardly a body to be critical of Scripture), p. 161 (1903 Bible Christian rite, where it appears, but prefixed by "The Lord has said"), and p. 238, n. 30 (Unitarian sensitivity on the matter).

31. See *Ordo Celebrandi Matrimonium* 13 (no. 26); although it could be argued that this item is a prayer, it lacks an "Amen" and seems more like the "declaration" Baxter proposed at the Savoy Conference in 1661, quoted in my *Nuptial Blessing* 156. I once had occasion to show the 1969 *Ordo* formula to Père I.-H. Dalmais at a meeting of the Societas Liturgica in Paris; he glanced at the book and grinned mischievously, "Oh! mais c'est une épiclèse, n'est-ce-pas?"

32. The British Methodist and the American Episcopal rites pioneered this structure, in parallel with the Roman Catholics. The American Episcopalians went further and adapted (consciously?) the old Metz tradition, by dividing consent and vow by the liturgy of the word; see my *Nuptial Blessing* 192ff.; the Metz 1543 rite is produced in full as *Ordo XIX* in Molin-Mutembe 317f. This structure had been considered by some of the Roman Catholic and Church of England revisers, but was rejected however; the New Zealand Anglican rite follows U.S.A.

33. This is discussed in my article in *Assembly* 9:4 (April 1983), and also in my book *To Join Together: The Rite of Christian Marriage*, Studies in the Reformed Rites of the Catholic Church, vol. 5 (New York: Pueblo Publishing Co., 1987), chapter 7. The German Roman Catholics similarly position the nuptial blessing after the consent. See *Die Feier der Trauung* (Einsiedeln and Cologne: Benziger, 1975) 28ff.

34. See Stevenson, "'Benedictio Nuptialis'" and *Nuptial Blessing* 187-189. The study-group was under pressure to preserve the bridal blessing (from some scholars) as well as to make the new blessing refer to both partners (from other scholars). In the end, three blessings were written, but only a compromise was reached on the rationale of the prayer.

35. See note 12 above.

36. This can be seen in the Gregorian Sacramentary's nuptial blessing (even when its ending is pluralized in order to refer to both bride and groom). It is also demonstrable in the handling of the

promise to obey from the Sarum Manual of the late Middle Ages, through Cranmer, down to the nineteenth-century British and American Methodist rites, when the word "obey" is dropped. The 1969 Roman Catholic *Ordo* permits the crowning of the bride only (*Matrimonium* 9, n. 15).

37. *The Book of Common Prayer* (New York: Seabury, 1979) 424; see Stevenson, *Nuptial Blessing* 192-194, which refers only to the consent (and not the vow) and first appears in 1928 (and not the recent revisions), so that my statement on p. 194 is inaccurate.

38. See note 11 above. See Robert Taft, "The Structural Analysis of Liturgical Units: An Essay in Methodology," *Worship* 52 (1978) 314-328 (reprinted in Robert Taft, *Beyond East and West: Problems in Liturgical Understanding* [Washington, D.C.: The Pastoral Press, 1984] 151-164]. See also Stevenson, *To Join Together* 56ff.

39. See note 12 above.

40. The Armenian rites shows features which are Byzantine, Syrian, and indigenous. (1) Euchologically, the parallels are much stronger with the Byzantine rite, as witness the *Barberini 336* prayer and the corresponding prayer from Conybeare's ninth-century text (see Stevenson, *Nuptial Blessing* 246, n. 3, for the Byzantine prayer, and F.C. Conybeare, *Rituale Armenorum* [Oxford: Clarendon, 1905] 109f.); moreover, in the marriage prayers in both rites, a pattern is discernible that juxtaposes one prayer based on the J creation narrative with another based on the P narrative (see Meyendorff, *Christian Marriage* 134-137; Conybeare, *Rituale Armenorum* 109-111). In the Byzantine case, we know that the J prayer is earlier than the P; moreover, both the P prayers begin with the pseudo-Jewish "Blessed are . . ." (2) The Armenians use Jn 2:1-11 at the marriage rite (as Byzantine) in the early texts, but it has been absorbed into the betrothal rite by the time of the more recent texts, leaving Mt 19:1-9 as the marriage-reading, which is a similar pericope to that contained in the three Syriac rites (Jacobite, Maronite, East Syrian). (3) But the Armenian rite also knows Syrian features, e.g., the use of the cross and the blessing of the robes.

41. See Stevenson, "Marriage Rites of Mediaeval Scandinavia." This prayer appears as an alternative collect in the 1969 *Ordo* (p. 31, n. 109); see P.-M. Gy, "Le nouveau rituel romain du mariage," *La Maison-Dieu* 99 (1969) 130, n. 106, for a list of sources. It is significant that the prayer is a collect (and not a *super oblata*, as of old), for the rite of consent in the new Roman *Ordo* takes place after the gospel and homily, and no longer before the Mass begins. The Gelasian-Fulda prayer in this new position "looks forward" to the entire celebration.

42. See note 26 above.

43. *Alternative Service Book 1980* 287-300.

44. *Book of Offices* (London: Methodist Publishing House, 1936) 86. Another bold step is that this rite begins with a prayer for the couple, thus at long last putting right an essential weakness in Cranmer's service, where there is no actual prayer until after the vows and ring-giving.

45. Gregory Dix, *The Theology of Confirmation in Relation to Baptism* (London; Dacre, 1946) 34.

46. See Leupold, ed., *Luther* 114f. For a discussion of Luther's rite, see also Bryan Spinks, "Luther's Other Major Liturgical Reforms: 3. The Traubüchlein," *Liturgical Review* 10 (1980) 33-38, but Spinks does not make the suggestion about linking "sacred reading" from the altar "over" the couple with the ensuing blessing-prayer, during which the pastor is to stretch his hands (again) "over" them.

47. See Stevenson, *Nuptial Blessing* 128f. and 259 in the Oxford edition. See also Martin Schwarz Lausten and Inger Bom, eds., *En Handbog for Sognepraester 1535, En Gudelig Formaning for Enfoldige Sognepraester 1530*, Skrifter fra Reformationstiden, vol. 1 (Copenhagen: Gads Forlag, 1970) 22-25, and nn. on p. 43.

48. Fuller, "Lectionary for Weddings," *Worship* 55 (1981) 244-259.

49. See texts from the period 1549-1662 in Brightman; see also Stevenson, *Nuptial Blessing* 149-152.

50. See Stevenson, "'Benedictio Nuptialis'"; the Syrian euchological and hymnic tradition, on the other hand, elaborates on the theme of the "spouse-Christ," for which see J.-Gh. van Overstraeten, "Les liturgies nuptiales des églises de langue syriaque et le mystère de l'église-épouse," *Parole de l'Orient* 8 (1977-1978) 235-310.

51. For freedom to write prayers, see *Alternative Service Book* 287, n. 7; see also the American Episcopal "Rite 3" in *The Book of Common Prayer* 435 (discussed in my *Nuptial Blessing* 194).

52. *The Celebration and Blessing of a Marriage* (Toronto: Anglican Book Centre, 1982) 5f. (introduction), 28-31 (readings). The draft Canadian rite is now superseded by *The Book of Alternative Services of the Anglican Church of Canada* (Toronto: Anglican Book Centre, 1985) 528ff.

53. Helen Kathleen Hughes, *The Opening Prayers of the Sacramentary: A Structural Study of the Prayers of the Easter Cycle*, Ph.D. Dissertation, University of Notre Dame, 1980).

54. A. Van Gennep, *The Rites of Passage* (Chicago: University of Chicago Press, 1960) esp. 116-145. See also my article, "Van Gennep and Marriage—Strange Bedfellows? A Fresh Look at the Rites of Marriage," *Ephemerides Liturgicae* 100 (1986) 138-151 (reprinted as Chapter 7 of this volume).

55. See note 11 above. See also my *Nuptial Blessing* 97-121 (chapter on the eastern rites).

56. M. Férotin, *Le Liber Ordinum en usage dans l'église wisigothique et mozarabe d'Espagne du cinquième au onzième siècle*, Monumenta Ecclesiae Liturgica, vol. 5 (Paris: Firmin-Didot, 1904) 434-441. There are a number of very archaic features in these rites; see my *Nuptial Blessing* 48-53. I am indebted to John Brooks-Leonard at the University of Notre Dame for a number of useful suggestions on the background of the *Liber Ordinum*.

57. See Ritzer 153; see also G.P. Badger, *The Nestorians and Their Rituals* (London: Masters, 1852) 2:253 (see 137n); see also the discussion in my *Nuptial Blessing* 117-119.

58. See the important study by J.-Gh. van Overstraeten, "Le rite de l'onction des époux dans la liturgie copte du mariage," *Parole de l'Orient* 5 (1974) 49-93.

ASHES AND LIGHT

9

Origins and Development
of Ash Wednesday

"DOUBLE EDGE" IS THE TITLE OF A PLAY BY LESLIE DARBON AND PETER Whelan. The entire action takes place in an imaginary college of Oxford University. The professor has been looking afresh at the events leading up to the death of the wife of a prominent politician. The play begins with her looking yet again at a series of slides depicting those events. A sound track gives an "official" version, that the woman's death was a mistake, and that the Prime Minister was the intended victim. The professor is skeptical. She turns off the sound track and looks afresh at the slides. By the end of the evening she has identified the murderer and the accomplice, who are the dead woman's husband and a journalist. She narrowly escapes being murdered herself.

I watched the play in the Yvonne Arnaud Theatre, Guildford, shortly before setting about writing this paper, and I took its message to heart as I marshalled my evidence, because liturgists, like any other researchers, suffer from the uncanny ability to produce their own sound track to fit in with the slides on the screen. When the evidence is as scanty as it is for our story of Ash Wednesday, the temptation is considerable to turn up our own sound track and elaborate upon it. It is, of course, the old story of continuities and discontinuities that reveals what one might judiciously call "what really happened," and I have seldom read someone's research without being aware of what the presuppositions were which lay behind the handling of the material and the arrival at conclusions.

With these cautionary remarks in mind, let me draw attention to four recurring themes that appear in different guises as the richness and complexity of Ash Wednesday make themselves felt.

The Nature of the Evidence

As with any study of a rite from biblical to late patristic times, the evidence varies from Old and New Testaments, through early writers such as Tertullian, and then arrives at the sacramentaries and the lectionaries, and carries on into the pontificals, with conciliar decrees giving voice to the official mind of the church. What we shall try to do is let that evidence speak for itself, and probe behind those texts, especially the liturgical texts, to see what made people want to pray those words, particularly when they were new.

The Symbolism of Ash

The use of ashes goes back to time immemorial. In antiquity it was as colorful as it is today, but with one essential difference: unlike modern western culture, ashes in antiquity were a symbol close to people's lives. In both settings it suggests destruction, humiliation, penitence, if given a religious setting. As ashes enter a religious milieu, the questions need to be asked, "Who is being given ashes?"—"Who (if anyone) gives the ashes?"—and (a difficult one to answer) "Where do ashes come from?"

Time and Repeatability

The nub of the matter is the transition of the Wednesday after Quinquagesima as the day when a special class of penitents received ashes and were excluded, temporarily, from communion with the church, to the ashing first of others, then of everyone, as part of the pious observance of Lent.[1] It is, in other words, part of a form of pressure exerted on Ash Wednesday to yield a liturgical symbol and piety for everyone.

Adaptability and Liturgical Units

The era of liturgical texts produces clusters of prayers and lessons that show signs of resistance to change. This is particularly the case with the prayers over the penitents and the blessing and imposition of ashes. Here is an example of Baumstark's Law, that the liturgy is at its most conservative on special occasions.[2] However, this does not necessarily mean that a given liturgy was always actually used. That question, therefore, needs careful pondering, and may be the reason for the transition from special to general ashing.

Biblical Background

There are four words for ashes in Hebrew.[3] By far the most frequent occurrence is *epher*, referring to fine, bruised dust. *Deshen* means ashes of fat, *aphar* means bruised, fine dust, and *piach* means dusty ashes. *Deshen* and *aphar* refer to the ashes of sacrificial victims, whereas *epher* refers to ashes of any kind, presumably of wood or vegetation, and it is in the context of *epher* (by far the largest number of occurrences) that we find penitence. Here are a few examples.

I am but dust and ashes.	(Gn 18:27)
Tamar put ashes on her head, and rent . . .	(2 Sm 13:19)
. . . and he sat down among the ashes.	(Jb 2:8)
. . . and I am become like dust and ashes.	(Jb 30:19)
I abhor . . . and repent in dust and ashes.	(Jb 42:6)
spread sackcloth and ashes	(Is 58:5)
sackcloth, and wallow thyself in ashes	(Jer 6:26)
covered . . . with sackcloth, and sat in ashes	(Jon 3:6)

From these quotations it becomes clear that ashes often went with wearing a hairshirt or rending one's clothes, and the purpose of the action was to make a firm public display of penitence, mourning, anger, frustration. Motives are not questioned, and the ashes do not appear to have been anything special. They were sprinkled over the head, in an act of deliberate disfigurement. It is hard to see it as a self-consciously cultic act. It is, rather, a personal response to sudden changes in circumstances, though the people concerned are undoubtedly pious. It is interesting to note that, whereas the Septuagint attempts to translate the four words differently (it does not always succeed), the Vulgate sticks almost exclusively to *cinis*. But *epher* is invariably translated as *spodos*. The Apocrypha's use of these terms is not significantly different from the Old Testament.

In the New Testament a more obvious ambivalence becomes apparent. On the one hand, Chorazin and Bethsaida are challenged to repent by Jesus (Mt 11:21 = Lk 10:13) and told that if the same things had happened in Tyre and Sidon, they would have repented in sackcloth and ashes. On the other hand, Jesus warns against public show in personal religion, and particularly topical in this regard is what he has to say against the hypocrites in the passage which later comes to be read on Ash Wednesday itself (Mt 6:16-21). The subculture Jesus is referring to is a highly stylized one: people disfigure their faces on fast days (Mondays and Thursdays, and other occasions). Commentaries assume that this involved the liberal use of ashes.[4]

Another important text is Hebrews 9:13, where reference is made to the custom of the High Priest sprinkling a person ceremonially unclean through touching a dead body with lustral water containing the powdered ashes of a red heifer. According to Maimonides (but not known from earlier surviving Jewish sources), the High Priest was sprinkled in this way on two of the days in the week in which he prepared himself for the Day of Atonement.[5] The reason for this practice may be to convey atonement in a tangible form as a result of the total destruction of the red heifer (including skin, flesh, blood, dung - Nm 19:5). Absolutely everything has been offered to God and there is nothing left except the ashes, which can then be regarded as graciously left by God, and therefore as a sign of atonement.[6]

Are these three strands of New Testament teaching reconcilable, without doing damage to their subtlety or ironing out their ambiguity? Jesus' teaching is clear. Sackcloth and ashes are accepted as signs of public penitence as a result of recognizing God's gift of salvation (Mt 11:21 = Lk 10:13), but the perversion of outward religion manifested in what are called "the hypocrites" is not acceptable because their motives are wrong. The atonement-motif (Heb 9:13) may be a pointer for things to come.

TOWARDS CANONICAL PENANCE

The question of post-baptismal sin is complex, and the path taken towards some form of public penance for certain grave sins is well-known. Both Tertullian and Cyprian reveal certain aspects of this procedure, though (as one would expect) Cyprian is less rigorist than Tertullian. In Tertullian's case, the penitents wore suitable garb, and asked for pardon and peace through the community's intercession. They knelt in sackcloth and ashes at the entrance to the place where the assembly met. Such prayer was done while they lay prostrate:

> *Exomologesis* requires that . . . you prostrate yourself at the feet of the priests and kneel before the beloved of God, making all the brethren commissioned ambassadors of your prayer for pardon.[7]

Cyprian emphasizes the role of the bishop (again, as would be expected of him), who lays his hand upon the penitent at the start of the time of penitence, as he does at the end, in the same way that he lays his hand upon a catechumen on admission to the catechumenate, and after baptism.[8] How far either Tertullian or Cyprian are describing a process that is, in modern parlance, "public" or "private" is hard to say. Perhaps the modern parlance is wrongly conceived, and does not fit into ancient categories.[9] But one senses a strong ecclesial approach to handling grave sin, which is regarded as social rather than individual. The sin is against the community and God. What is interesting to note is that in the east, already by the third century, a more relaxed attitude is developing towards penance, with a careful balance between the role of the spiritual director and the presbyter/bishop in the whole process. It may be the result of this more wholesome approach which rendered the giving of ashes superfluous in any of the eastern rites.

The fourth century built on these foundations in the west. Strict rules began to be imposed, at least theoretically. For example, the Synod of Elvira (dated 294-314) required those who missed three consecutive Sunday eucharists to be temporarily excluded.[10] Penitential letters circulated, embodying practical advice as to how to regulate the flock of Christ. We are now ready to look at our first proper liturgical texts.

THE GELASIAN SACRAMENTARY
AND RELATED DOCUMENTS

As Patrick Regan and Thomas Talley have shown,[11] the origins of Lent in the west are far from simple and uniform. By the late fourth century, preparation for the Pasch consisted of six weeks and was called "Quadragesima," i.e., the forty days, beginning on the First Sunday of Lent. Maundy Thursday was thus the last day of Lent. Regan uses Leo the Great's homilies as evidence for the way in which Lent was used by the devout, primarily as a time of spiritual renewal, and of entering more fully into the Christian faith, which means discipline. It was only the need to observe forty days of fasting which required the start of Lent to become fixed on the Wednesday before Quadragesima, because, with Sundays not being fast days, that only left thirty-six days altogether for a Lenten fast. Through the fifth century, infant baptism was replacing adult baptism, and Lent was taking on a more penitential character. How far public penance was part of a local congregation is hard to tell. But the Gelasian Sacramentary contains some interesting material which is an amalgam of different elements.[12]

First, there are five *orationes et preces super paenitentes*. The first is a general prayer for forgiveness for those who confess. Then come four quite specific prayers for one person (*hunc famulum*), which pray for deliverance from the consequences of sin and pray for a proper use of the time of penitence. The last prayer comes in the first person singular, a prayer by the priest for the pardon of the penitent.

Such prayers would have fitted well in the context suggested by Tertullian and Cyprian, even with the hand-laying. They are of such importance that the Gregorian Sacramentary keeps them (omitting the last, and splitting the second last into two), adding the direction "confessing his sins in the customary manner on the Wednesday after Quinquagesima" after *orationes et preces super paenitentes*.[13]

Immediately following the prayers in the Gelasian Sacramentary comes a title *Ordo agentibus publicam paenitentiam*, which is followed by a direction to the priest in the second person singular (a sure sign of antiquity): "you receive him early on the Wednesday at the start of Quadragesima and cover him with a hairshirt, you pray for him and extrude him until Maundy Thursday." Shortly after comes a mass-set directed to be used "in the fast on the first station on Wednesday," which looks forward to the coming fast as a time of spiritual energizing and renewal.

What does this give us? Quite a lot. The Wednesday before Quadragesima is labelled the *caput quadragesima*, i.e., the start of Lent. People who do public penance are given a hairshirt, prayed for, and excluded until Maundy Thursday. If the studies of Chavasse and others are right, what we have here reflects Roman practice in the sixth century, and it may even be earlier. There is no mention of ashes, but, on the other hand, it would have been quite possible for a penitent to have ashed oneself. Just because the Sacramentary mentions the hairshirt being put on, it does not preclude other symbolism, even a penitent arriving in church already ashed. But this, of course, is a tentative suggestion, even an *argumentum ex silentio*. Liturgical historians shrink from such a course, but it is a least a remote possibility.

What of the readings? The gospel reading[14] traditional to Ash Wednesday is Matthew 6:16-21, which Talley thinks goes back to at least the fifth century, as Maximus of Turin scolds some of his faithful for starting their Lent fast on this Wednesday, in their enthusiasm for Jesus' words about fasting. The other weekday lessons do not reflect any pattern. The previous reading for Quinquagesima is Luke 18:31-43 (the sower), and Thursday has Matthew 8:5-13 (the healing of the centurion's servant), whereas Friday has Matthew 5:43-6:4 (love your enemy . . .). It is hard to avoid the suggestion that the reading was put there deliberately, with at least some reference to fasting. Perhaps it was meant to signal the start of a period of fasting soon afterwards.

The epistle-cycle[15] is more interesting. Quinquagesima has 1 Corinthians 13, the hymn to love. Wednesday has Joel 2:12-19 (rend your hearts, not your garments), followed on Thursday—the epistle series has a Thursday, a sign of including later material—by Isaiah 38:1-6 (Hezekiah's repentance), and Friday and Saturday with Isaiah 58:1-9 and 9-14 (The Lord will guide you, no obstacle in the way). It would be hard not to see in the Isaiah sequence a deliberate series, and the Ash Wednesday pericope from Joel fits well with its gospel.

THE GREGORIAN SACRAMENTARY
AND RELATED DOCUMENTS

The lectionaries have been looked at in connection with the Gelasian Sacramentary for the sake of convenience. They could equally well be matched with the Gregorian Sacramentary, a discussion of which follows.

The Gregorian Sacramentary[16] has a mass-set entitled *Feria IIII* in the Padua version, which begins with the ominous *Collecta ad sanctam Anastasiam*, which means that the papal procession gathered at St. Anastasia and, following the next direction, the Mass was celebrated at St. Sabina's. There were three original *collectae* before the end of the seventh century: Ash Wednesday, Greater Rogation, and St. Caesarius.[17] On this occasion the procession to St. Sabina, near the left bank of the Tiber, involves a church which was a *titulus*, named after the donor and transformed into a basilica in the early fifth century. It has been described as "the best-preserved witness of the post-Constantinian worship arrangement."[18] It is much smaller than the other basilicas. The mosaics in the apse portray the unity of Jew and Gentile, not a theme directly covered in either of the lessons, though one notes the presence of an Old Testament prophecy instead of the epistle. In his study of processional liturgy in antiquity, Baldovin concludes that the procession from St. Anastasia to St. Sabina must have been determined after fixing Wednesday as the start of the Lenten fast. Ordo Romanus XXII, a Gallicanized text from the end of the eighth century, describes the processional liturgy for this day, which fits the Gregorian texts.[19]

The *collecta* appears in the Gelasian Sacramentary at the head of an alternative mass-set for the vigil of Pentecost. It is a bold prayer, asking for God's grace on the Christian *militia* as it begins the fast. The collect of the day and the postcommunion offer the fast to God, whereas the *super oblata* speaks in general rather than in seasonal terms. The *super populum* prays for God's protection. This is the format of prayer, generally speaking, of the eighth-century Gelasian Sacramentaries,[20] since they follow the Gregorian rather than the Old Gelasian at this point.

What can we make of this?

First, the differences between the Gelasian and the Gregorian betray underlying attitudes to Lent that may be distinct.

The Old Gelasian accommodates the start of Lent in its very pages as a gradual process, whereas the Gregorian has it already in hand, tucking away the rite of public penance in its hinder pages.

Second, whereas the Old Gelasian calls this Wednesday the *caput ieiunii*, the Gregorian only gets there in the second half of the ninth century. This is probably an archaism.

Third, the Gregorian, by awarding Ash Wednesday a special part in Roman stational liturgy—which lingers on in the Roman tradition beyond the Alps for centuries to come—opens the way for the next step, the blessing of ashes.

Fourth, there is as yet no mention of ashes, even though the Old Gelasian mentions the hairshirt. But this does not preclude penitents and others coming to Mass already downcast and ashen. Blessing candles, palm branches, and ashes is not yet done in the Roman liturgy.

FROM CANONICAL PENANCE TO TARIFF PENANCE

There is no need to dwell on the gradual change from canonical to tariff penance in the sixth to the ninth century. Various factors were at work. Canonical penance, described earlier, with its unrepeatable character, was not meeting the needs of ordinary people, who wanted a pastoral approach which suited them more. Perhaps under indirect eastern influence, Celtic monks produced a more mobile approach, whereby, through using penitentials, penitents were given practical tasks that balanced the sins committed, thus ensuring some kind of "satisfaction." There were attempts to revive canonical penance, for example, at the behest of Theodulf of Orleans, but the tide was turning, as in so many other matters. The link with the church in canonical penance, which was created by its corporate context, was, in tariff penance, made through the priestly ordination of the confessor. This change in what might be called consumer demand was bound to have repercussions elsewhere. If canonical penance in the traditional Lenten way was seldom if ever carried out (Jonas of Orleans, who died in 843, described it as "rare in the church today"[21]), what happened to help make Lent so penitentially focussed? To that we must now turn.

BLESSING OF ASHES
IN THE LATE NINTH AND TENTH CENTURIES

The early sacramentaries do not contain any blessings of ashes. But among the later texts of the Gregorian Sacramentary[22] are to be found three manuscripts which contain the same prayer: the Sacramentary of St. Amand (ninth-century additions to the main text written c. 870-880); in the Aniane tradition (additions made at the end of the ninth/beginning of the tenth centuries); and the Sacramentary of St. Aubin's Abbey, Angers (tenth century). Too much should not be made of this prayer appearing in all three of these texts because, from the lists given in the Deshusses edition, they are clearly a minority. But the fact that it appears, and at about the same time as the other blessings associated with the liturgical year, such as candles on 2 February and palm branches on Palm Sunday, suggests that there was a new need. People carried candles and branches in procession long before the ninth and tenth centuries. And penitents ashed themselves long before this, too. What is new is that these objects should be *blessed*.

The St. Amand Sacramentary entitles the prayer the "blessing of ashes with which the penitents should be sprinkled," a slightly more prescriptive title than the others in the manuscript, which suggests mild self-consciousness. The style and content of the prayer is thoroughly Carolingian. God is asked to bless these ashes with his angel, so that they may be a remedy for all who call on God's name as they accuse themselves of their sins. The revealing feature in this prayer, however, is the reference to "whoever will have sprinkled these (ashes) over themselves for the redemption of their sins . . ." at the end. These are hardly words that apply to ashes being blessed by a priest for him to impose on a special category of the faithful. They evoke, rather, the practice of self-ashing, and although *paenitentes* is the term in the title of the prayer, one wonders just how restrictive that term was in Northern France at the end of the ninth century. One suspects that it could refer to anyone going through the tariff system of penance as part of the Lenten observance. The fact, too, that the prayer appears (with minor variants and errors) in all three books suggests, further, that this prayer was already something of a standard formula. As we shall see, it comes at the head of a group of four blessings of ashes in the Romano-Germanic Pontifical.

Other such rites are to be found from around the same time in the early pontificals, which have been studied by Rasmussen. The Pontifical of Sens[23] (variously dated between the ninth and tenth centuries) and the Pontifical of Beauvais[24] (ninth or tenth century) both contain a prayer for blessing the ashes. Sens places it on its own, long after the Ash Wednesday order for penance, which includes the four Old Gelasian prayers found in the Gregorian Sacramentary, together with two others. This separate item is entitled *benedictio cinerum*. Beauvais, on the other hand, inserts it at the end of the "orations over a penitent after he has confessed." These prayers, though they come from other sources, form the same kind of liturgical unit as Sens, and one senses that the classical sacramentary prayers "over penitents" in public have now entered a more private milieu, as the method of performing this liturgy has altered—another symptom of the change from canonical to tariff penance.

The blessing of ashes that is in question, like the one just looked at in the sacramentaries, appears frequently in later books, and comes second in the Romano-Germanic Pontifical sequence. Although covering similar ground, it differs in tone. God prefers penitence rather than the death of a sinner. God is to bless (sign of the cross inserted here) these ashes, which for humility and pardon we resolve (*decernimus*—a very deliberate verb) to have placed on our heads, that we who know we are dust, and will return to dust, may be granted pardon of sins. Like the sacramentary prayer, there is detectable a slight self-consciousness, as if praying about ashes were something new.

Among the books in which the Sens-Beauvais prayer appears is the tenth-century Benedictional of Canterbury, known as the Claudius Pontificals. In the second of these (both are tenth century) is a full rite for public penance, with penitential psalms, and before the solemn extrusion of the penitent(s) from the church at the end, our prayer is used for the blessing of ashes, followed by the direction "here the ashes are cast over their heads with blessed water, and they are expelled from church."[25]

The Sens-Beauvais books are fragmentary by comparison, but it is tempting to suggest that all three texts betray different stages of evolution, with Sens-Beauvais adapting to wider penitential usages, and Claudius adhering to the old canonical penance, the church building taking over the role of the Christian community as the embodiment of the community from which the penitent(s) is/are expelled. It is interesting to observe that the Claudius rite (tenth century) closely resembles that of Senlis (fourteenth century).[26] Pontificals, unless they are in the state of evolution, are not always typical of what the church is actually doing on the ground.

The third pontifical in Rasmussen's study is that of Reims,[27] which comes from the tenth century, but may be slightly earlier. At the end of the rite of public penance, by the bishop, there comes the *benedictio cinerum*, which consists of three items: first, a blessing; then the imposition of ashes; and finally, a prayer for perseverance in the Christian life. The blessing dwells on the theme of humility and the grace of God in the believer, working in the same way as the ashes which touch the head (there is a delightful matching of *attactis* ["touched"] of the heads and *intactos* ["untouched"] of the faithful). This prayer also appears in the Sacramentary of St. Thierry, Reims, written about 869, so that it was probably well-established in the Reims tradition. It also appears as the third in the series of four blessings of ashes in the Romano-Germanic Pontifical (c. 950). The formula at the giving of ashes is the well-known quotation from Genesis 3:19, preceded by the imperative *memento*. It is the first appearance we have encountered so far. Jungmann[28] regards it as the earliest, although that does not mean that it was the first time the formula was used, since it is just the sort of text that would suggest itself at this point, if a formula were sought after. Indeed, an allusion to Genesis 3:19 has already been seen at the end of the blessing of ashes in Sens-Beauvais. The concluding prayer is the Old Gelasian collect for the vigil of Pentecost, the Gregorian *collecta*.

What are we to make of these texts?

First, we need to note the obvious need to compose blessings of the ashes, at a time when "things had to be blessed."

Second, a clear consequence of this development was that, as with blessing candles and palms, the method of distribution (in the case of ashes, their imposition) would have to be ritualized. I would hazard a guess that the Genesis 3:19 formula, or something like it, is at least as old as the blessing (if not older still), which would place it somewhere toward the latter part of the ninth century.

Third, who exactly is receiving the ashes? Superlative episcopal rites, like the Claudius Pontifical, are clear that it is still public penitents undergoing a form of canonical penance. But under the surface, something more subtle is going on. There is a shift from canonical to tariff in pastoral practice, and with it a more varied approach to who the Lenten penitents are. The sacramentaries and early pontificals seem to suggest a distribution of ashes linked with the season of Lent, and in practice opening out to a wider group of people.

Fourth, as with the blessing of candles and palms, and anything else for that matter, an increasing repertoire of prayers produces an increasing exploration of the theological and devotional images in these prayers. We have seen three. Others appear in time, including two in the Canterbury Benedictional (eleventh century) not known elsewhere.[29]

BACK TO THE PONTIFICALS: FROM "POITIERS" TO THE ROMANO-GERMANIC PONTIFICAL

The so-called Pontifical of Poitiers,[30] which is in fact a large all-purpose liturgical book from about the year 900, from northeast of Paris, has no ashing rite, but produces a grandiose pattern of canonical penance, adapted to the elaborations of the liturgy. It serves as an important source for the Romano-Germanic Pontifical, which does have an ashing rite, hence (for our purposes) its importance.

First, there is the Ash Wednesday confession. Second, the Mass for penitents. Third, the prayers for reconciling penitents (on Maundy Thursday).

The confession is lengthy, and is followed by instruction on the seven deadly sins, followed by seven prayers (some go back to the Old Gelasian; all of them are used in the Romano-Germanic Pontifical), followed by seven psalms, each with a collect (all appear in the Fulda Sacramentary[31]), followed by the extrusion from the church.

The Mass for the penitents has three collects, *super oblata*, and post communions: some are from the Old Gelasian, most appear in Fulda. The epistle is Romans 6:19-23 (set free from sin), the gospel is Luke 15:1-7 (the lost sheep). The reconciliation of penitents precedes the Mass, and consists of another seven prayers, all of them (except the last, in Fulda) from the Old Gelasian.

In his review of Martini's edition of Poitiers, Jounel tries to conceal a slight doubt as to whether all this would ever have been celebrated,[32] since it looks somewhat dinosaur-like when set against the other books that we have looked at from around this time. It is a stubborn affirmation of canonical penance.

When we turn to the Romano-Germanic Pontifical (redacted in Mainz about the year 950), we find an even more curious rite, something of an synthesis.[33] Most of it consists of the Ash Wednesday confession, but with the Mass immediately afterwards, and the ashing and extrusion at the end. The confession and prayers for forgiveness follow almost exactly the Poitiers order. Then come the seven penitential psalms and a series of prayers, some of which come from the Poitiers sequence following the seven deadly sins, and some of them from the prayers for reconciling penitents on Maundy Thursday. In the Mass (altered from Poitiers' *pro paenitentibus* to *post confessionem*, presumably because it now comes immediately after confession), the collect, *super oblata*, and postcommunion all come from Poitiers, but the epistle and gospel are not those of Ash Wednesday from the classical lectionaries. Instead of Joel 2:12-19, we have Isaiah 1:16-19 (wash and be clean); instead of Matthew 6:16-21, we have Luke 18:10-14 (the Pharisee and the publican). Although the latter is an obvious choice (read at the time on Pentecost 10), the former is somewhat out-of-the-way; its choice in all probability rests on Poitiers, where it appears as the lesson for the first nocturn on Maundy Thursday.

Ashes are placed on the head of the penitent with the formula from Genesis 3:19, and a hairshirt (which we have not encountered since the Old Gelasian) is also placed on the penitent with a composite formula, ending in Psalm 51:17. A Poitiers prayer follows, after which the penitent is escorted out of church while a chant, inspired by the extrusion of Adam and

Eve from the Garden of Eden (again Genesis 3:19), is sung. Poitiers' influence on this part of the rites is abundantly clear.

But there then follows an altogether different rite, beginning with the very Gregorian-sounding *Collecta ad S Anastasiam*. Immediately, the ashes are blessed, with three prayers we have already seen.[34]

Omnipotens sempiterne deus, parce	St. Amand Sacramentary
deus qui non mortem	Sens-Beauvais
deus qui humiliatione	Reims (Pontifical Sacramentary)

A short prayer, not known from elsewhere and alluding to Jonah in Nineveh (Jonah 3:6), rounds off the section in a neat conclusion. All four prayers survive together into the 1570 Missal.

Chants follow during the imposition of ashes, though no formula is actually suggested. The Gregorian *collecta*, also found in Reims in a comparable position, leads into the procession. At this point, the service breaks off, though one assumes the procession concludes at St. Sabina with the Mass for Ash Wednesday, at which—among other traditional items— the readings would be Joel 2:12-19 and Matthew 6:16-21.[35] And so this pontifical concludes Ash Wednesday.

It is clear that what we have are two quite different rites which are aimed at two different clientele. The former is the old canonical penance, dressed in tenth-century form, quarried largely from the Poitiers Pontifical in terms both of its content and overall shape, although adjustments and simplifications have been made; and the distribution of ashes has been properly incorporated at the end, but only for the old class of penitents. Around the start of the tenth century, Reginon of Prüm[36] mentions sprinkling of ashes on penitents at the enrollment on Ash Wednesday, a germ, surely, of things to come, but perhaps a summary of a slow development, as both the order of penitents and the ashing widens in scope.

The second rite adapts the Gregorian Sacramentary's Ash Wednesday stational liturgy so that the blessing and imposition of ashes precede the procession. The rite itself is, once more, a synthesis, bringing together prayers that are still fairly new and in varying stages of circulation, to bolster up a more popular approach to ashing (there is no hint of restriction in the directions—one is to assume that ashing is for anyone who wanted it). The compiler took the best of what he could procure: Poitiers for the older rite, and the local, more modern approaches for the new rite which is now to start off the Gregorian Mass. It reads a little like some of the new service-books of the western churches today, with their double provision for Christian initiation, both of adults and of infants. Consumer demand, pastoral variation, and liturgical creativity all play their part. In the older rites unblessed ashes (as of old?) and a hairshirt occur, whereas in the newer rite there are only ashes, but they are blessed, in line with more recent and popular practice. The rite is no muddle, but deliberate.

It remained for legislation to catch up with this shifting scene. Traces of the Romano-Germanic Pontifical's double rite persist through the Middle Ages, though it is clearly the second rite which wins the day.[37] Later in the tenth century, in the famous Anglo-Saxon *Regularis Concordia*, there is a general ashing of the whole community of monks, after the abbot has blessed the ashes at the conclusion of none (before High Mass); this will reflect English monastic practice of the time, but may also reflect Continental practice, in view of the general influences on the *Regularis Concordia* as a whole. In the following century the Council of Benevento (1091) under Pope Urban II dealt with three matters of clerical procedure, about the election of bishops, and travelling clergy, before decreeing that all clergy and laity, men as well as women, are to receive ashes on the head on Ash Wednesday.[38] Lanfranc made a similar decree for his monks in Canterbury c. 1070.[39]

* * * * * *

The subtitle of this investigation might well be "From Job 42:6 to the Romano-Germanic Pontifical." It has indeed been a rich and varied picture. To revert to the theatrical analogy made at the outset, there have been many slides to glance at, and I know that my sound track has been not only lengthy but overladen with presuppositions.

The evidence is indeed of a diverse character. The symbolism of ashes is too powerful to be confined to one group of people, or even to one meaning, as the prayers show. The pressure to make ashing available more widely was bound to be one of the consequences of the move from canonical toward tariff penance. And the genius of liturgical texts is that they demonstrate the extraordinary adaptability of prayers and customs either to fall victim to what might be called "arrested evolution," or else to travel in the direction of where the wind is blowing at a given time.[40]

But a more detailed analysis can be offered in conclusion.

1. *The Overall Story: Restrictive or Open?*

A restrictive interpretation would suggest a limited sound track between the slides on display in their sequence. The biblical background would be acknowledged, and set firmly as fitting in with canonical penance, perhaps as glimpsed at in the writings of Tertullian and Cyprian (and others). The Old Gelasian Sacramentary's rite, with the giving of the hairshirt, would interpret this, as reflecting Roman practice, perhaps from the fifth century, at the start of Lent.

When, around the same time, the Lenten fast came to be begun on the Wednesday before Quadragesima (causing, or caused by, the Joel 2:12-19 and Matthew 6:16-21 readings?), it was inevitable that the major step of inaugurating canonical penance, with the giving of the hairshirt, should also take place on this day. It is this which moves north, and is reflected in the Gelasians of the eighth century.

The next piece of evidence is the Gregorian Sacramentary, which lacks any reference to ashes or hairshirts, but has a mass-set for Ash Wednesday, preceded by a *collecta*, fitting in with the solemn stational liturgy that was evolving. This is exported north of the Alps as well. But canonical penance was already breaking down by the ninth century; it was exceptional. Toward the end of that century, the blessing of ashes began to appear in local service-books, both sacramentaries and pontificals. On the face of it, such ashing was for penitents, and it might well be asked who these penitents were. If they were part of the growing class of beneficiaries of tariff penance, they would, presumably, be ashed after receiving absolution.

Finally, the Romano-Germanic Pontifical in the tenth century provides a fulsome rite, which includes not only elements of the penitential liturgies that have been evolving (seven deadly sins, seven psalms, seven prayers), but a Mass, with special readings, leading into the extrusion from the church. Another rite follows on the same day (*eodem die*) with another ashing rite, incorporated into the Gregorian-type pre-Mass rite.

But is there a more open interpretation of this evidence? I would suggest that there are three places where this might be the case. First, early Christian piety, for all that it was aware of Jesus' critique of formal religion (like the prophets before him), took sackcloth (i.e., the hairshirt) and ashes into its personal practice, so that it was already familiar before canonical penance was formally established. That supplies a link between the Bible and the Fathers.

Second, although there is no evidence for the specifically *liturgical* use of ashes in Lent in either the Gallican or Visigothic liturgies,[41] it seems likely that the custom was already established, at least in Gaul at the time of Romanization. There are no signs of editorial alterations in the eighth-century Gelasian Sacramentaries, whereas there *are* when it comes to the Ash Wednesday Mass, which is uniformly the Gregorian Mass, complete with *collecta*.[42]

Third, and most important of all, the need to bless ashes in the ninth century, so far from being exclusively for a small group of people, after penance, appears equally to have been a pre-Mass custom for anyone who wanted it, at whatever stage or degree of tariff penance, and even beyond that category. These blessings are sometimes hidden away among other pre-Mass blessings (the three sacramentaries cited above), or else are followed by the Gregorian *collecta*, presumably to start the Mass (the Reims Pontifical). Such a wider interpretation would explain the need for the Romano-Germanic Pontifical to opt for its dual-rite synthesis in the following century.

2. *Ashes: Their Provision, Blessing, and Use*

It is not till the thirteenth century that we come across the direction that the ashes should be made from the previous year's palm branches, if there exists a sufficient number of these.[43] The custom, of course, might be much earlier. Moreover, the blessing of palms, as we have observed, dates from around the same time (ninth century) as the blessing of candles and ashes. "Palms" were usually branches of any tree available.[44] Modern "palms"—as is well-known—need to be burnt in larger quantities than virtually any other branches in Northern Europe to produce anything like enough ashes for even a small group of people. In the ninth century, in Europe, people depended on wood (and possibly peat) for cooking and heating. It is likely that these were the ashes used, and the custom of burning "palm" (i.e., any) branches came in sooner rather than later.

The early prayers all explore humiliation and spiritual growth as underlying themes, but one cannot fail to notice the subtle way in which the tactile character of the ashing is developed, particularly in the prayer from the two Reims books.[45] The precise method of ashing is not entirely clear. Perhaps self-ashing, in the old Jewish piety, was done by throwing ashes into the air, for them to fall over the head of the penitent, and this is what is eventually taken over by the church when ashing became a distinctive liturgical act. This suggests a fairly thorough amount of ashes on the head—a pointer to the lavish use of a symbol that was basically familiar to people.[46]

3. A Theology for Ash Wednesday?

The historian cannot ignore another factor in the complex story of unravelling the liturgical use of ashes. Whereas the ashing of penitent Christians is a peculiarity of the Roman rite at the start of Lent, two other liturgical uses of ashes must not be ignored.

One is the custom in the East Syrian Church of preserving the *henana*, ashes of the saints, and mixing such ashes with water and wine for couples to drink at the liturgy of betrothal. Such a practice was established by the eighth century.

The other is the practice of the old Visigothic Church to make the sign of the cross with ashes on a penitent *in extremis*, after giving a hairshirt. This is possibly part of a still older rite, though Férotin's supporting sources (like the Old Gelasian

Sacramentary) mention only the hairshirt, and not the ashes. Be this as it may, from these two uses it becomes apparent that ashes are indeed an ambiguous liturgical custom, which may be compared to the practice of footwashing, which takes on different meanings, whether on Maundy Thursday or at paschal baptism.[47]

Does this throw any further light upon *Lenten* ashing? To ash penitents *as a specific order* at the enrollment is indeed a rite of passage, pointing to internal-individual and external-community attitudes towards sin. It provides a powerful "marker" for those undergoing a special kind of experience on the edges of the church. But to ash *anyone*, including penitents of the tariff (and later) kind, is less a "marker" within the community, and more a devotional practice of an individual nature. This paper suggests that the move from the one to the other may be earlier than has been accepted hitherto. Actions in the liturgy are notoriously difficult to date in absolute terms, because liturgical books are notoriously slippery material on which to base firm hypotheses. A case in point is the very term "Ash Wednesday," which we have used indiscriminately throughout this study. The tradition of the Roman Missal does not actually use the term *feria IV cinerum* ("the Wednesday of ashes") until 1474,[48] though the First English Prayer Book (1549) sees fit to ignore the Sarum Missal's *feria iiii in capite ieiunii* ("the Wednesday of the start of the fast") to "The First Day of Lent, *commonly called* Ash Wednesday."[49] That "commonly called" probably points back to a long vernacular use which the official Latin books never quite caught up with.

Our story, moreover, seems shot through with paradoxes, the two chief being the remarkable survival on this day of two somewhat fierce bible-readings that warn against outward show (on the one hand), while the church wrestles with the need to ritualize penitence and how to reconcile the death-throes of canonical penance with the growth of a much looser approach to the ritual expression of forgiveness (on the other hand).

It will belong to a further study to take up the tale from the Romano-Germanic Pontifical through the Middle Ages, the Reformation, and down to our own day.[50] Suffice it to say for now that the synthesis made by that pontifical is nothing short of superb as a way of starting Lent and looking forward to Easter, with its ritual blessing, and aspersion of ashes on the whole congregation (?) as it gathers at St. Anastasia (or its equivalent); and then, after the *collecta*, with its prayer asking for grace to persevere, processes for the eucharist to St. Sabina (or its equivalent), singing about human penitence and divine forgiveness. Word, action, song, and Scripture mingle creatively as the church gradually articulates the way in which God speaks to its particular and general areas of need. Such is the liturgy's genius for bringing light and shade into its celebration of time before God.[51]

Notes

1. This point is made by Thomas J. Talley, "The Liturgy of Reconciliation," in *Worship: Reforming Tradition* (Washington, D.C.: The Pastoral Press, 1990) 62ff.

2. A. Baumstark, *Liturgie comparée: principes et méthodes pour l'étude historique des liturgies chrétiennes* (Paris: Editions de Chevetogne, 1953) 17ff.

3. See Robert Young, *Analytical Concordance to the Holy Bible* (London and Redhill: United Society for Christian Literature, 1939) 56. See in general R. De Vaux, *Ancient Israel: Its Life and Institutions*, 2d ed. (London: Darton, Longman, and Todd, 1965).

4. See, for example, A.H. McNeile, *The Gospel According to St. Matthew* (London: Macmillan, 1915) 83f.

5. Maimonides, *Mishneh Torah* VIII, viii, 1.4. See also Barnabas Lindars, *The Theology of the Letter to the Hebrews* (Cambridge: University Press, 1991) 89, and n. 90.

6. I am indebted to the late Professor Barnabas Lindars for help in this part of the discussion.

7. Tertullian, *De Paenitentia* 9.

8. Cyprian, *Epistolae* 15 and 16.

9. See, for example, James Dallen, *The Reconciling Community: The Rite of Penance*, Studies in the Reformed Rites of the Catholic Church, vol. 3 (New York: Pueblo Publishing Co., 1987) 29ff.

10. Quoted in Dallen, *The Reconciling Community* 59.

11. See Patrick Regan, "The Three Days and the Forty Days," *Worship* 54:1 (1980) 2-17; and Thomas J. Talley, *The Origins of the Liturgical Year* (New York: Pueblo Publishing Co., 1985) 163ff,

12. L.C. Mohlberg, E. Eizenhöfer, and P. Siffrin, *Liber Sacramentorum Romanae Aecclesiae Ordinis Anni Circuli "Sacramentarium Gelasia-*

num", Rerum Ecclesiasticarum Documenta, Fontes, vol. 4 (Rome: Herder, 1968) 17ff, nos. 78-93. See also A. Chavasse, *Le Sacramentaire gélasien: Sacramentaire presbyteral en usage dans les titres romains au VIIè siècle*, Bibliothèque de théologie série IV, Histoire de la théologie, vol. 1 (Paris: Desclée, 1957) 147ff.

13. See J. Deshusses, *Le Sacramentaire grégorien: ses principales formes d'après les plus anciens manuscrits*, Spicilegium Friburgense, vol. 16 (Fribourg: Editions Universitaires, 1971) 451ff, nos. 1379-1382.

14. W.H. Frere, *Studies in Early Roman Liturgy II: The Roman Lectionary*, Alcuin Club Collections, vol. 30 (London: Milford, 1934) 6, 34.

15. W.H. Frere, *Studies in Early Roman Liturgy III: The Roman Epistle-Lectionary*, Alcuin Club Collections, vol. 32 (London: Milford, 1935) 4; and A. Wilmart, *Le Lectionnaire d'Alcuin*, Bibliotheca "Ephemerides Liturgicae," vol. 2 (Rome: Ephemerides Liturgicae, 1937) 152.

16. Deshusses, *Le Sacramentaire grégorien*, vol. 1, 130f., nos. 153-157.

17. See G.G. Willis, "Roman Stational Liturgy," in *Further Essays in Early Roman Liturgy*, Alcuin Club Collections, vol. 50 (London: SPCK, 1968) 11.

18. John F. Baldovin, *The Urban Character of Christian Worship: The Origins, Development, and Meaning of Stational Liturgy*, Orientalia Christiana Analecta, vol. 228 (Rome: Pontificium Institutum Studiorum Orientalium, 1987) 112.

19. M. Andrieu, *Les Ordines Romani du Haut Moyen Age*, vol. 3, Spicilegium Sacrum Lovaniense, vol. 24 (Louvain: Spicilegium Sacrum Lovaniense, 1957) 259f.

20. A. Dumas, *Liber Sacramentorum Gellonensis*, Corpus Christianorum Series Latina, vol. 159 (Turnholt: Brepols, 1981) 33f., nos. 265-271; for comparative table, see vol. 159 A, 19f. See also O. Heiming, *Sacramentarium Augustodunensis*, Corpus Christianorum Series Latina, vol. 159 B (Turnholt: Brepols, 1986) 34f., nos. 279-289 (Phillipps Sacramentary); and A. Hänggi and S. Schönherr, *Sacramentarium Rhenaugiense*, Spicilegium Friburgense, vol. 15 (Freiburg: Universitätsverlag, 1970) 100, nos. 193-197 (no form of public penance, only the Mass).

21. Jonas of Orleans, *De Institutione Laicali* 1, 10.

22. See Deshusses, *Le Sacramentaire grégorien*, vol. 3, Spicilegium Friburgense, vol. 28 (Fribourg: Presses Universitaires, 1982) 41, 53. The manuscripts are: Paris, Bibliothèque Nationale, ms. lat. 2291, 9th century additions, fo. 2r; Florence, Biblioteca Medicea Laurenziana, ms. Edili 121, 9th-10th century additions, fo. 166v-167. See also V. Leroquais, *Les Sacramentaires et les missels manuscrits des bibliothèques*

publiques de France (Paris, 1924) 72: Angers, Bibliothèque Municipale 91 (83), fo. 74v-75. For the third manuscript mentioned by Deshusses, *Le Sacramentaire grégorien* 38 (the Sacramentary of St. Thierry, Reims) see below note 27.

23. N.K. Rasmussen, *Les Pontificaux du haut moyen âge: Genèse du livre de l'évêque* (thèse présentée en vue du doctorat avec spécialisation en liturgie et en théologie sacramentaire, Paris, Institut Catholique, 1977) 146. (Forthcoming posthumous publication under the editorship of P.-M. Gy, in *Spicilegium Sacrum Lovaniense*, 1992.)

24. Ibid. 176.

25. D.H. Turner, *The Claudius Pontificals*, Henry Bradshaw Society, vol. 97 (1971) 83-85.

26. Text in E. Martène, *De Antiquis Ecclesiae Ritibus*, vol. 3 (Antwerp: Novelli, 1764) 53 (Ordo VII). (= Martène) See A.-G. Martimort, *La Documentation liturgique de Dom Edmond Martène*, Studi e Testi, vol. 279 (Vatican City: Biblioteca Apostolica, 1978) 458. (= Martimort)

27. Rasmussen, *Les Pontificaux* 293. The St. Thierry Sacramentary is Reims, Bibliothèque Municipale 213 (fo. 184).

28. J.A. Jungmann, *Die lateinischen Büssriten in ihrer geschichtlichen Entwicklung*, Forschungen zur Geschichte des innerkirchlichen Lebens, vol. 3/4 (Innsbruck, 1932) 48.

29. R.H. Woolley, *The Canterbury Benedictional*, Henry Bradshaw Society, vol. 51 (1916) 16 and 144 (notes).

30. A. Martini, *Il Cosidetto Pontificale di Poitiers*, Rerum Ecclesiasticarum Documenta Series Maior Fontes, vol. 14 (Rome: Herder, 1979) 12-50, nos. 29-90.

31. See the corresponding rite in G. Richter and A. Schönfelder, *Sacramentarium Fuldense Saec. X* (Fulda: Actiendrückerei, 1912) 42ff.

32. P. Jounel, in *La Maison-Dieu* 142 (1980) 140 ("Une liturgie aussi développé a-t-elle pu jamais été célébrée? Cela est peu probable.") The whole review, 138-140.

33. C. Vogel and R. Else, *Le Pontifical Romano-Germanique du Dixième Siècle*, vol. 2, Studi et Testi, vol. 227 (Vatican City: Biblioteca Apostolica, 1963) 14-23, XCIX, 44-80. Few of the sources are given in the notes. The bulk of them indicated in this study (see appended chart) are supplied by the author.

34. See above.

35. This is perhaps a better explanation than one which might suppose that the apparent change of readings in the Mass was because the traditional Gospel (Mt 6:16-21) attacks the outward show of religion, which might be taken as a criticism of the practice of ashing. Talley is intrigued by the Romano-Germanic rite (see his *Worship: Re-*

forming Tradition 62f.). Our view is that this pontifical has two rites and the new readings are chosen out of sheer need, because the two Masses would (ideally) be celebrated on the same day, and a duplication of readings was regarded as inappropriate. Ironically, Luke 18:9-14 is now an alternative gospel to Matthew 6:16-21 for Ash Wednesday in the Church of England; see *Alternative Service Book* (London: SPCK, 1980) 502f.

36. Reginon of Prüm, *De Ecclesiasticis Disciplinis* 1. 291. (See Talley, *Worship: Reforming Tradition* 63, 73 n. 7.) The question is, how widely was this "order" of penitents interpreted, and how retrospective were these directions on developing practice?

37. Another transitional rite is that of Narbonne (12th century), where there are two separate ashings at the same service, first of the penitents who are extruded, and then of the clergy and the rest of the congregation; see Martène 50f. and Martimort 457.

38. See T. Symons, ed., *Regularis Concordia* (London: Nelson, 1953), para. 34, pp.32-33. The Benevento decree is quoted by Martène 57, and alluded to by Talley, *Worship: Reforming Tradition* 63. The full text of the council is to be found in J.D. Mansi, *Sacrorum Conciliorum Nova et Amplissima Collectio, Tomus Vicesimus* (Venice: Zatta, 1775) 739. This council was a general council of the church and took place at Benevento because Urban II was at the time in exile from Emperor Henry IV.

39. Quoted in Woolley, *The Canterbury Benedictional* 144.

40. On liturgical evolution, see the important essays by Robert F. Taft, "The Structural Analysis of Liturgical Units: An Essay in Methodology" and "How Liturgies Grow: The Evolution of the Byzantine Divine Liturgy," in *Beyond East and West: Problems in Liturgical Understanding* (Washington, D.C.: The Pastoral Press, 1984) 151ff, 167ff.

41. See, for example, L.C. Mohlberg, *Missale Gothicum*, Rerum Ecclesiasticarum Documenta, Series Maior Fontes, vol. 5 (Rome: Herder, 1961) 46-48 for the Masses at the start of Lent.

42. See note 20 above.

43. "Feria quarta cinerum ante missam benedicuntur cineres facti de ramis benedictis preteriti anni, si habentur, in medio ante altare . . ." in S.J.F. van Dijk, ed., *Ordines of Haymo of Faversham*, Henry Bradshaw Society, vol. 85 (1953) 1. This dates from the mid-thirteenth century.

44. J.W. Tyrer, *Historical Survey of Holy Week: Its Services and Ceremonial*, Alcuin Club Collections, vol. 29 (London: Milford, 1932) 55f.

45. See note 27 above. The prayer also refers to the *aspersio* of ashes, a further indication of its tactile associations, and proof that it was sprinkled over the head, rather than rubbed on the forehead.

46. On the possibly earlier date for the Genesis 3:19 formula at the imposition of ashes, see the comparable case argued by Paul De Clerck for the "ego-" baptismal formula going back as far as the fifth century, "Les origines de la formule baptismale," in Paul De Clerck and Eric Palazzo, eds., *Rituels: Mélanges offerts au Père Gy, O.P.* (Paris: Editions du Cerf, 1990) 199-214. I owe the suggestion of the ashes thrown into the air to the Rev. Dr. A. Gelston.

47. For the eastern rite, see Kenneth W. Stevenson, *To Join Together: The Rite of Marriage* (New York: Pueblo Publishing Co., 1987) 67ff.; for the Visigothic, see M. Férotin, *Le Liber Ordinum en usage dans l'église wisigothique et mozarabe d'Espagne*, Monumenta Ecclesiae Liturgica, vol. 5 (Paris: Firmin-Didot, 1904) col. 87-92. See the discussion about the symbolism of the footwashing in exegesis and in the Maundy Thursday liturgy ("exemplum humilitatis") and North Italian-Gallican baptism ("mysterium sanctificationis") in P.F. Beatrice, *La lavanda dei piedi: Contributo alla storia delle antiche liturgie cristiane*, Bibliotheca Ephemerides Liturgicae "Subsidia", vol. 28 (Rome: Edizioni Liturgiche, 1983).

48. See Dom P. Bruylants, *Les Oraisons du missel romain: Texte et histoire*, vol. 1, *Tabulae Synopticae Fontium Missalis Romani Indices* (Louvain: Abbaye du Mont César, 1952) 17f. But see above, note 43, for Haymo of Faversham, a century earlier, for the use of "feria quarta cinerum."

49. See comparative tables in F.E. Brightman, *The English Rite*, vol. 1 (London: Rivingtons, 1915) 288f. 1549 and 1662 are the same, though 1552 omits "commonly called Ash Wednesday."

50. For a study of the rites of penance from around this time, see A. Nocent, "La pénitence dans les *ordines* locaux transcrits dans le *De Antiquis Ecclesiae Ritibus* d'Edmond Martène," in Guistino Farnedi, ed., *Analecta Liturgica 10: Studi in memoria dell'abate Prof. Salvatore Marsilli (1910-1983)*, Studi Anselmiana, vol. 91 (Rome: Pont. Ateneo S. Anselmo, 1986) 115-138. I plan a corresponding study of the Ash Wednesday rites.

51. See our study "The Origins and Development of Candlemas: A Struggle for Identity and Coherence?", *Ephemerides Liturgicae* 102 (1988) 316-346; reprinted in J. Neil Alexander, ed., *Time and Community: In Honor of Thomas Julian Talley* (Washington, D.C.: The Pastoral Press, 1990) 43-76. I would like to record my gratitude to Professor Thomas J. Talley for his assistance in several aspects of this study.

Ash Wednesday: Possible Development

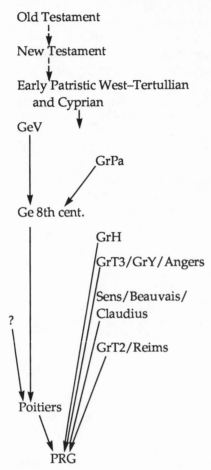

Old Testament	ashes and hairshirt accepted form of penitence
New Testament	ditto, but note Jesus' warning about fasting (Mt 6:16–21)
Early Patristic West–Tertullian and Cyprian	beginnings of canonical penance– ashes (?) and hairshirt (?)
GeV	5th cent. Rome: (ashes?), hairshirt for canonical pen.
GrPa	6th cent. Rome: Ash Wed. collecta, procession + Mass
Ge 8th cent.	synthesis of GeV and GrPa
GrH	as GrPa
GrT3/GrY/Angers	9th/early 10th cent. blessing of ashes
Sens/Beauvais/ Claudius	Pontificals with simple rite of blessing: after pen. or before Mass?
GrT2/Reims	9th cent. blessing of ashes/Pontifical with blessing, imposition (Gn 3:19), and Gr "collecta" [–Mass?]
Poitiers	c. 900 elaborate form of public penance
PRG	two rites: –public penance (like Poit.) but with ashing–hairshirt after Mass at end –blessing and general ashing, followed by "collecta" (and Mass)

***

GeV=Old Gelasian (n. 12); GrPa=GrH (for Ash Wed.)=Gregorian Sacramentary (n. 13); Ge 8th cent.=Gelasians of 8th century (n. 20); GrT2 (Deshusses' term)=Sacramentary of St. Thierry, Reims (n. 27); GrT3 (Deshusses' term)=Sacramentary of St. Amand (n. 22); GrY (Deshusses' term)=N. Italian Sacramentary in Aniane tradition (n. 22); Sens/ Beauvais=Pontificals (nn. 23,24); Claudius=Claudius Pontifical, 10th century, Canterbury (n. 25); Reims=Pontifical (n. 27); Poitiers=Pontifical (n. 30); PRG-Romano-Germanic Pontifical (n.33)

Ash Wednesday in the Romano-Germanic Pontifical and Its Sources

44	Ordo feria quarta in capite ieiunii	
	address re. extrusion	
45	concede deus omnipotens propitius esto	Poit (=Poitiers) 19
46-49	address re. sins	
50	credis in Deum patrem	
	vis dimittere . . . peccata vestra	Poit 31
50a	confiteor tibi	Poit 34
51	misereatur tui omnipotens Deus	Poit 35
52	penitent kneels before celebrant	
53	multa quidem et innumerabilia sunt	Poit 36
54	penitent prostrates	
55	provision for servants still to be penitents	
56	seven penitential psalms	
57	exaudi, domine, preces nostras	Poit 50 GeV 78
		GrH 1379
58	da quaesumus domine huic famulo	Poit 52
59	preveniat hunc famulum	Poit 53 GeV 79
		GrH 1380
60	adesto domine supplicationibus	Poit 54 GeV 80
		GrH 1381
61	domine deus noster qui peccatis	Poit 55 GeV 81
		GrH 1382 GeG 1861
62	exaudi quaesumus omnipotens deus	
	preces	
63	adesto domine supplicationibus . . .	
	et huius	?
64	precor domine clementiae tuae	Poit 294 GeV 82
		GeG 271
65	penitent recites 5 psalms, entering church	
66	deus cuius indulgentiae cuncti indigent	Poit 299
67	Missa post confessionem: introit	
	omnipotens sempiterne deus	Poit 79 GeV 360
	OT lesson: Isaiah 1:16–19	Poit 209a
	gradual and tract	
	Gospel lesson: Lk 18:10–14	(Pentecost 10)
	offertory	
68	praesta quaesumus omnipotens	Poit 84
69	communion	
70	omnipotens et misericors deus	Poit 88

71	ashes on head:	GeV 83?
	memento, homo (Gn 3:19)	Reims
	hairshirt: convertere . . .cor enim . . .	GeV 83–not formula
72	assit quaesumus domine huic famulo	Poit 51
73	extrusion: ecce eiceris hodie . . .in sudore	
74	Collecta ad S. Anastasiam	GrH 153
	blessing of ashes: omnipotens . . .	GrT3/GrY/Angers
	parce metuentibus	
75	deus qui non mortem sed paenitentiam	Sens/Beauvais/
		Claudius
76	deus qui humiliatione flecteris	GrT2/Reims
77	omnipotens sempiterne deus, qui Ninivitiis	?
78	antiphon: exaudi nos domine quoniam	
	Ps. 69: Immutemur	
	ashing	
79	concede nobis domine praesidia militiae	GrH 153/Reims
80	procession. antiphons: juxta vestibulum.	
	parce domine. emendemus. peccavimus.	

Numberings: from C. Vogel and R. Elze, *Le Pontifical Romano-Germanique du Dixième Siècle.* vol. 2, 14–23 (XCIX. 44–80); see note 33.

Some Notes:

Shape

44-46	=	full form of public penance: confession / psalms / prayers

67-70   =   Mass after confession

71-73   =   public ashing and hairshirt giving, and extrusion

74-80   =   Ash Wednesday stational Mass, with blessing of ashes and general ashing before *collecta* and processional chants

Sources

44-66   influence of Poitiers is strong, both from public penance (45-61) and (slightly) from public reconciliation (64; 66).

N.B. strength of the unit of Old Gelasian prayers over penitents.

63 is unknown, but has a familiar structure.

GeG (=Gellone) appears twice–62 and 64.

67-70   influence of Poitiers is strong–all three Mass prayers and OT lesson.

71-73   If the Reims Pontifical predates PRG, then influence is direct, or based on a common growing tradition of ashing with formula.

GrT2, the Sacramentary of St. Thierry, Reims, dates from c. 869, so the prayer antedates PRG.
N.B. The public giving of the hairshirt goes back to GeV.

74-80   In essence, the GrPa/H stational Mass, but with four ash-blessings, three from 9th/10th century local rites.
N.B. The sacramentaries have the same prayer, pontificals don't.

77 is unknown, but explores the biblical theme of Jonah in Niniveh.

Motivation

44-73   is a contemporary synthesis of canonical penance, using the church building where "community" would have sufficed of old. No phasing through different rites at different times.

74-80   is a contemporary synthesis of growing general ashing, incorporated into the procession.

10

The Ceremonies of Light: Their Shape and Function in the Paschal Vigil Liturgy

LITURGISTS ARE FREQUENTLY TOLD BY OTHERS (AND SOMETIMES THEY even tell themselves) that they tend to look at the subject of their trade entirely through the eyes of the "professional."[1] It is, perhaps, appropriate that a brief examination of that most conservative of liturgies (the Easter Vigil) should begin with a description by a layperson, in this case, that of Bernard Montgomery ("Monty"), who was in Jerusalem in an official capacity (with the august title of "Officer Commanding, the Holy Land") in 1931. His description does not survive in a letter, but (as his biographer, Nigel Hamilton notes), in "an anonymous transcript which he sent to his mother, perhaps intending that she should get it published somewhere."[2] It wasn't published at the time, but here is part of his extraordinary account from the biography itself:

> The ceremony is conducted by the Greek Orthodox Patriarch; and a Bishop of the Armenian Churches goes with him into the Holy Sepulchre . . . Every available piece of sitting or standing room in the church is packed with young people for several days before the event, fabulous sums are paid for balconies, and people camp out in them: babies are frequently born in the church while waiting. This is very lucky and is much sought after . . .

189

... the Shebals (young men) enter in procession, singing songs. They sing that they are happy now; as Christ who was killed is soon to rise again, the Jews who killed Him are sorrowful at yon wall, and so on. The singing is very uproarious, and they all get worked up into a high pitch of excitement.

The Patriarch appears, is disrobed, and enters the Sepulchre.

The whole of the onlookers now get fearfully excited: everyone has a bundle of candles and they get them ready to light from the Holy Fire when it is passed out.

Meanwhile, the Patriarch calls upon God to provide the Fire, and he comes out.

Runners are waiting and seize it and run up to the top galleries with it, others pass it round the people on the floor.

In about 30 seconds every single person in the Church (about 16,000) has a lighted candle, and the effect is wonderful: as is the grease, as the people get over-excited and wave the candles about. (After the ceremony, my tunic was covered with grease, and also my hair.) Then suddenly the doors of the Sepulchre are opened and the Patriarch emerges holding a lighted torch in each hand . . . He then tries to get up to the Altar in the Church to light the candles on it. But everyone wants to light his candle from the torch, and the crowd surged in on the old man, and he got pushed backwards and forwards, and almost trampled on. The whole crowd is shouting and singing and is worked up to a fever of excitement. Finally a squad of police picked him up and rushed him through the crowd up to the altar. I bet he was glad when he got there.

Monty was known not to waste a word in his descriptions; he was in Jerusalem to keep the peace; he was an Anglican (son of a bishop of Tasmania, and grandson of the famous Dean Frederic Farrar of Canterbury), whose Anglo-Saxon spirit no doubt entered strangely into the atmosphere of this fantastic liturgy. He is struck by the mood of the crowd (no less than four times does the word "excite"—or one of its cognates—appear in the narrative), and for him the climax of the service is the sudden burst of light.

The Easter Vigil is about that light, a symbol of the risen Christ. The same basic symbolism applies to the current Eastern Churches, certainly the Byzantine.[3] It is really rather amazing that, except in a few "modern" places, ancient wax or oil lights should persist in liturgical symbolism.

The Easter Vigil has figured prominently in twentieth-century western liturgical thinking. In 1951 Roman Catholics were permitted to celebrate the Vigil during the night, rather than on the morning of Holy Saturday, thus restoring the original character of a nocturnal service, and (it was hoped) restoring it to being a *popular* liturgy.[4] Then, in 1956, a revised Holy Week rite appeared, which pioneered the way subsequently taken by the (more radical) revisions of all the Roman Catholic services after the Second Vatican Council.[5] It is no coincidence, then, that it all began with the Vigil. The Constitution on the Sacred Liturgy (1963) has a strongly paschal flavor to it, thanks to the work of such scholars as Casel and Bouyer.[6] Moreover, much of their work was mediated to several of the Western Churches not in communion with Rome, who had begun to find their sixteenth- and seventeenth-century liturgical books too austere in their celebration of Holy Week.[7]

But the essential *shape* of the Vigil in 1951, 1956, and 1970 is the same as it was, consisting of four main sections: the ceremonies of light, the vigil readings, the baptismal liturgy, and the eucharist. The only main variants in this shape are that (1) in 1951 a new feature, the renewal of baptismal vows, appeared in order to stress the baptismal character of the rite,[8] and (2) in 1970 the baptismal liturgy, whether celebrated in whole or in part, i.e., only with the renewal of vows, should follow the liturgy of the word in the eucharist, thus bringing together in close relation the two main units of Scripture, the vigil readings and the readings from the eucharistic synaxis.[9]

By contrast, the (ecumenical) British Joint Liturgical Group, both in 1971 and in 1983,[10] produced in its *Holy Week Services* a rite which appeared at first sight to be entirely new, but which—as we shall see—is a variant on a Jerusalem experiment of the tenth century;[11] this new feature is the reversal of the traditional order, so that the liturgy *begins* with *all* the readings (vigil and synaxis), and then leads into light, the first part of the service being in some degree of darkness. English Roman Catholics followed this inversion,[12] so that it is important to study both precedent and meaning in the development of this complex and ancient liturgy. It is, perhaps, worth pointing out that many non-Roman Catholic churches have experienced difficulty in popularizing the entire Easter Vigil,[13] partly because of the strangeness of a late-night or early-morning act of worship on such a day, and partly because of a traditional attachment to Easter *morning* as the occasion for the Easter eucharist. Many of these Churches have sought to adapt the Vigil in various ways. Two predominate: one is to curtail the Vigil before the eucharist in order not to detract from it the next day; the other is to begin the main Easter morning eucharist with some ceremonies of light, which of course cannot possibly be functional (unless the weather is particularly inclement), but are exclusively symbolic.[14]

MEANING OF THE VIGIL

But what are the "precedent" and "meaning" of the Vigil? It is necessary, first, to try to probe behind the different kinds of Holy Week ceremonies down the ages in order to distinguish between *three* kinds of liturgical celebration

Unitive Celebrations

The first is what may be termed "unitive."[15] By this is meant precisely the vigil rite, in its ancient form, which, allowing for certain of its own developments, existed on its own, without any preparatory "historical" rites till the fourth century. The "unitive" celebration is, in essence, the all-night vigil, which culminated in the Easter eucharist, of which we have early testimony. By the third century it had strong baptismal associations, and it may well have had special ceremonies of light, but whether these were only that of Lucernare (to introduce a vigil) or a simple lighting of the lamps (to introduce vespers) is not clear from the evidence. The point is, however, that the "unitive" celebration is one of the death *and* resurrection of Christ.

Recent studies, particularly by Talley and Taft, have offset the assumption of Dix that we must drive a wedge between ante-Nicene "eschatological" celebration in the liturgy, and post-Nicene "historical" celebration.[16] There is evidence for the growth of some "historicism" of what later became Holy Week in the third century. But the main liturgy is the vigil: it shows signs of conservatism already; it is sufficiently important to become baptismal (for obvious reasons); and, above all, its liturgical paraphernalia at this early stage are in a kind of *code*. You celebrate the death and resurrection in light, then in word, then in baptism, then in eucharist; that is how it evolves, although word and eucharist form the primitive core. It develops some days of preparation and fasting, especially for the baptizands. But it can stand on its own.

Rememorative Celebrations

The second is what may be termed "rememorative."[17] By this is meant a liturgy which is part of a series of "events," which belong to one another, and which are celebrated in such a way that they have a direct relationship to each other; but the key to their style is important, because they reflect on different aspects of the mystery of salvation, without re-enacting them. "Rememorative" Holy Week liturgy is exactly what Egeria encounters at Jerusalem.[18] On the afternoon of Palm Sunday, the crowd walks down the Mount of Olives, but there is no donkey in sight. On Thursday before Easter, there were, probably, two eucharists, but there is no attempt to locate them at the purported point at which the Last Supper happened.[19] Indeed, one of the striking features of that singularly fatiguing liturgical program which she witnesses is that it resembles more a lengthy play, with some intermissions for sleep and food here and there, with a vague connection between them. Still, there is the element of code, for the relic of the cross is venerated for what it symbolizes, not what it represents.

Representational Celebrations

The third is what may be termed "representational."[20] By this is meant a liturgy which deliberately and consciously seeks to "re-present" a past event in a dramatic manner. Although there are many later medieval examples of it, particularly in developments like the stations of the cross, it is hard to know precisely when "representational" Holy Week liturgy begins. Perhaps the (later) Georgian Lectionary gives us a glimpse of the phenomenon on Good Friday, where the veneration has been dropped in favor of the rite of the "burial of the cross"; certainly the (even) later Byzantine "burial of *Christ*" with the *epitaphion* is representational.[21] But what of the west, in the Vigil? A fine example is to be found in the drama of the *quem quaeritis*,[22] a charming tenth-century case of what we used to call "making the liturgy meaningful," in which different robed persons act out the parts of the women coming to the tomb, and the angel tells them that the Lord is risen. The important innovation, however, is that the *quem quaeritis* not only appeared in several versions, but occupied varying positions in the Easter liturgies, whether at the vigil or elsewhere. Frere saw it in the tenth-century *Winchester Troper*, at the start of the vigil.[23] For dramatic and liturgical reasons, the popularity of this drama is connected with another representational ceremony, the deposition of the cross, which may well have started in Jerusalem and been taken west in the liturgical trade-route. As part of the vigil, whether at the start, or (as sometimes was the case) elsewhere, the *quem quaeritis* is not in any form of code, but is intended to dramatize, and it would mix strangely with the archaic nature of the vigil, although this, in itself, would serve to heighten the "realism" of the meaning of the drama. The reason for such representational liturgy is well-known, and is described in a contemporary document as "strengthening of the faith of the unlearned common persons and neophytes."[24]

Various criteria could be employed to assess these three modes of liturgical celebration. "Unitive" is austere, primitive, and (if you are liturgically patient) the kind of celebration which is theologically least demanding. "Rememorative" is, as we have seen, mid-way, still employs code, but requires elaboration, preparation, and, most important of all, a vibrant community, in order to provide concentration. "Representational" is the culmination of the pictorial mind, the result of popular piety, potentially vulgar, and perhaps appealing to the "cathedral" rather than the "monastic" type of spirituality. In spite of all that we liturgists keep saying, I suspect that in both Roman Catholic as well as Protestant traditions, "representational" spirituality, with all its theological demands on the *cognoscenti*, is far more common than "rememorative," even though the classical liturgical reforms of the west in recent years have provided us with "rememorative" rites.[25] But it should be no surprise that the twentieth century should, in some way, contain a sort of liturgical and spiritual residue of two millennia of history. The Easter mystery is something bigger than any conciliar definition, much more elusive of meaning than the most speculative theologians can express.

Set in this wider historical context, the vigil assumes a variegated form, and the question of its appropriateness, effectiveness, and (indeed) its popularity today only serves to heighten the question of its inner meaning, for the more encoded a liturgy is, the more flexible it can be; contrariwise, the more precisely defined it is (and "representational"), the less flexible it can be, and, perhaps, the more likely to be discarded when it runs out of inner resources to convey meaning to a fresh generation. The popularity of piety that is "representational" rather than "rememorative" in its style may account for the failure of the vigil, in its original, lengthy, and demanding form to commend itself to may Christians, past as well as present. This may explain why some celebrations today follow, in their own way, the lead taken by those medievals who incorporated the *quem quaeritis* into the vigil; thus the vigil lessons are sometimes supplemented and interpreted by different forms of drama, mime, and dance, often subtly rememorative, often outlandishly representational. On the other hand, many people who have totally imbibed the spirit of the renewed liturgies prefer the vigil to remain in its archaic code, void of any "spelling out" whatever.

HISTORY

The vigil, down through history, has been the object of accumulation, adaptation, and anticipation, as the eastern and western evidence demonstrates. Looking first at the east, it is clear from Egeria's account that what took place at Jerusalem differed little from back home in Spain (or Gaul), but the fifth-century Armenian Lectionary tells us that the vigil begins in the evening with the lighting of a candle, continues with twelve lessons, during which (one assumes) the baptisms take place; then at midnight the newly-baptized enter with the bishop, and the eucharist is celebrated.[26] There are three manuscripts of the Lectionary, two of which imply the

same practice with the lights as Egeria observed of the Lucernare, namely, that the light was taken from a lamp kept burning permanently in the tomb, a custom easily associated with
Jerusalem, but not readily imitable elsewhere, for the third
manuscript (which perhaps represents a later usage, outside
Jerusalem) makes something of a symbolism of three lights.
Moreover, the Lectionary implies an abbreviation of the Jerusalem light since the time of Egeria, in line with the other services, and perhaps not unconnected with the demise of Cyril.
In all the other documents, the light-ceremony is followed by
the vigil-readings, in which there are few variants, though
Bertonière has shown the way in which the original twelve
differed from Constantinople, which in turn left its imprint
on Jerusalem later on.[27] The Georgian Lectionary,[28] written in
the tenth century but reflecting liturgical practice perhaps as
far back as the eighth, begins the liturgy with three processions, the kiss of peace, the blessing of one candle, the lighting of other candles, and the opening of doors. The processions involve three thuribles. The candle-ceremony has been
elaborated with a single candle; and many others, perhaps for
functional as well as symbolic purposes. At any rate, the
threefold procession may well symbolize the three days in the
tomb, as Bertonière suggests. It is in the document called *Hagios Stauros 43*[29] that we find the most radical development,
for not only do we find a combination of the vigil with Saturday evening vespers (the liturgy of the word includes the
opening and concluding formulas for vespers, *Nunc Dimittis*
and all), but the structure of the whole liturgy is a superb example of an all-embracing accumulation:[30]

1. Beginning of Vespers of Burial of Christ
2. Sharing of light, with *phos hilaron*
3. Vigil-readings
4. Incensing of shrines
5. Patriarch's entry to tomb and sharing of holy fire among
   all
6. Procession from Anastasis to Basilica (this had been earlier Jerusalem practice)
7. Conclusion of Vespers
8. Patriarch goes to baptistery for baptisms

9. Return to Basilica for synaxis-readings and remainder of liturgy

10.Concluding lesson (Jn 20:1-18) and incensing and anointing of tomb (Orthros follows).[31]

It will be apparent that this liturgy, which is monastic in origin, distinguishes between vesper-light and paschal-light, in that the former precedes the vigil-readings, and the latter follows it, so that it occupies a position in direct relation to the liturgies of baptism and eucharist. Moreover, the theology behind this differentiation appears to be suggested by the connection between baptism and the eucharistic lessons which follow, in particular, the traditional Jerusalem epistle, Romans 6:3-11.[32] The whole service points to the tomb, for that is where the eucharist is celebrated, using the Jerusalem liturgy, that of St. James.

The relationship between vespers and vigil is outside the scope of this study.[33] What surprises the western reader is that the light-ceremony as it developed at Jerusalem does not appear either in the Constantinople liturgy, nor in the various monastic rites studied by Bertonière, and he gives as his reason the special Jerusalem association of the light with the resurrection of Christ, and the special tales associated with the miraculous provision of this light.[34] Current Byzantine practice begins the second eucharist (at midnight) with the Good Friday "Canon" (repeated from Good Friday); which is followed by some light-ceremonies; which lead into matins, and the liturgy, which is celebrated during vespers. The president chants a long prayer, lights his candle, from which everyone else's candles are lit, and there is a procession.[35]

Not so in the west. In (what we may take to be) the seventh-century Visigothic rite, we already find an adaptation of the Jerusalem rite. The bishop and clergy gather together in the sacristy whose door is firmly shut; a light is struck from flint; a lamp is lit, with which the paschal candle is lit; the bishop blesses both lamp and candle; all clergy light their own candles from it; a deacon carries the candle through the door, now suddenly opened, for maximum dramatic effect; the people light their candles now. The procession moves to the altar, where both lamp and candle are solemnly blessed, each by a deacon.[36] In this old Spanish cathedral liturgy[37] are to be seen the three stages of the light-ceremonies which become predominant in the west, namely: a) the provision of the light; b) the bearing of the light into the church; and c) the sharing of the light among the faithful.[38] Most texts which have come down to us presuppose a single initial candle (a "paschal" one), which is treated dramatically, but older Roman usage is perhaps reflected in *Ordo Romanus* 23 (probably eighth century), where two large standard candles are carried into church, and remain on either side of the presidential chair, wherever that might be placed in the course of the liturgy (these candles are lit from a candle kept secretly lit since Good Friday).[39] *Ordo Romanus* 17 (late eighth century), on the other hand, is Gallicanized, and assumes a special paschal candle.[40] In fact, evidence for the special candle of this kind emanates from the north of Italy, thanks to some chance references, and two texts surviving and attributed to Ennodius of Pavia (513-521).[41] Schmidt's chart of light-ceremonies in his study of Holy Week texts shows that the use of a special paschal candle comes from north of Rome,[42] as none of the Gregorian documents mentions it (adhering in one case to the older tradition of the standard candlesticks). However, Northern Italy, Gaul, and Spain all knew elaborate paschal proclamations, which set out the Easter victory in rich rhetorical terms, with Old Testament typology. The Spanish doublet of lamp and candle is intriguing; the diaconal prayers are in preface-form, but only the candle-prayer has an invocation, for God's blessing on the candle, the Easter celebration, and the whole church.[43]

All three stages of the light-ceremonies in the west, however, betray Jerusalem influence. The provision of light is occasionally from a lamp kept lit from two days before. The procession fits in with what we have already seen, as does the sharing of the light. The difference, however, is that the western texts more self-consciously theologize about these inventions. And two quite different approaches to the entry of the light can be discerned, Spanish drama (from Jerusalem), and gradual sharing of the light (either with the threefold cry of *Lumen Christi* or the singing of the Prudentius hymn *Inventor Rutuli*).[44] And in the west, these special ceremonies assumed an exclusively paschal symbolism and association, whereas in the east, light-symbolism is more naturally part of liturgical tradition, because of its use at festal vespers, with *phos hilaron*. But the vigil is increasingly anticipated in the west. As early as the eighth century, it is celebrated in the afternoon of Holy Saturday; in the twelfth, it starts at noon, paving the way for the ultimate curtailment of its meaning, Holy Saturday morning.[45]

From this brief and selective historical survey, a number of fundamental issues can be observed.

1. The vigil sticks out, on its own, from the rest of Holy Week, especially if it is celebrated in an authentic way, i.e., it is a lengthy service, without much omission of lessons, and it begins late at night or very early the next morning.

2. Eastern practice blesses the light in order to share it, whereas later western practice blesses a "paschal" candle as a special focus.

3. Western light-ceremonies elaborate through duplication (the source of light, as well as the special candle), and dramatic considerations.

4. The ceremonies of light *either* become specifically paschal (as in the west); *or* are moved to a special position in the liturgy in order to be distinctive from vesper-light (*HS* 43); *or* they follow a short liturgy of "darkness," burst out in an epiphany of light, and lead into eucharist (later Byzantine).

5. Where the light is provided from a lamp kept lit from Good Friday (or, in some cases, Maundy Thursday), we see the phenomenon of linking together different aspects of the mystery of salvation, in a "rememorative" type of liturgy.

6. Distinctive theologies of light can be discerned from euchology, for whereas paschal proclamations cry out with the deliverance from sin and death (in the west), Byzantine Christians pray for illumination and renewal, as an epiphany.[46]

CONFLICTS AND COMPLICATIONS

What, then, of the apparent conflict between the Missal of

1970 and the Joint Liturgical Group's inversion of the traditional order? A conservative response would be that the west has only known the sequence of light-word-eucharist-baptism. But the issues are more complex than that. *HS 43* is a document which arose out of a complex situation, probably copied in the first part of the twelfth century, but reflecting earlier Jerusalem usage; evidence suggests that, thanks to the destruction of the Holy City in 1009, it was long out of date, and was only copied in order to demonstrate past practice. Nonetheless, the fact that it was deemed worthy of copying is itself witness to the importance of the tradition it represents. It is, in fact, the most carefully thought-out of all the rites we have so far seen, as well as being the most inclusive. But the major difference between it and the trend to invert light and word is that *HS 43* divides the vigil readings from the eucharistic synaxis by the light-ceremonies and the baptism, whereas, in the Joint Liturgical Group proposals, *all* the lessons are read in semi-darkness, which (of course) is in line with the Joint Liturgical Group's previous work, which has tended to assume that office and synaxis readings are the same.[47] Thus, there is a theological weakness in such a drastic streamlining, in that the Easter gospel, which in *HS 43* is read in a blaze of light, is in the Joint Liturgical Group's proposals to be read in semi-darkness.[48]

But there is a further complicating factor. Those who have participated in the vigil with the readings before the light-ceremonies observe that the light-ceremonies come as a climax, with a strongly Easter symbolism (the rationale of *HS 43*), and also remark on the fact that the lessons "feel" like a vigil,[49] since they are read in darkness. In other words, the inversion results in the lessons providing an atmosphere of waiting, whereas the traditional western order appears to give the impression that the "waiting" is over and done with; an impression heightened if liberties are taken that result in the number of readings being reduced to only a few. It is a mark of the poverty of our new liturgies that we are not able to have lessons in two different places at the same service, although the American Episcopal Prayer Book of 1979 (which also allows for prefixing the Easter morning eucharist with light-ceremonies) in fact keeps a more traditional order in the full text of the vigil rite, where the eucharistic synaxis comes only after the baptism.[50]

Even in the Roman Catholic Church, after 1951, we are still dealing with a *revival* of something old, which sometimes will need adaptation in order to fit appropriately into the needs and temperaments of different cultures. This is bound to be as true of "rememorative" rites as of "representational," though (perhaps fortunately) "representational" rites do not become embedded in official liturgies as easily as the "rememorative" ones. And a concomitant difficulty here is how to make new liturgies which can find their own climate, so that the "official" text is not composed in order to define too closely exactly what the people are meant to experience. In this sense, modern rites are sufficiently flexible in the content of the liturgy of light (in theory at least) that it can be performed in various ways, to suit local circumstances, the emphasis falling on the *thanksgiving* over light, rather than its *provision*.[51]

The Paschal Vigil's structure, however, depends not on the light-ceremonies, but on our deployment of the "word" in the Easter Vigil. Both the Missal of 1970 and the Joint Liturgical Group of 1971 and 1983 have produced vigil liturgies that are just a bit too "logical" and "clean," in which "structure" dominates rather than "shape." The secret of the Easter Vigil liturgy, surely, lies in its combination of "watching" and "renewal," which is a strong argument for separating the vigil-lessons and those of the eucharistic synaxis. For this reason, the American Episcopal Prayer Book (1979) and the Missal of 1970 provide the most flexible and at the same time most archaic vigil liturgies, consisting of light (in a simple form), vigil-lessons, baptism, and eucharist (starting with the synaxis). If the *HS 43* solution is to be tried, then its shape should be followed more closely, with vigil-readings leading into a feast of light, leading into baptism, leading into eucharistic synaxis and celebration of the Mass.[52] Although light-symbolism may flit around and suggest new experiences of the risen Lord, it is firmly in the "light of Christ" that the gospel of his resurrection should be read. Theology must not predefine liturgy, otherwise liturgy becomes cumbersome and didactic; but liturgy should be theological, in having an inner logic which points us again and again, at Easter, to our rebirth as children of God.

Comparative Chart: East, West, and Modern West

1. EAST

Egeria (4th c.)	Armenian Lect. (5th c.)	Georgian Lect. (8th-11th c.)	HS (10th-11th c.)	Modern Byzantine
Vigil "like us"	Candle lit (P adds "3")	Candle lit (L adds)	Vespers of Burial	Good Friday Canon
...with light?	Vigil R's: 12, w. prayers	3 processions	"phos hilaron"	bl. of light
Readings		bl. of "new" candle	Vigil R'S	procession
		opening of doors	Light: from tomb	Mattins
		"phos hilaron"	end of Vespers	
Baptisms (during R's)	Baptisms (during R's)	Vigil R's	Baptisms	Synaxis
Synaxis	Synaxis	Baptisms (during R's)	Synaxis	Eucharist
Eucharist	Eucharist	Synaxis	Eucharist	
		Eucharist		

2. WEST

Liber Ordinum (7th c.)	GeV	OR 17 (c.790 "Ga-Rom")	OR 23 (700-50 "Rom")	PRG (c.950 Mainz)
bl. of lamp/candle	Lighting of P candle	Lighting of P candle	2 standard c's	Candle blessed, lit
ministers share light		(from Good Friday light)	(from Good Friday)	(GeV Prayers, + alt.)
sudden opening of doors		Sol. blessing		Proc. into Ch:
sharing		new procession of entry,		(silent, or hymn)
sol. blessing; lamp, candle	sol. bl.	with candles		7 acolytes' torches lit
				Exsultet
				Everything lit
Vigil R's	Vigil R's	Vigil R's	Vigil R's	Vigil R's
Baptisms	Baptisms	Baptisms	Baptisms	Baptisms
Synaxis	Synaxis	Synaxis	Synaxis	Synaxis
Eucharist	Eucharist	Eucharist	Eucharist	Eucharist

3. MODERN WEST

MR 1570	MR 1970	JLG (1971, 1983)	American BCP (1979)	C of E (1986)=MR 1970
bl. of new fire	bl. of new fire	Vigil R's	bl. of new fire	Vigil R's
lighting of 3-candle	lighting of P candle	Synaxis	lighting of P candle	lighting of candle
Lumen Xti proc.	Lumen Xti proc.	lighting of candle	Lumen Xti proc.	Lumen Xti proc.
(gradual sharing)	(gradual sharing)	Lumen Xti proc.	(gradual sharing)	(gradual sharing)
Exsultet: P candle lit	Exsultet	(gradual sharing)	Exsultet	Exsultet
(everything lit)	(everything lit)	Exsultet	(everything lit)	(everything lit)
Vigil R's	Vigil R's	(everything lit)	Vigil R's	Synaxis
Bl. of Bap. water	Synaxis	Baptism/vows	Baptism/vows	Baptism/vows
Synaxis	Baptisms/vows	Eucharist	Synaxis	Eucharist
Eucharist	Eucharist		Eucharist	

1. EAST: light is vesperal, and is eventually "rationalised" into being paschal in HS 43.
2. WEST: drama (showing light/processions) and duplication (blessings): some rationalisation (OR 23's "2' candles'); NB Spanish lamp.
3. MODERN WEST: reintroduction of baptismal character; questionable relationship of Vigil R's/synaxis; flexible texts (and timing);...but where does the light come, before or after the Vigil lections?

Notes

1. See, for instance, Paul Bradshaw's excellent paper, delivered at the Ninth Meeting of the *Societas Liturgica*, Vienna, 1983, "Patterns of Ministry," reprinted in *Studia Liturgica* 15 (1982/1983) 49-64 (French translation in *La Maison-Dieu* 154 [1983] 127-150).

2. N. Hamilton, *Monty: The Making of a General 1877-1942* (London: Hamish Hamilton, 1981) 224ff.

3. See E. Mercenier, *La Prière des églises de rite byzantin*, vol. 2 (Monastère de Chevetogne, 1948) 267ff.

4. Text in H. Schmidt, *Hebdomada Sancta*, vol. 1 (Rome: Herder, 1956) followed by full study, vol. 2 (1957) with texts on the 1951 and 1956 rites. (= Schmidt). See also the various articles in *La Maison-Dieu* 37 (1954) and 41 (1955), both of which were devoted to the Holy Week liturgy.

5. See note 4 above.

6. Two (now dated) studies were O. Casel, "Art und Sinn der Ältesten Christlichen Osterfeier," *Jahrbuch für Liturgiewissenschaft* 14 (1934) 1-78 (French tr. = *La Fête de Pâques dans l'église des pères*, Lex Orandi, vol. 37 [Paris: Editions du Cerf, 1963]) and L. Bouyer, *Le Mystère pascal*, Lex Orandi, vol. 4 (Paris: Editions du Cerf, 1947); on the Decree and its background, see P. Jounel, "La Constitution sur la liturgie: De sa préparation à sa mise en application," *La Maison-Dieu* 155 (1983), e.g., p. 14, where Jounel draws attention to the "compétence et ferveur" with which Archbishop H. Jenny, of Cambrai, stressed the importance of the paschal character of the liturgy.

7. J.T. Martin, *Christ Our Passover: The Liturgical Observance of Holy Week* (London: SCM, 1958), with texts, adapted modern Roman/ English medieval; and R. Greenacre, *The Sacrament of Easter*, Studies in Christian Worship, vol. 4 (London: Faith Press, 1965), commentary-type sermons; revised edition coauthored with Jeremy Haselock, *The Sacrament of Easter* (Leominster: Gracewing, 1989).

8. The entirely new character of this ingredient is frequently overlooked; David Tripp draws a parallel between the modern fashion for baptismal-vows-renewal and the traditional (eighteenth century) renewal of the "covenant" in the Methodist Churches, see D.H. Tripp, *The Renewal of the Covenant in the Methodist Tradition* (London: Epworth, 1969) 116-118, 123-124, 140-141, 148, 149, 159-161, 184-185, 212. It is interesting to note that the Covenant renewal is made the basis for the British Joint Liturgical Group's (see note 10 below) service for the Tuesday of Holy Week, pp. 24-26 (1971) and pp. 36-39 (1983), but a specifically baptismal character is introduced, which does not appear in the British Methodist Covenant service, which

normally takes place on a Sunday near the beginning of the calendar year, see *The Methodist Service Book* (London: Methodist Publishing House, 1975) D 1-11.

9. *Missale Romanum*, editio typica (Vatican City: Typis Polyglottis Vaticanis, 1970) 266ff. Some years ago Hermann Schmidt indicated to me in correspondence that no proper study of the new Roman Catholic rites of Holy Week had yet appeared; nothing in the meantime has been published.

10. R.C.D. Jasper, ed., *Holy Week Services* (London: SPCK and Epworth, 1971[1]) 34ff; and D.C. Gray, ed., *Holy Week Services* (revised and expanded) (London: SPCK, 1983[2]) 76ff. The JLG was formed in 1963, with representatives from the major Churches of the U.K.; by 1971 the Roman Catholics were full members.

11. The idea for reversing light and word became popular in the Church of England in the 1960s in the Diocese of Southwark, see Gerald Hudson, "A Diocesan Lead," in C.P.M. Jones, ed., *A Manual for Holy Week* (London: SPCK, 1967) 83ff., where Hudson writes: "So . . . we come in the late evening to a church in darkness to await the good news of Easter." (See Gordon Wakefield's introductory essay to the first edition of the Joint Liturgical Group services, p. 15: "The key to the understanding of the whole service is not in the fact of our entrance into the Church but of Christ's entrance into the world. Therefore the readings have been placed first . . .") The writer knew this reversal of the order at Theological College, in Salisbury: by 1970 it was traditional, although he was responsible for changing back to the older western order in 1972. On the Jerusalem orders, see below.

12. The influence of the JLG proposals is clear, since Roman Catholics were full members (and no longer "observers") by 1971, and both the 1971 and 1983 vigil rites employed adapted versions of the 1970 Missal texts. See *Lord, by Your Cross and Resurrection: Celebrating Holy Week* (St. Thomas More Centre for Pastoral Liturgy, 1979).

13. This problem is shared by many, Roman Catholics too, as witness the (relatively) few numbers who attend the Vigil Eucharist, in comparison with the crowds who come on Easter morning; cathedrals, monasteries, and special parishes appear to be an exception, for obvious reasons.

14. See *The Book of Common Prayer* (New York: Seabury, 1979), American Episcopal, which has the entire vigil liturgy (pp. 285-295), but the preceding notes permit that "When the Vigil is not celebrated, the Service of Light may take place at a convenient time before the Liturgy on Easter Day" (p. 284). This is increasingly popular in Anglican circles, even when the vigil is celebrated in such a way that

it terminates before the eucharist. The permutations are endless: in one old English parish church, where Easter Sunday Evensong is still the popular service, the liturgy on Easter Sunday evening would conclude with a procession to the font, for the renewal of baptismal vows. One Anglican Theological College starts the vigil with the liturgy of light, late on the Saturday evening, continues through the night with an extended "watch" (with readings at certain points), and concludes with a baptismal eucharist at dawn. This is perhaps the most authentic of all, because the vigil is hard work, rather than a liturgical "dessert." The practice at Taizé has been to make every weekend a "mini"-paschal celebration, and to connect all the Holy Week liturgies together during Holy Week itself, as witness their *Liturgies pascales à Taizé* (Taizé, 1971). The Swiss Reformed church has tried to introduce the vigil, see B. Bürki, "La célébration de l'aube de Pâques à la Collégiale de Neuchâtel," *Questions liturgiques* 1982, 195-216. All these development are witness to the ecumenical potential of Holy Week, in its many forms.

15. See Casel, "Art und Sinn."

16. T.J. Talley, "History and Eschatology in the Primitive Pascha," *Worship* 57 (1973) 212-221, and "Liturgical Time in the Ancient Church: The State of Research," *Studia Liturgica* 14 (1982) 34-39; see also R.F. Taft, "Historicism Revisited," *Studia Liturgica* 14 (1982) 97-109 (reprinted in Robert Taft: *Beyond East and West: Problems in Liturgical Understanding* [Washington, D.C.: The Pastoral Press, 1984] 15-30). These views *contra* G. Dix, *The Shape of the Liturgy* (London: Dacre/Black, 1945) 333ff.

17. See O.B. Hardison, Jr., *Christian Rite and Christian Drama in the Middle Ages* (Baltimore: Johns Hopkins Press, 1969[2]) 139ff; see p. 141, "Placing major emphasis on nonrepresentational modes, the early Christian liturgy solved the problem by making the Resurrection as vivid as the Crucifixion through the ceremonies of Holy Saturday."

18. See text and commentary, J. Wilkinson, *Egeria's Travels* (London: SPCK, 1971) 138f., and 2d edition (Warminster: Aris and Phillips/Jerusalem: Ariel Publishing House, 1981) 138 f.; this second edition contains a list of addenda/corrigenda (pp. 311-333), preceded by a new essay, "Jewish Influence on the Jerusalem Liturgy" (pp. 298-310).

19. See Taft, "Historicism" 105, quoting from John F. Baldovin's study of stational Liturgy (Yale University Ph.D. Dissertation), published as *The Urban Character of Christian Worship: The Origins, Development, and Meaning of Stational Liturgy*, Orientalia Christiana Analecta, vol. 228 (Rome: Pontificium Institutum Studiorum Orientalium, 1987) 87ff.

20. See note 17 above.

21. C. Kekkelidze, *Jerousalimsky Kanonar VIIIe véka* (Tiflis, 1912) (this is what used to be referred to as the *"7th Century Canonarion"*; but see also G. Bertonière, *The Historical Development of the Easter Vigil and Related Services in the Greek Church*, Orientalia Christiana Analecta, vol. 193 (Rome: Pontificium Institutum Studiorum Orientalium, 1972) 10 ff. (and passim).

22. See Hardison, *Christian Rite* 178-219.

23. W.H. Frere, *The Winchester Troper*, Henry Bradshaw Society, vol. 8 (London, 1894) xvi (quoted in Hardison, *Christian Rite* 182, n. 12).

24. Quotation from the *Regularis Concordia*, of the "Depositio Crucis" ceremony, quoted in Hardison, *Christian Rite* p. 192, but used by him about the *quem quaeritis*, p. 196.

25. See A. Verheul, "Le mystère du Samedi Saint," *Questions liturgiques* (1984) 19-38, on the origin of the "burial of Christ" and its possible (re)-introduction as a fitting office for the morning of Holy Saturday.

26. Wilkinson, *Egeria's Travels* 270.

27. Bertonière, *Historical Development* 38-62.

28. Ibid. 25-27.

29. Ibid. 12-18, and 37 ff.

30. Ibid. Chart A 1-4.

31. It would be difficult to translate this order into western liturgical parlance in order to give it is proper "ambience." Roman Catholic procedure might look like this:

    Dne, ad adiuvandum me festina (opening of vespers)
    Office hymn (?)
    Psalmody
    Vigil-readings
    Ceremonies of light
    Magnificat
    Collects and conclusion of office

For Anglicans, the same, except, perhaps, substituting "Nunc Dimittis" for "Magnificat." Another change in *HS 43* is that the baptisms do *not* take place during the vigil-lessons, but happen between light-ceremonies and eucharist, which may also have been because of the need to associate the ceremonies of the new light with baptism.

32. The light-theme for vespers could be described as "doxology-illumination" (as is apparent from the hymn *phos hilaron*), whereas the Easter-light theme is one of spiritual illumination and renewal, in the Byzantine tradition; see also R.F. Taft, "Thanksgiving for the

Light: Towards a Theology of Vespers," *Diakonia* 13 (1978) 43ff. (reprinted in *Beyond East and West* 127-150).

33. See P.F. Bradshaw, *Daily Prayer in the Early Church*, Alcuin Club Collections, vol. 63 (London: SPCK, 1981; New York: Oxford University Press, 1982) 68-69, 84-87, 96-98, 100-110; see also R.F. Taft, *"Quaestiones Disputatae* in the History of the Liturgy of the Hours: The Origin of Nocturns, Matins, Prime," *Worship* 58 (1984) 130-158 (see esp. 151, n. 56).

34. Bertonière, *The Historical Development* 40ff.; but the later western development is less concerned with the *provision* of light from the *tomb* (and its accompanying drama), and more concerned with paschal typology, as the "paschal proclamation" shows.

35. See note 3 above. The procession involves the whole congregation, an imitation, perhaps, of earlier Jerusalem practice; whereas the western processions (including the Jerusalem-inspired Visigothic one) is for the dramatic showing of the light; see B. Capelle, "La procession du *Lumen Christi* au Samedi Saint," *Travaux liturgiques*, vol. 3 (Louvain: Centre Liturgique, 1967), 221-234; see also D.R. Dendy, *The Use of Lights in Christian Worship*, Alcuin Club Collections, vol. 41 (London: SPCK, 1959) 128ff.

36. See Capelle, "La procession" 223-224, and M. Férotin, *Le Liber Ordinum en usage dans l'église wisigothique et mozarabe d'Espagne du cinquième au onzième siècle*, Monumenta Ecclesiae Liturgica, vol. 5 (Paris: Didot, 1904) col. 208-211.

37. See Migne, PL 85:436ff. for the *Missale Mixtum* text.

38. The Old Gelasian (*GeV*) has a simple form, with the entry of ministers, signing and lighting of paschal candle, and the "Gelasian" proclamation (*ds mundi conditor*); one assumes that the congregation's candles were lit thereafter, prior to the vigil-lessons. The sharing of the light among the whole congregation only took place after the *Exsultet*, whether the procession into the church involved the paschal candle or not, and whether the procession was accompanied by the threefold cry of *Lumen Christi* or the hymn *Inventor Rutuli*; see Schmidt 812ff. The *Lumen Christi* procession takes over in the papal liturgy of the twelfth century (Schmidt 822), which Capelle traces *Ordo Romanus* 13A, an eighth-century Gallicanized Roman order ("La procession" n. 35).

39. Schmidt 512.

40. Ibid. 509.

41. Ibid. 633-637.

42. Ibid. 810.

43. See texts in Schmidt from *GeV*, 362-363 and 637-638; see also note 38 above; Ambrosian, 645-647; the "old Italian" recension, 824-

826; as well as the (much Gallicanized) later Roman version, 639-645. Why the Spanish doublet? Perhaps because the *source* of light for the paschal candle (and, one may conjecture, subsequent lightings at Easter services) should be given prominence, too. (See the new Swiss Reformed text used at Neuchâtel, quoted fully by Bürki, "La célébration" 205, n. 28.)

44. See Capelle, "La Procession," note 35 above and note 38. There was considerable local variety over this, for example in late medieval Scandinavia, which may have had to do with the size of the church; see B. Strömberg's detailed study of the available documents in his introduction to *The Manual from Bystorp*, Bibliotheca Liturgica Danica, vol. 2 (Egtved: Edition ApS, 1982) 32-43; whereas Odense has nine strophes, Bystorp (following Copenhagen) has the first three, omitting the last; Notmark, a small church building, omits it altogether, see K. Ottosen, *The Manual from Notmark*, Bibliotheca Liturgica Danica, vol. 1 (Copenhagen: Gad, 1969) 69, and noted by Strömberg (p. 37).

45. Schmidt 873-877.

46. One salient exception is the prayer *exaudi nos lumen indeficiens*, whose western archetype is in the old Spanish rite (bishop's blessing of the "lamp" in the sacristy), and which next appears as a blessing of "light" (*luminis*) in the (early eleventh-century) Sacramentary of Vich, but here it precedes a shorter version (*domine deus pater omnipotens, exaudi nos*), which also appears (in slightly varying forms) in the Pontificals of Albi and of Egbert, as well as the Romano-Germanic Pontifical (but here, for use on Maundy Thursday evening); the twelfth-century Roman pontificals place it back at the beginning of the vigil, as does the thirteenth-century Lateran Missal; texts in Schmidt 427, 555, 573, 610, 822; the later version appears in the 1570 Missal, and that of 1956, but not in 1970; see J. Bernal, "Vicisitudes literarias e históricas de la oración hispana 'Exaudi nos, Lumen indeficiens'," in *Miscellanea Liturgica in onore di Sua Eminenza il Cardinale Giacomo Lercaro*, vol. 2 (Rome, 1967) 1033-1044; see also N.K. Rasmussen, *Les Pontificaux du haut moyen-âge: Genèse du livre de l'évêque*, Thèse présentée en vue du doctorat avec spécialisation en Liturgie et en Théologie Sacramentaire (Århus, Denmark, 1977), vol. 1, 90. The Spanish archetype bears a striking resemblance in structure, theme, and through repetition of "light" (and cognates) with the Byzantine light-blessing (see note 3 above), although this latter is addressed to Christ; I strongly suspect a Jerusalem (common) origin for the Spanish vigil rite.

47. See R.C.D. Jasper, ed., *The Daily Office* (London: SPCK/Epworth, 1968); this book together with the earlier Sunday proposals

(also edited by Jasper), *The Calendar and Lectionary* (London: Oxford University Press, 1967) had a marked influence on subsequent liturgical revision in Britain, in the 1975 *Methodist Service Book*, the 1979 *Book of Common Order* (Presbyterian, Church of Scotland), and the 1980 *Alternative Service Book* (Church of England).

48. "The church is in complete darkness, except for a light to enable the readers to see the Bible on the lectern" (*Holy Week Services*, 1971, p.34); cf. "This service may be held either after dark on the Eve of Easter or in the morning of Easter Day. The Church shall if possible be in darkness, except for a light to enable the readers to see the Bible on the lectern" (*Holy Week Services*, 1983, p. 76; see also note 14 above).

49. Conversations with several colleagues.

50. See M. Hatchett, *Commentary on the American Prayer Book* (New York: Seabury, 1980) 243-250; Hatchett points out (p. 248) that the baptismal liturgy *may* (alternatively) come *after* the vigil-lessons and the eucharistic synaxis, but there is no further and more drastic alteration in the shape of the rite.

51. See notes 4 and 9 above for Roman Catholic texts.

52. The Church of England Liturgical Commission has produced official Holy Week services, in which the vigil operates on precisely this basis, beginning with Old Testament lessons, moving into light-ceremonies, and thereafter into the eucharistic synaxis; but provision is made for the old western structure, following the new Roman Catholic order, as well as some of the options mentioned above in note 14. (Bürki ("La célébration" 201) suggests that the vigil-liturgy should associate the reading of the Easter gospel closely with the liturgy of light, and for the same theological reasons we suggest.) For the Church of England texts, see *Lent, Holy Week, Easter: Services and Prayers* (London: Church House Publishing, 1986) 223ff. See also my own "On Keeping Holy Week," *Theology* 89, no. 727 (January 1986) 32-38.

11

Prayer over Light:
A Comparison between
the Easter Vigil
and Candlemas

A CURSORY GLANCE AT THE NEW SERVICE BOOKS OF THE WESTERN churches and their supplementary texts will reveal the growing popularity of the ceremonies of light. In this brief survey I want to concentrate on two important festival liturgies that use light in very special ways. One of them, the Easter Vigil, is deeply embedded in the liturgical year and is perhaps the oldest ingredient of it. The other, Candlemas (and for convenience I shall use the late medieval English title here) is usually relegated to the calendar, and has its own muddled history, being sometimes a feast of the Lord (and his Presentation in the temple), sometimes a feast of the Virgin Mary (and her Purification), and sometimes even a feast of Simeon. In providing a sort of extended comment on two lengthy essays,[1] I hope to show certain points of comparison of various kinds. But before looking in detail at both feasts in turn, it is worth drawing attention to the underlying issues.

The Easter Vigil, in its traditional western and eastern forms owes its origin to the early, "unitive" celebration of the death and resurrection of Christ that we can glimpse at from the ante-Nicene evidence. Light was provided because it was evening and therefore dark. One theological mystery, recounted in four Gospels in different ways, dominated the occasion, usually preceded by a lengthy series of Old Testament lessons.

Candlemas, on the other hand, is a late beginner. It was an important Jerusalem festival at the time of Egeria (end of the fourth century), but it is not until about three hundred years later that it appears to have been introduced at Rome. Although candles were carried in procession at the time of the Venerable Bede, the earliest texts for blessing the candles do not appear until the ninth century. The gospel for Candlemas is rich indeed, but it occurs only in Luke. And unlike the Easter Vigil, the candle ceremonies and procession do not have the close connection with the celebration of the day; the Gregorian Sacramentary simply has a *collecta* to start off the procession. To summarize history somewhat cavalierly, the Easter Vigil celebrates the death and resurrection in light, word, baptism, and eucharist, whereas Candlemas originally celebrates Presentation/Purification/*Hypapante* in a eucharist and then prefixes a penitential procession with a candle blessing.

The Easter Vigil

The blessing and provision of light at the Easter Vigil are a fascinating and complex story. In the east, light has never been *blessed* as such, but instead there is "thanksgiving over light," in a prayer which asks for spiritual illumination.[2] In the west, however, considerable variety is apparent. From the sixth century (perhaps earlier) texts appear for the *laus cerei* in the north of Italy, and, later, in the Gallican service books.[3] The two prayers attributed to Ennodius of Pavia (d. 521) open on the theme of fire and heat, continue in light, rejoice in the gift of salvation after offering the wax light to God, and end with an insistence that the church is not making a pagan sacrifice, nor a Jewish one, but celebrating the resurrection. The Visigothic rite has a doublet, first blessing the lamp, then the candle. The lamp blessing is more general, giving thanks for lights at a wedding, and with general themes of salvation. The candle prayer is a prolix affair, rich in imagery.

To this type of prayer, with its *sursum corda* opening, the seventh/eighth-century Gallican *Exultet* is prefixed. What becomes the standard Roman text is strongly paschal in its overtones, dwelling on the Passover typology, and even including one or the other of the two optional elements, the *felix culpa* section, or the *laus apium*. The old Ambrosian text goes off on its own, even bringing in the virgins bearing their lamps as they await the bridegroom. Beneath such later overlay there may lie an old, simple, "pure" Roman light prayer in the form of the Gelasian text, *deus mundi conditor*, which some of the Gregorian books include as an extra after the *Exsultet* and sits following prayer.[4] The next stage in the sequence of elaboration is the addition of the prayers for blessing the new fire. Local texts vary considerably, but it would seem that these are originally functional, as if (to use twentieth-century terms) it were a case of saying a short prayer when striking a match with which to light the candle. From the late eighth century onwards, directions and prayers begin to appear. In the late tenth century, the Sacramentary of Vich has the Visigothic blessing of a lamp in addition to the candle, and uses a prayer that is very similar to the Byzantine rite on this day, and which also resembles a prayer frequently used in the Candlemas light-prayer sequence.[5] But in many places, instead of the new fire being "struck." it was kept in a special place from Maundy Thursday or even Good Friday.

Nowadays we have trained ourselves in that lamentable presupposition that nothing must ever be said more than once in a liturgy. Our forebears did not approach God with that premise. More to the point, they were happy to mix together different light themes. The *Exsultet* family of prayers over the paschal candle is usually accentuated toward Passover. In fact, they often read a little like a sort of Christian Haggadah over Easter. Later individual prayers of the collect type that were used over the lamp or the new fire were obviously shorter, and therefore lacked the requirement to argue a particular case at some length.

Thus, the Easter Vigil remains essentially a vigil, with a small processional element within it.[6] The function of the light prayers is to give focus to the paschal candle, in the first instance, and only thereafter to the blessing of the new fire, whether the paschal candle was actually borne into church in procession, or (as in some places) convenience took over, and the new fire itself was carried in procession, to be used to light the paschal candle, already on its stand, only during the *Exsultet*. Euchology and dramatic action walk step by step, together.

Candlemas

We have already pointed out how the earliest light prayer for Candlemas dates from the ninth century. Toward the end of that century, the Sacramentary of St. Martin's Abbey, Tours, has some extra items. These ninth-century additions include, both here and in other books of this type, prayers over the ashes at the start of Lent and prayers over the palm branches on the Sunday before Easter.[7] The prayers thus belong to a growing need in liturgical development. The one in question, used as a source for one of the two candle prayers on this day in the 1970 Missal, does not actually *bless* the candles, but prays that they may light up the temple of God to his glory.[8] Most other individual pre-Mass prayers that are extant *do* bless the candles, and some of them stumble through the diverse themes of this day, whether of presenting Jesus, purifying Mary, or of Simeon (and Anna) greeting Jesus. One prayer, which occurs in the Collectar-Pontifical of Baturich of Regensburg (817-848), makes a brief mention of Simeon, but is more interested in the protection of the faithful by the blessed candles (cf. palm-bearing on Palm Sunday) and the prayers of Mary and the saints. The prayer also refers to wax as *apium liquor*, a theme known in some of the earlier *laus cerei* formulas in the Easter Vigil. The later pontificals and service books add further prayers, so that they begin to appear in clusters, moving in and out of related themes to do with the feast, as well as other features not directly connected (such as the one already noted like protection from evil and the prayers of the saints). The Romano-Germanic Pontifical produces a grandiose rite, with a lengthy procedure for the *preparation* of the candles (cf. the preparation of the oils on Maundy Thursday, and other special occasion rites). There are no fewer than seven blessings, one of which mentions Moses' use of oil-lamps. The twelfth-century Roman Pontifical has only five prayers, but the *Nunc*

Dimittis is included for the first time. The Narbonne Pontifical (same century) has a blessing of the new fire, rephrasing the corresponding prayers from the Easter Vigil. Such a development would seem to bring the medieval tendency to its peak. But there are further anomalies.

In many medieval rites, black or penitential colors are worn on this day, and yet this background is not allowed to affect the ideas of new prayers as they appear in the texts. There is, too, a growing preoccupation with the *source* of light, before the candles. Perhaps this is related to the fact that the procession and Mass had moved from its (original) pre-dawn position to much later in the morning. One might have expected the judgment theme, which is so strong in the second oracle of Simeon ("a sword shall pierce . . ." Lk 2:35), and those dark vestments to have had some effect on the prayer compositions. But that, perhaps, would be to expect too much. After all, no local light-prayer for the Easter Vigil takes up the theme of the disciples journeying to Emmaus.

Comparison 1 - Structural

In the Easter Vigil, the emphasis is on the provision of light. One paschal candle becomes the source from which all other candles are lit, for a dramatic entry into church during which (in some places in the Middle Ages) a hymn, *Inventor rutuli*, was often sung, instead of the threefold *Lumen Christi* cry. As usual, it is in secondary matters such as the initial provision of light (whether from flint or from a candle kept in a special place) that the most variety is to be found. At Candlemas, however, the original structure of providing candles, followed by a *collecta*, followed by a procession to the stational church for Mass, gives way to an increasingly elaborate series of blessings prior to the distribution. The *distribution* of *blessed* candles takes on an importance of its own, corresponding with the Easter Vigil's lighting candles through a chain of other candles, tracing origin to a prominently blessed, single source. In this respect, Candlemas has as much in common with Ash Wednesday and Palm Sunday, a pre-Mass rite. But it is to be expected, since the rites are of the same post-Carolingian vintage. It should also be noted that the entrance procession at the vigil eventually keeps the old Jerusalem *Lumen Christi* cry, whereas the Candlemas procession in its fullest form always has a chant.

Comparison 2 - Euchological

This is harder to be precise about, since a case could be argued for connecting any light prayer with another. We have noted the sporadic use of the blessing of new fire at Candlemas in a prayer borrowed from the Sacramentary of Vich for the blessing of fire at the Easter Vigil.[9]

But the prayer-themes, apart from this, are distinct. Easter light is about light in darkness, but for the Passover, celebrating the fact of the resurrection, sometimes taking in eschatological symbolism of waiting for the bridegroom's appearance. Candlemas light, by contrast, dwells more on the individual dramas of the gospel pericope, with its rich character portrayal. We take this for granted, but it needs to be noted, especially as the Easter Vigil has *four* gospels for its story, Candlemas has only *one*.

Comparison 3 - Inculturation

Both the Easter Vigil and Candlemas use light, but each uses it in a different manner, and the later overlay of the centuries fails to obscure the original reasoning behind each feast. For Easter, it is a case of the Easter community celebrating the resurrection and affirming that the light shines in the darkness, illuminating the meaning of the Old Testament lessons. For Candlemas, it is a case of the community rising before dawn in order to take the Roman stational liturgy on a solemn occasion to its proper place. The use of candles at both is probably originally eastern,[10] but each has survived by careful adaptation and revival in the west.

But we live at a critical times in the development of the western liturgies, and it is important to see in *both* of these venerable rites the essential role of ambiguity in the celebration and the danger of attempting to resolve the ambiguities. The Easter Vigil ought to be hard work, not domesticated into a slick easy service, with as few Old Testament lessons as possible, perhaps culminating in an all-night champagne party.

Similarly, the trouble with the revised Candlemas rites is that they concentrate exclusively upon the Christmas aspect of the feast, and avoid the darker feature, which really replaces Candlemas as the hinge between Christmas and Easter. It is interesting that the Easter Vigil and Candlemas should have developed separately the practice of using dark-colored vestments for the first part, and changing into white for the Mass. Yet in the twentieth-century revisions, with their passion for systematic thought, white has been substituted throughout. Perhaps this was a wise move, as there are few things more fussy than seeing clergy change their clothes half-way through a performance. But as both these rites become increasingly popular (the era of evening eucharists has made Candlemas a winner in some circles), there is a danger of eliminating ambiguity from both these rites. At the risk of sounding just like the very systematically minded people I frequently criticize, the abiding lesson of prayer over light in both these venerable liturgies is that they keep exploring new light themes, biblical as well as experiential. In an age that rejoices in highly developed technology that so frequently goes wrong, perhaps it is our primeval instincts that enable us to delight in primitive symbolism. God's marvelous light is indeed a gift for thanksgiving, but rather than something cozy, sentimental and nice, it is also a terrifying indication of judgment. Perhaps when prayers are next written, some of that rich ambiguity might come through, so that we do not have to leave it all to scripture readings and clerical attire.

Comparison 4 - Theological

In his classic work of Christian apologetics, *The Foolishness of God*, John Austin Baker begins by referring to "the indescribably exciting, rewarding, and privileged vocation of theology,"[11] and goes on to say: "In talking about God, as in so many other fields, we need to ask where we have come from, if we would rightly understand where we are going and why."[12] In this brief comparative analysis of two distinct but related uses of the symbolism of light in the liturgical year, it will have become apparent that history and theology intermesh, and that light shining in darkness, whether at the paschal celebration or at the Presentation in the Temple, is not just a quaint survival of an archetypical custom for the High Church-minded, but it is a proclaiming, in the darkness of this world, of where the key to *all* illumination ultimately comes from—Jesus Christ, the true light. The function of the liturgical historian is, as always, to tell the story and to illuminate its meaning.

But there is one theological sideline, often forgotten, that recurs on both the feasts under scrutiny—sacrifice. The *Exsultet* prays that "in the joy of this night receive our evening sacrifice of praise, your church's solemn offering" and goes on to hail Christ as "that Morning Star, who came back from the dead, and shed his peaceful light on all . . ."[13] The Candlemas liturgy is saturated with sacrificial allusions, in Byzantine hymnody, and patristic preaching delights in this motif, too, for example, in the following memorable lines from Ephrem: "But Simeon the priest, when he had received Christ in his arms so that he might present him to God, understood when he beheld him that he was not offering Christ but was himself being offered."[14] Here, it would seem, is abundant proof that the sacrificial aroma is not to be fumigated away. Light, then, is a symbol far more wide ranging than its mere function.

Notes

1. See Kenneth Stevenson, "The Ceremonies of Light: Their Shape and Function in the Paschal Vigil Liturgy, *Ephemerides Liturgicae* 99 (1985) 170-185 (reprinted as Chapter 10 in this volume), and "The Origin and Development of Candlemas: A Struggle for Identity and Coherence?, *Ephemerides Liturgicae* 102 (1988) 316-346 (reprinted in J. Neil Alexander, ed., *Time and Community* [Washington, D.C.: The Pastoral Press, 1990] 43-76). In addition to the full documentation in these two articles, attention needs to be drawn to Eileen Roberts, "The *Exultet* in Twelfth Century Sicily as an Indicator of Manuscript Provence," *Ecclesia Orans* 5 (1988) 157-164.

2. See, in general, Robert F. Taft, "Thanksgiving for the Light: Towards a Theology of Vespers," in *Beyond East and West: Problems in Liturgical Understanding* (Washington, D.C.: The Pastoral Press, 1984) 127-149.

3. Hermann Schmidt, *Hebdomada Sancta*, vol. 2, *Fontes Historici Commentarius Historicus* (Rome: Herder, 1957) 627ff. for texts. (= Schmidt)

4. See ibid 362f. This would allow for the fact that the original Roman custom at the vigil was not to bless *one* large candle, but to carry *two* processional candles; see Schmidt 442.

5. See below, note 9.

6. The processional element was stronger at the entry into church in the old Jerusalem rite; see Gabriel Bertonière, *The Historical Development of the Easter Vigil and Related Services in the Greek Church*, Orientalia Christiana Analecta, vol. 193 (Rome: Pontificium Institutum Studiorum Orientalium, 1972).

7. See Jean Deshusses, *Le Sacramentaire Grégorien: Ses principales formes d'après le plus anciens manuscrits*, vol. 3, Spicilegium Friburgense, vol. 28 (Fribourg: Presses Universitaires, 1982); text in Edmond Martène, *De Antiquis Ecclesiae Ritibus*, vol. 3 (Antwerp: Novelli, 1764) 45f.

8. *Missale Romanum* (Vatican City: Typis Polyglottis, 1970) 523.

9. See Schmidt 427, where it appears in two versions. See also Martène, *De Antiquis* 46 (Narbonne), 47 (Arles Pontifical, first quarter of the fourteenth century), *not* at blessing of fire, but over candles, just before distribution.

10. See Kenneth Stevenson, *Jerusalem Revisited: The Liturgical Meaning of Holy Week* (Washington, D.C.: The Pastoral Press, 1988) 71ff. on the origins of the vigil.

11. J.A. Baker, *The Foolishness of God* (London: Darton, Longman and Todd, 1970) 10.

12. Ibid. 13.

13. *The Sacramentary* (New York: Catholic Book Publishing Co., 1974) 186.

14. Rowan Williams, tr., *Eucharistic Sacrifice: The Roots of a Metaphor*, Grove Liturgical Study, vol. 31 (Bramcote: Grove, 1982) 21. See also Kenneth Stevenson, *Eucharist and Offering* (New York: Pueblo Publishing Co., 1986) 33ff.